Other Insight Guides available:

Alaska
Amazon Wildlife
American Southwest
Amsterdam
Argentina
Arizona & Grand Canyon
Asia, East
Asia, Southeast
Asia's Best Hotels
 and Resorts
Australia
Austria
Bahamas
Bali & Lombok
Baltic States
Bangkok
Barbados
Belgium
Belize
Berlin
Bermuda
Brazil
Brittany
Buenos Aires
Burgundy
Burma (Myanmar)
Cairo
California
California, Southern
Canada
Caribbean
Caribbean Cruises
Channel Islands
Chicago
Chile
China
Colorado
Continental Europe
Corsica
Costa Rica
Crete
Cuba
Cyprus
Czech & Slovak Republic
Delhi, Jaipur & Agra
Denmark
Dominican Rep. & Haiti
Dublin
East African Wildlife
Eastern Europe
Ecuador
Edinburgh

Egypt
England
Finland
Florida
France
France, Southwest
French Riviera
Gambia & Senegal
Germany
Glasgow
Gran Canaria
Great Britain
Great Railway Journeys
 of Europe
Great River Cruises
 of Europe
Greece
Greek Islands
Guatemala, Belize
 & Yucatán
Hawaii
Hungary
Iceland
India
India, South
Indonesia
Ireland
Israel
Istanbul
Italy
Italy, Northern
Italy, Southern
Jamaica
Japan
Jerusalem
Jordan
Kenya
Korea
Laos & Cambodia
Lisbon
Madeira
Malaysia
Mallorca & Ibiza
Malta
Mauritius Réunion
 & Seychelles
Melbourne
Mexico
Montreal
Morocco
Namibia
Nepal

Netherlands
New England
New Mexico
New Orleans
New York State
New Zealand
Nile
Normandy
North American and
 Alaskan Cruises
Norway
Oman & The UAE
Oxford
Pacific Northwest
Pakistan
Peru
Philadelphia
Philippines
Poland
Portugal
Provence
Puerto Rico
Rajasthan
Rio de Janeiro
Russia
Sardinia
Scandinavia
Scotland
Seattle
Sicily
South Africa
South America
Spain
Spain, Northern
Spain, Southern
Sri Lanka
Sweden
Switzerland
Syria & Lebanon
Taiwan
Tenerife
Texas
Thailand
Trinidad & Tobago
Tunisia
Turkey
Tuscany
Umbria
USA: On The Road
USA: Western States
US National Parks: West
Utah

Venezuela
Vienna
Vietnam
Wales

INSIGHT CITY GUIDES
(with free restaurant map)

Barcelona
Beijing
Bruges, Ghent & Antwerp
Brussels
Cape Town
Florence
Hong Kong
Las Vegas
London
Los Angeles
Madrid
Moscow
New York
Paris
Prague
Rome
St Petersburg
San Francisco
Singapore
Sydney
Taipei
Tokyo
Toronto
Venice
Walt Disney World/Orlando
Washington, DC

INSIGHT **CITYGUIDE**

MIAMI

APA PUBLICATIONS
Part of the Langenscheidt Publishing Group

※ INSIGHT GUIDE
MIAMI

Project Editor
Martha Ellen Zenfell
Picture Editor
Hilary Genin
Art Director
Klaus Geisler
Cartography Editor
Zoë Goodwin
Production
Kenneth Chan
Editorial Director
Brian Bell

Distribution

UK & Ireland
GeoCenter International Ltd
Meridian House, Churchill Way West
Basingstoke, Hampshire RG21 6YR
Fax: (44) 1256-817988

United States
Langenscheidt Publishers, Inc.
36–36 33rd Street 4th Floor
Long Island City, NY 11106
Fax: (1) 718 784-0640

Australia
Universal Publishers
1 Waterloo Road
Macquarie Park, NSW 2113
Fax: (61) 2 9888 9074

New Zealand
Hema Maps New Zealand Ltd (HNZ)
Unit D, 24 Ra ORA Drive
East Tamaki, Auckland
Fax: (64) 9 273 6479

Worldwide
Apa Publications GmbH & Co.
Verlag KG (Singapore branch)
38 Joo Koon Road, Singapore 628990
Tel: (65) 6865-1600. Fax: (65) 6861-6438

Printing

Insight Print Services (Pte) Ltd
38 Joo Koon Road, Singapore 628990
Tel: (65) 6865-1600. Fax: (65) 6861-6438

ABOUT THIS BOOK

Insight Guides pioneered the use of creative photography in travel books in 1970. Since then, we have catered for our readers' need not only for excellent information, but also for an understanding of the destination. When the internet can supply inexhaustible (but not always reliable) facts, our guides marry text and pictures to provide more elusive qualities: knowledge and discernment.

How to use this book

The book is carefully structured both to convey an understanding of the city and its culture and to guide readers through its sights and activities:

◆ The Best of Miami at the front of the book helps you to prioritize. Unique experiences, the best events, best beaches and family attractions are listed, plus money-saving tips.

◆ To understand Miami, you need to know something of its past. The Big Orange's history and culture are described in several authoritative essays written by specialists in their fields who have lived in and documented the city for many years.

◆ The Places section details all the attractions worth seeing. The main places of interest are coordinated by number with the maps.

◆ A list of recommended restaurants, bars and cafés is printed at the end of each significant chapter. Some of these are also described and plotted on the pull-out restaurant map that accompanies the guide.

◆ Photographs throughout the book are chosen not only to illustrate local buildings and geography, but also to convey the moods of the city and the spirit of its people.

◆ The Travel Tips section includes all the practical information you will need for a visit, divided into four sections: transportation, accommodations, activities (including nightlife, shopping and sports), and an A–Z of practical tips. Information can be located quickly by using the index printed on the back cover flap.

◆ A detailed street atlas is included at the back of the book, complete with a full index.

The contributors

This new edition was project edited by **Martha Ellen Zenfell**, and builds on the original, also edited by Zenfell, which conveyed the excitement of the emerging Art Deco District. An American based in London, England and a frequent visitor to Miami (she was married in South Beach's Art Deco

city hall, and honeymooned in a friend's beach penthouse), Zenfell has observed the city's changes with an attentive and informed eye.

It is Insight Guides' policy to use local contributors whenever possible. The on-site editor of the original edition, **Joann Biondi**, wrote the essay "The Many Faces of Miami" and provided on-the-spot support for this edition. Biondi's recent projects include 100 first-hand interviews with people recounting their memories of old Miami. **Fred Wright Jr** is an Insight Guides stalwart. Having updated *Insight Guide Florida*, he was the logical choice to bring the Places and Travel Tips sections up to date.

Victoria Pesce Elliott is the restaurant critic for the *Miami Herald*, and editor of *Zagat Miami/South Florida*. When recommendations for the city's eateries were required, Victoria dipped into her personal files to come up with the selection here.

Contributors to earlier editions – and much of their work still appears – include noted historian **Arva Moore Parks**, *Miami Herald* reporters **Yves Colon** and **Melissa Moonves**, plus **Fred Mawer, Cindy Rose Still, Alex Stepick, Geoffrey Tomb, Patrick May, Ian Glass, Sandra Dibble, Alice Klement, Ivan A. Rodriguez** and **Herb Hiller.** This edition uses many bold and beautiful images of the city taken by, among others, Florida-based **Tony Arruza, Catherine Karnow, Marcus Wilson Smith** and **Graeme Teague**. The spirit of the city was enlivened by **David Whelan**, and proofreading was done by **Penny Phenix**.

CONTACTING THE EDITORS

We would appreciate it if readers would alert us to errors or outdated information by writing to:

Insight Guides, P.O. Box 7910, London SE1 1WE, England. Fax: (44) 20 7403-0290. insight@apaguide.co.uk

NO part of this book may be reproduced, stored in a retrieval system or transmitted in any form or means electronic, mechanical, photocopying, recording or otherwise, without prior written permission of *Apa Publications*. Brief text quotations with use of photographs are exempted for book review purposes only. Information has been obtained from sources believed to be reliable, but its accuracy and completeness, and the opinions based thereon, are not guaranteed.

www.insightguides.com
In North America:
www.insighttravelguides.com

Travel Tips

THE BEST OF MIAMI

Setting priorities, saving money, unique attractions...
here, at a glance, are our recommendations, plus some
tips and tricks even many in Miami won't know

BEST FESTIVALS AND EVENTS

- **Miami/Bahamas Goombay Festival** Coconut Grove's Grand Avenue transforms into Nassau's Bay Street during this summer party, one of the largest black heritage festivals in the United States. Early June. *See page 152.*

- **Columbus Day Regatta** Spectator boats outnumber participant boats in this good-natured weekend that turns Biscayne Bay into one huge party space. The regatta dates from the 1950s. Mid-October. *See page 64.*

- **Calle Ocho** Also called Carnaval Miami, this week-long event in Little Havana celebrates with good concerts, great food, and the longest conga line in the world. Mid-March. *See page 63.*

- **Orange Bowl Festival and King Orange Jamboree** Football fans go crazy in a month-long hoopla leading up to the Orange Bowl, the college football classic, on New Year's Day. There's a sailing regatta, fashion shows and other events, but the best is the family-oriented King Orange Jamboree Parade held on New Year's Eve. December to January. *See page 64.*

- **NASDAQ-100 Championships** Stars of the tennis world take over Key Biscayne for two weeks as top players compete for millions of dollars in prizes. March. *See page 163.*

- **White Party Week** One of many gay events held in the year, the party includes dancing on the sand in South Beach and a fund-raising dinner at Vizcaya. November. *See page 85.*

- **Art Deco Weekend** Deco enthusiasts dominate this event in the pastel-painted architectural district, which features lots of lectures, lunches, parties and vintage cars. Mid-January. *See page 65.*

BEST FOR PEOPLE WATCHING

- **Ocean Drive**
  Anytime is fine, but try after midnight to check out the classiest clubbers; Winter Party Week for near-naked men; and the SoBe Wine & Food Festival for a sophisticated crowd. *See page 81.*

- **Art Basel**
  During December's premier art event, the galleries are hopping and the champagne corks are popping. *See page 64.*

- **Lincoln Road**
  With scores of outdoor cafés (some with sofas) and umbrella-bedecked tables, you'll end up meeting everyone in Miami. *See page 92.*

- **Coconut Grove**
  A lively bar and café scene – the Grove groove – is played out against the rhythms of a sexy Latin beat. *See page 149.*

- **Ortanique**
  In Coral Gables, Caribbean cooking is as upscale as the clientele at Cindy Hutson's temple to the taste buds. Try the lobster and mango. *See page 147.*

- **Hotel Victor**
  With glowing jellyfish tanks, thumping DJs and an open-air lounge, the Victor plays host to one of the hottest scenes on the beach. *See page 95.*

ONLY IN MIAMI

- **Art Deco District**
  This world-class collection of pastel-painted buildings brought renewed fame and major bling to Miami. *See page 79.*

- **Vizcaya**
  Tycoon James Deering built this bayside winter retreat in 1916. See it by day or stroll by moonlight. *See page 158.*

- **Little Havana**
  Saturated with Cuban culture and fueled by the bitter-but-best coffee imaginable. *See page 121.*

- **Coral Gables**
  Designed in the 1920s, this is a lush village with Mediterranean-style homes and the elegant 1926 Biltmore Hotel *(above).* *See page 139.*

- **Little Haiti**
  Vividly colored houses and high-energy music point the way to this vibrant Caribbean community. *See page 133.*

- **Design District**
  Miamians call it "one square mile of style." Need we say more? *See page 131.*

BEST FOR KIDS

These attractions are popular with children, though not all will suit every age group.

- **Miami Seaquarium** Home of Lolita, the Killer Whale and TV's *Flipper*. Visitors can also get up-close and personal with dolphins. *See page 163.*
- **Children's Museum of Miami** Hundreds of interactive exhibits keep kids happy for hours and hours. *See page 99.*

- **Miami Metrozoo** This huge, cageless zoo showcases more than 1,300 animals. There's also a kids' zoo and talks by the zookeeper. *See page 169.*
- **Monkey Jungle** It's monkey business here: escape on a wild jungle safari or watch monkeys dive for treats. *See page 171.*
- **Wings Over Miami** Classic aircraft and flying war-birds will delight kids who have their heads in the clouds. There's a good gift shop. *See page 168.*

- **Gold Coast Railroad Museum** Kids clamor to play with wooden model train sets, like Thomas the Tank Engine, while parents enjoy the old-fashioned, full-scale trains. *See page 169.*
- **Cape Florida Lighthouse** Built in 1884 at the southern tip of Key Biscayne, getting there by hiking or biking is fun. *See page 165.*
- **Museum of Science & Planetarium** There's a wildlife center with rare birds of prey, laser shows once a month and live science demonstrations daily. *See page 156.*
- **Parrot Jungle** Florida's most famous feathered friends get their own attraction in Miami, with ape and monkey exhibits to visit along the way. *See page 99.*

BEST BEACHES FOR

- **Posing** *South Beach* Pack a suitcase of sequined bikinis and join the beautiful people as they lounge, luxuriate, tan, talk and do everything but swim. *See page 79.*
- **Picnics** *Matheson Hammock Park* This little beach not far from Coral Gables has pleasant picnic pavilions, but if packing lunch is too arduous, there's a restaurant and snack bar carved into a coral-rock building. *See page 146.*
- **Families** *North Shore State Recreation Area* With a boardwalk, showers, picnic tables and restrooms, this beach keeps both kids and parents happy. *See page 105.*
- **Fishing** *South Pointe Park* Try the little fishing pier at the southern tip of South Beach. South Pointe is also a good place to wait for sunrise or to watch giant cruise ships sail through the narrow channel of the bay. *See page 89.*
- **Being Naked** *Haulover Beach* The northern part of the park is the domain of naturalists who like to be sun-kissed all over. *See page 106.*
- **Watersports** *Key Biscayne* Just over the Rickenbacker Causeway are Jet Ski Beach and Windsurfer Beach; no prizes for guessing what fun-seekers flock here for. *See page 162.*
- **Tranquility** *Bill Baggs Cape Florida State Park* On the very tip of Key Biscayne and with a view of Cape Florida Lighthouse, this beach has few facilities and little shade – just peace, silence and solitude. Leave all your worries, and your cell phone, behind. *See page 164.*

BEST BUILDINGS OF THE QUIRKY KIND

- **MiMo Architecture**
Miami Modern
(MiMo) buildings are
known for asymmetric
angles, kidney shapes
and cheesehole
cutouts. North Beach
has the best collection.
See pages 103–5.

- **Ancient Spanish
Monastery**
This 12th-century
monastery from Spain
was reassembled in
Miami stone by stone.
See page 135.

- **Coral Castle**
This mansion made of
coral rock was built
by a Latvian immi-
grant to his unrequited
love. *See page 171.*

- **Jules' Undersea
Lodge** Swim to
dinner in the world's
first underwater
resort. *See page 207.*

- **Stiltsville**
Houses perched on
stilts; see them now
before they fall into
the bay. *See page 165.*

BEST EXCURSIONS

- **The Everglades**
Covering over a
million acres west of
Miami, the park is
home to a rare com-
munity of plants and
endangered animals.
See page 197.

- **Florida Keys**
This string of islands
in the turquoise sea
has much to offer
snorklers, wildlife
lovers, clubbers
and culture-seekers.
See page 205.

- **Palm Beach**
Manicured, moneyed
Palm Beach seduces
with class and cachet.
See page 187.

- **Fort Lauderdale**
Gardens, museums and
outdoor dining draw
visitors. *See page 181.*

Please Do Not Feed
the Crocodiles.
THEY MIGHT BITE!

BEST SWIMMING POOLS

- **Venetian Pool**
Possibly the most
beautiful public pool
in America, the Venet-
ian earns its position
on the National Regis-
ter of Historic Places
with vine-covered
loggias and three-
story observation
towers. *See page 143.*

- **The National**
A long, tree-lined Deco
beauty, the hotel's
signature silver-
domed tower
is framed the
entire length
of the pool.
See page 90.

- **The Biltmore**
Kings and queens,
Judy Garland and Al
Capone flocked to
float at the Biltmore.
Synchronized swim-
ming was practically
invented here, and
Johnny Weissmuller
(*Tarzan*) was an
instructor. *See pages
143 and 145.*

- **The Raleigh**
As curvaceous as Sir
Walter Raleigh's
shield, this Art Deco
gem with a waterfall
and porthole-window
bar is serene and sexy.
See pages 74 and 90.

MONEY-SAVING TIPS

Miami is not a discount town. In fact, during "the season" (November to March), it's not uncommon for hotels to charge a rate at weekends that is high-er than the weekday rate, even if you are already a guest. Taxes swell the bill even more. Restaurants often include an "optional" tip of between 15 and 20 percent in the total. Visitors are under no obligation to pay this, but always check before leaving an additional tip. With a little local knowledge, however, there are different ways to save:

Museum Admission Some muse-ums have a "donation" day, when the fee is decided by the visitor; these include the Museum of Contemporary Art (Tuesday) and the Jewish Museum of Florida (Saturday). Others offer a "Free for Families" rate, such as the Miami Art Museum (second Saturday, afternoons), and the Miami Children's Museum (third Friday, 6.30–8.30pm)

Special Passes The "Go Miami" card is an all-inclusive ticket to 25 local attractions including Vizcaya, Metrozoo, Parrot Jungle and cruises on the *Island*

Queen. The more days you use the pass, the more money you save. For information, contact the Miami Beach Visitors Center, tel: 305-672-1270.

Transportation To save on Metrobus and Metrorail journeys pay with transit tokens, available from machines at most stations, instead of cash. The air-conditioned, pastel-colored South Beach Local bus travels the length of the Art Deco District, stopping at or near 20 points of interest. Using the bus saves a fortune in taxi fares, as each journey costs just 25¢.

THE MAGIC CITY

In many ways the most foreign of US cities,
this frontier town is coming of age.
It's still young enough to party all night,
but old enough to do it in style

Reflecting in the shining seas of the Atlantic, tall, glittering neon towers are evocative emblems of Miami's nickname, "the Magic City." Order a rum punch at a table in the Ocean Drive sunshine and kick back. Take in the waves of lithe models, wrapped in floating colors of fabric light as air, tanned, muscled hunks posing and prowling in their path. Right across the street, the aquamarine ocean teases with breezes rustling in the palm fronds, as swimmers paddle in pools caressed by waterfalls. Sleek boutiques and restaurants line Lincoln Road and Collins Avenue, tantalizing with tropical decadence. Night falls and sensual rhythms of salsa and *compas* roll out of the South Beach clubs, with parties that go on until dawn.

Over MacArthur Causeway, below the high-lit skyline, is another Miami. This is where deals are made, and from where a *de-facto* US capital of Latin American and Caribbean business operates. Finance flows from across the globe into banks, condominiums and hotels. This tropical frontier town is coming of age with its own ballet, symphony and professional sports teams. In December, the grown-up art world holds its second largest annual get-together, Art Basel, in Miami Beach.

"Greater Miami," within Miami-Dade County, comprises 31 different municipalities, sprawling over 500 sq. miles (1,300 sq. km), including a 15-mile (24-km) stretch of golden Miami Beach. A topographically two-dimensional town, Miami has no hills, but a lush foliage of orchids, bougainvillea, hibiscus and palms more than makes up for it.

In many ways the most "foreign" of all US cities, dark eyes and heavy accents make Miami feel more like a Caribbean cousin than an Indiana in-law. Spanish is the second language, but only just. Close to fifty precent of Miami residents are Spanish-speaking, as are many of the radio stations. An invitation for dinner at 8 begs the question: is that American time (8 o'clock exactly), or Latin time (about 10)? And the music; even the techno has a little Latin slink about it, and neighborhoods each have their own distinct tropicana rhythms, sliding from the storefronts and the cars.

If Miami *were* an automobile, it would be a white soft-topped Corvette, chasing to the beach for sunrise after a night on the town.   ❑

PRECEDING PAGES: a seagull checks out the scene in South Beach; pastel-painted retro-kitsch in a cool café.
LEFT: warm breezes and delectable drinks in a neon Nirvana.

BIRTH OF A CITY

**South Florida has always drawn settlers,
first from far-flung lands, later from Europe.
They all battled the mosquitos for this rich, remote
coastal area. Then, in 1896, the railroad came to town**

Pasqua Florida – *a feast of flowers* – was the name that Juan Ponce de León gave to the unruly peninsula he accidently discovered while on a quest for eternal youth on the nearby island of Bimini. From then and for the next 400 years, South Florida was the ground and the prize for continuous wrestling by the Spanish, the British, the Creek and the Seminole Indians, all of them struggling against the only regular victor, the mosquito. It wasn't until the beginning of the 20th century that the tropical playground of modern Miami made a dent in the public consciousness.

For 10,000 years people have been coming to South Florida. Indians, who may have migrated from Alaska and Siberia seeking the sun, settled along the river banks in a tropical Garden of Eden. Lacking metal, they fashioned their tools from sea shells. A Spanish adventurer brought the European intrusion to their simple way of life.

Fountain of youth

Juan Ponce de León traveled the world in search of glory. What he hoped to discover, sailing north from Puerto Rico on March 3, 1513, was an island called Bimini and a fabled spring that gave eternal youth. What he found instead, and named "Pascua Florida" (which has also been translated as "Easter") was the tip of a huge new continent. Three months after landing somewhere between today's St Augustine and Jacksonville, Ponce de León sailed

into Biscayne Bay, noting in his journal that he had reached Tequesta (present-day Miami).

For the next half-century, Spaniards tried to conquer the wild peninsula. They were no match for the native people – or for the ubiquitous mosquito. Later, in 1562 the French established an outpost named Fort Caroline near present-day Jacksonville. King Philip II of Spain sent Pedro Menéndez de Avilés as governor to secure Florida. By 1565, Menéndez had routed the French and founded the first permanent settlement in what is now called the United States at St Augustine.

A Jesuit mission at Tequesta flourished briefly, failed, reopened, and failed again, but

LEFT: poster for the "world's greatest playground."
RIGHT: Ponce de León "discovers" Florida, 1513.

the Spaniards and the native Indians formed an alliance. Over the years, Spanish ships and sailors shipwrecked on the Tequesta coast had friendly receptions from the natives.

Slowly, Spain began to cede to England its claims over the New World. As the English took over Creek Indian land, renegade Creeks crossed over the border into Spanish Florida, plundering and burning as they went. The native Indians, who were now Spanish allies, fled before them. The Spanish, unhappy about a hostile Creek population in Florida, made another attempt to settle South Florida, sending Father Joseph María Mónaco and Father Joseph Xavier de Alana to Tequesta in the

summer of 1743. They established a triangular fort with mortared corners, and called it "Pueblo de Santa María de Loreto" – Miami's second name. By this time though, the Indians had grown unfriendly, the settlement did not flourish, and the King ordered the mission to be abandoned.

A British colony

In 1763, the Treaty of Paris ended the Seven Years' War (the "French and Indian War" to Americans) and two centuries of Spanish rule. Florida was a British colony. When the Spanish left, the remaining Indians followed them to Cuba, and Britain became proud owner of a new land with very few inhabitants. The British were quick to map the area (the entire east coast of Florida was surveyed between 1765 and 1771) and changed the Spanish names to English ones. At the stroke of a pen, Biscayne Bay became "Sandwich Gulf."

The 20 years of British rule brought grand plans for settling South Florida, "the most precious jewel of His Majesty's American dominion," but none succeeded. British Tories, who poured into Florida during the American Revolution, were shocked by the announcement that Florida was to be exchanged with Spain for the Bahamas. Loyalists fled to the Bahamas, as Florida's second Spanish period (1784–1821) began.

One Pedro Fornells was granted 175 acres (70 hectares) on "Cayo Biscaino" (today's Key Biscayne), and John Egan received 100 acres (40 hectares) on the north bank of the "Rio nombrado de aqua dulze" (now the Miami River). They became Florida's first landowners. The small oasis of "civilization" in South Florida was called the Cape Florida Settlement. Though officially Spanish, South Florida was really more a part of the Bahamas, linked through trade and sentiment. Florida was also a haven for runaway slaves – one in a number of sources of tension between Spain and the US.

By 1819, the Spanish cut the losses on their Florida adventure, and by 1821 – a deal struck – the Stars and Stripes fluttered over the US's most tropical territory. The US confirmed the Egan family's land claim; Mary Ann Davis received title to land she had bought from Pedro Fornells on Key Biscayne; and land was granted to Polly and Jonathan Lewis along the banks of the bay and the river, called the "Miami" from this time on. In all, a little over 3,000 acres (1,200 hectares) of South Florida was now privately owned.

In the 1830s, Richard Fitzpatrick dreamed of recreating his South Carolina plantation. He bought all the land grants on the mainland and campaigned for the development of the Miami area. But Indian troubles intervened, and Fitzpatrick sold his land for $16,000 to his nephew, William English. Within a year of his arrival in 1842, English had settled the village of Miami on the river's south bank. He was the first to call the area "Miami."

The Seminole Wars

In Florida, as in the rest of the US, the history of settlers and Indians was of broken promises and dishonored treaties. Land-hungry whites wanted the Indians moved West to reservations, and a group of Seminoles refused to go.

In December 1835, Major Francis Langhorne Dade (for whom Dade County is named) and 109 of his men died in a bloody Seminole attack, known as the Dade Massacre, and the Seminole Wars continued until 1857. The US sent troops and built Fort Dallas as a defense on the north bank of the Miami River. Many died in the wars, including New York horticulturalist Henry Perrine. Though

SCORES TO SETTLE

The Seminole Wars of the mid-1800s are not officially over. The Seminole people claim that no valid peace treaty has yet been signed and enacted, and they remain in a state of war with the US.

South Florida sat out the war in isolation.

William Gleason was a carpetbagger who came to Miami in 1866, liked what he saw, and decided to have it for himself. He foiled a plan to settle former slaves in South Florida under the 1862 Homestead Act, which granted 160 acres (65 hectares) of land free to any citizen who would live on it for five years and

Perrine was able to save his wife and children, he was killed in the Seminole attack at Indian Key, in August, 1840. The US Coastal Survey first mapped the new town in 1849, but continuing Indian problems took a toll, and by 1860 Miami and its handful of inhabitants had disappeared from public records.

The Civil War that tore the rest of the nation apart barely touched Miami. Florida joined the Confederacy, but Key West remained in Federal control. The monthly mailboat, Miami's link with the outside world, was suspended and

improve it. Gleason maintained almost total control of the area for many years, to the point that when a land dispute forced him to leave the Miami River area he took Miami with him – that is, the Miami post office, whose name he changed to "Biscayne."

Early snowbirds

Settlers began to come into the area, and long-time resident Edmund Beasley filed a claim in 1868 for the land that is now Coconut Grove. Two years later William B. Brickell and Ephraim T. Sturtevant arrived from Cleveland, Ohio. Brickell bought land and built a home and trading post on the banks of the Miami

LEFT: Seminole man in traditional dress.
ABOVE: Fort Dallas, built during the Seminole Wars.

A DIM LIGHT

A lighthouse at Cape Florida, built by Bostonian Samuel Lincoln, began operating in 1825. Its light was so ineffective that sailors said they would "go ashore looking for it."

River. Sturtevant acquired land in Biscayne, which his daughter, the influential pioneer Julia Tuttle, visited. In 1873, settlers opened a post office in the bayfront community called Cocoanut Grove (as it was spelled then). Government engineers completed Fowey Rock lighthouse in 1878, and the old Cape Florida Light, now redundant, was darkened.

Miami's mild winters attracted northern visitors, the first fully-fledged tourists. Among them was Ralph M. Munroe of Staten Island, who stayed with friends Charles and Isabella Peacock at the Bay View House in today's Peacock Park, overlooking the bay from the bluff. This became the city's first lodging place.

Club for women

Coconut Grove became a community of "firsts," as civilized institutions began to thrive on the Florida frontier. Ralph and Kirk Munroe (no relation) founded the Biscayne Bay Yacht Club in 1887. A school was opened the following year, and in 1891 Ralph

Munroe donated a parcel of land for the Union Chapel to be built. This became Plymouth Congregational Church, which can still be visited. The area's first woman homesteader, schoolteacher Flora McFarlane, organized a library in Charles Peacock's store, and the Housekeepers Club for women, out of which came the Pine Needles Club for young girls.

The dream of a city

The city of Miami, however, was still only an idea – an idea in the mind of the recently widowed Cleveland matron, Julia Sturtevant Tuttle. She started her new life in Florida, not on her late father's homestead, but on the "best" property available, on the north bank of the Miami River. On November 13, 1891, she brought her 23-year-old daughter and 21-year-old son, and began to plan her city, hoping that railroad magnate Henry Plant would extend his line, which reached as far south as Tampa in 1893, to tiny Miami, but she was disappointed. Another railroad man, Henry M. Flagler, who made his first millions in Standard Oil with John D. Rockefeller, had fallen in love with Florida. His railroad inched southward from St Augustine, reaching Palm Beach by 1893. He, too, wasn't interested in bringing it the last 66 miles (106 km) to Mrs Tuttle's doorstep. Until the winter of 1894–95.

As popular Miami mythology has it, a killer freeze hit Florida, destroying most of the area's citrus crops. But in semi-tropical Miami, orange blossoms still bloomed. The part of the story where Mrs Tuttle offered Flagler half her land, plus some of Brickell's, is true, however, and as a result, the railroad was extended to Miami.

Pulled by a locomotive and greeted wildly by the populace (all 300 of them), the new era arrived on April 15, 1896. The engine's bell clanged the end for a sleepy frontier town, and the beginning of modern Miami.

Within a month the first newspaper, the *Miami Metropolis,* rolled off the press. On July 28 citizens voted to incorporate the city, never officially a town, and elected John B. Reilly, Flagler's man, as mayor. The city fathers laid out streets, rather poorly, and founded churches and schools. Then, on Christmas morning, a fire started in Brady's grocery store at what is today Miami Avenue and SW 2nd Street and destroyed 28 buildings, the destruction wiping out almost the entire business district.

Just three weeks later, energetic rebuilding underway, Flagler's enormous, elegant Royal Palm Hotel opened with a gala dinner. The city began to proclaim itself "America's sun porch" to tourists, and hosted very different visitors in the scorching summer of 1898: American troops billeted on their way to fight the Spanish in Cuba after the sinking of the battleship *Maine* in Havana harbor. But 7,000 bored soldiers plus humidity plus swarms of mosquitoes did not add up to tranquility. One

Evening Record, edited by Frank Stoneman.

Until 1909, Miami's downtown area and outlying communities like Coconut Grove and Larkins (today's South Miami), huddled on the narrow, 4-mile (6-km) wide coastal ridge between the Atlantic Ocean to the east and the Everglades to the west, beginning at today's NW 27th Avenue. The governor, Napoleon Bonaparte Broward, campaigned on a promise of draining Florida's vast wetlands to create an "Empire of the swampy Everglades," and government engineers dug the Miami Canal to drain the Everglades.

They also dug "Government Cut," which later became the Port of Miami, across the

frustrated soldier said, "If I owned both Miami and Hell, I'd rent out Miami and live in Hell."

Early growth

In the early years of the 20th century, Miami began a modest boom. The Tatum brothers built a toll bridge across the river at Flagler Street and began to develop the Riverside subdivision. A new business district included Seybold's ice-cream parlor, two rival Burdines department stores, banks, saloons, movie theaters and another newspaper, the *Miami*

LEFT: Julia Sturtevant Tuttle, influential pioneer.
ABOVE: Flagler's railroad pulls into town, 1896.

FLAGLER'S FOLLY

Henry Flagler was a true father of tourism in Florida. With resources and experience from his first career, founding Standard Oil, he not only pioneered the remarkable Florida East Coast Railway, but also had the vision to build plush hotels along the route.

William Krome, just 28 years old, spent two years surveying for the 100-mile (160-km) Key West Extension and was made assistant construction engineer for the project, known locally as "Flagler's Folly." In the face of the doubters, and in the teeth of three hurricanes which took 144 lives, Krome completed the railroad in 1912, a year ahead of schedule, in time for Flagler's 82nd birthday.

lower end of the future Miami Beach, improving access to Miami's harbor and creating Fisher Island. Florida began its tradition of selling wetlands and, as developers dreamed of profits from land where none existed, dredges began to hum in the wilderness west of Miami. It was not until 1916 that the Florida Federation of Women's Clubs acquired a large tract of land, which they called Royal Palm State Park,

to conserve the wildlife-rich Everglades.

Miami attracted visionaries like John Collins, a New Jersey Quaker who became sole owner of Ocean Beach in 1909. He borrowed money and began to build a bridge to connect Miami with the beach. Halfway through, his money ran out. Fortunately, the man with land and a grand dream met a man with hard cash, Carl Graham Fisher, who had made his mint with Prest-O-Lite, the first really bright automobile headlight. Fisher loaned Collins $50,000 to finish his bridge. In return, Collins gave Fisher a piece of land on the island that became Miami Beach.

On June 12, 1913, a long line of motor cars

rattled over the wooden planks of Collins' bridge. When they got to Bull Island (now Belle Isle), where the bridge temporarily ended, the drivers hopped out, lifted their lightweight automobiles, turned them around, and headed back to the mainland. That same summer workmen leveled the beach's native mangroves which allowed Fisher's dredge to go to work, throwing up sand and shells from the bay bottom to create Miami Beach.

In 1915, the citizens of the city voted to incorporate, and elected J.N. Lummus their first mayor. Ocean Beach, on the south end of the island, became a "people's playground," with casinos, swimming pools and cabana complexes, as well as a restaurant that Joe and Jennie Weiss ran out of their home. This became Joe's Stone Crab, which is still wildly popular today. Farther north, Fisher envisioned an exclusive playground for the wealthy, with golf, tennis and polo.

Back in Miami pioneer merchant Ev Sewell, became the city's first great promoter. His nationwide advertising campaign lured the rich and famous, many of whom built homes on Brickell Avenue, Coconut Grove's "Millionaires' Row." The most lavish of these was Vizcaya, a European-style palace with formal gardens by James Deering of International Harvester, which was finished in 1916.

Sewell convinced Glenn Curtiss, a pioneer in the aviation industry and a pilot himself, to open a flying school in Miami. When Congress declared war on Germany in April 1917, Sewell promoted the idea of a naval aviation school. In October 1917, the US government bought land in Coconut Grove and built Dinner Key Naval Air Station. By the end of the war, 128 seaplanes were based here, filling Miami's once peaceful skies with noise.

The Roaring Twenties

Nowhere did the 1920s roar louder than in Miami. The war was barely over when developers began carving orange groves and tomato patches into subdivisions. In 1921, the city tried to solve the jumble of street names and numbers with the Chaille Plan, a new naming system. Avenue D became Miami Avenue, 12th Street became Flagler Street, and streets and avenues were renumbered outwards.

Between 1920 and 1923 the population doubled. City fathers approved a grand plan for modernization, including a large new bayfront park and a skyscraper courthouse. Downtown parking became disastrous, but downtown land became a gold mine, and the real boom was yet to come. By 1925, the frenzy, fueled by Miami's superb climate and tracts of available land, was out of control. The list of new subdivisions grew; Hialeah, Biltmore, Melrose Gardens, Flagler Manor, Miami Shores, Miami Beach, Central Miami and dozens of others.

One neighborhood stands out: George Merrick's "Coral Gables, Miami's Master Suburb," a planned community of Mediterranean-style homes, graceful plazas and wide boulevards. Unlike many developers, Merrick delivered on his promises. He made huge profits and poured them back into his suburb. He spent millions on advertising, and hired silver-tongued orator William Jennings Bryan for $100,000 for promotional speeches at Coral Gables' Venetian Pool on DeSoto Boulevard. Few structures exemplified the flamboyance of the period better than this architectural whimsy. Once a rock pit, the pool featured extravagant waterfalls, coral caves and landscaping on a grand scale.

Real estate boom

The buzz all over Florida was real estate. Everyone seemed to be making a bundle as land changed hands once, twice, many times at ever-spiraling prices. "Binder boys" flocked to the state, real estate salesmen who sold "binders" (10 percent deposits) on land, then resold them, though the profits were mostly on paper.

Three replicas of Spain's Giralda Tower were under construction (the Biltmore Hotel, the *Miami News* Tower and Miami Beach's Roney Plaza Hotel) and the University of Miami was on the drawing board. But the bottom started to fall out of the boom. In August 1925 the Florida East Coast Railway stopped all but essential freight to repair its tracks, cutting off the supply of building materials by land. Developers turned to the sea, using anything that would float to transport lumber and supplies. The flotilla was interrupted in Janu-

AN ADMAN'S DREAM

Between 1925 and 1926, at the peak of the city's boom, the *Miami Herald* ran more pages of advertising copy than any other newspaper in the world.

ary 1926 when the *Prinz Valdemar* overturned in Miami's shipping canal and closed the port for more than three weeks. Anti-Florida campaigns in northern states hurt, too. Still, the Biltmore Hotel opened on January 16, 1926, and in February workmen began construction of the University of Miami.

For the time being, though, the Miami property boom was clearly over. By the middle of

that summer, even Coral Gables' previously excellent sales were slipping.

Few people paid attention to the newspaper headlines on September 17, 1926, warning of an impending tropical storm. They were awoken in the middle of the night to a city without electricity, and storm gusts screaming past their windows. The winds were measured at 128 miles (206 km) per hour before the wind gauge blew away. At dawn the torrents of rain and tidal surge abated, and many people ran from their homes to survey the terrible destruction, unaware that they were in the eye of the storm. The hurricane resumed, this time from the opposite direction, stranding thousands, and more than 200 people lost their lives. By the following afternoon, when the brutal storm had blown itself away, Miami was in chaos. Houses were left in pieces and businesses destroyed. Boats had been thrown on to dry land. Miami had been reeling before the hurricane. Afterwards, it was ruined.

Growing pains

National headlines proclaimed "Miami is Wiped Out!" The damage was great, but so was the spirit of the stricken city. Within a week Mayor Ed Romfh was talking about Miami's comeback. The University of Miami gave South Florida hope for the future when it

opened its "cardboard college" on October 15, 1926. It converted a bankrupt apartment hotel into classrooms with thin cardboard partitions. It was a start.

The next couple of years brought a few bright spots, like the opening of the Everglades and Robert Clay hotels and the completion of the Tamiami Trail, the first major road across the Everglades, in 1928. But for the first time the majority of traffic was flowing north, out of Miami, away from the stark skeletons of buildings rising against the sky – ruined by the winds of the storm.

With the passage of the 18th Amendment in 1920, the US had become officially dry.

Miami hardly noticed. Rumrunners loved the canals and coves of South Florida and soon the area had acquired yet another nickname, "the leakiest spot in America." Miami's reputation for winking at both the liquor and the gambling laws attracted new and less desirable residents, including the infamous gangster Al "Scarface" Capone, who bought a mansion on Palm Island in 1928.

Most of the local civic leaders, including the Sewell brothers and George Merrick, were bankrupt. Much-needed cash injections came from Miami outsiders with their eyes on a sunny future, like Joseph Widner, who purchased Hialeah racetrack in 1932, and the Phipps family, who completed Biscayne Boulevard in 1927. Miami's aviation industry was born. What began as Florida Airways Corporation, founded by the air ace Eddie Rickenbacker in 1926, became Eastern Airlines by 1930, and Pan Am began its Key West–Havana service in 1927. Airports were built, and in 1929 Miami hosted both Charles Lindbergh and Amelia Earhart at the "Olympics of Aviation."

In 1932, America elected Franklin D. Roosevelt as president, hoping that he would lead the country out of the Depression. His New Deal programs launched an "alphabet soup" of agencies. The CCC (Civilian Conservation Corps) put young men to work in the nation's parks. In Miami they worked on Matheson Hammock and built Greynolds Park. The PWA (Public Works Administration) constructed new buildings, including the Coral Gables Fire Station and Liberty Square, Florida's first public housing project.

The government also hired unemployed World War I veterans to build an overseas highway to Key West. Many of them met a tragic fate when a monster hurricane struck on Labor Day in 1935, killing more than 400 people and wrecking both the uncompleted highway – which didn't open until 1938 – and Flagler's Overseas Railroad.

But tourists, many from Latin America, were again flocking to Miami. In 1933 the Palm Fete, which had been sporadically celebrated in the past, put on a New Year's Day football game between the University of Miami and Manhattan College. Against all predictions, the local team won, and the success of the event prompted the organizers to schedule a game for the following year, at the site of the future Orange Bowl. The newly named "Orange Festival" held its first New Year's Eve parade in 1936. A Miami tradition was born, one that all of America still watches.

The Miami Beach economy was looking up, too. New "modern" hotels and apartments sprang up along Collins Avenue. Unhappily, anti-Semitism flourished. Carl Fisher and John Collins had developed the north part of the beach as a "restricted" area, and "Gentiles Only" signs appeared in hotels and apartments. Across the ocean, an Austrian paperhanger named Adolf Hitler took power in Germany. A second world war was on the horizon.

of 1942, the military had turned 147 Miami hotels into barracks. GIs drilled on golf courses and exercised on wide sandy beaches. Even the country's ultimate matinée idol, Clark Gable, came to Miami Beach in uniform. Before the war was over, one-fourth of the officers and one-fifth of the enlisted men in the US Army Air Corps had trained in Miami Beach.

The Navy took command of Miami's only post-boom skyscraper, the Alfred I duPont Building, promptly nicknamed the "USS Neversink." Still, as most American ships were in the Pacific Ocean, German submarines roamed the Florida Straits almost at will. During 1942,

World War II

Tourism, already the mainstay of Miami's economy, plunged when the Japanese bombed Pearl Harbor and the US declared war. A tanker torpedoed by German submarines in full view of Florida's coast in February 1942 didn't help. The city's hotels suddenly emptied – but not for long.

American soldiers, lots of them, filled the suites. City fathers convinced the government that warm and deserted South Florida would make a good training ground, and by the end

LEFT: the hurricane of 1926 devastated the city.
ABOVE: soldiers in gas masks train on Miami Beach.

ROOSEVELT'S CLOSE SHAVE

Franklin D. Roosevelt, who had been vacationing in South Florida, agreed to make an appearance in Bayfront Park on February 15, 1933. Miami's voters had supported him in the previous year's election and he came to thank them. It nearly cost him his life. Among the 18,000 people there was an unemployed bricklayer named Guiseppe Zangara, who resented people with wealth and authority. Zangara fired an $8 pawn-shop pistol five times, wounding four people and hitting Chicago mayor Anton Cermak, who stood only inches from Roosevelt. Cermak died on March 6, and Zangara went to the electric chair soon afterward.

German submarines torpedoed four tankers in full view of Miami, and 25 more along the coastline between Key West and Cape Canaveral. Many hotels became hospitals for wounded soldiers, and after the war, the Biltmore Hotel continued to be an Army hospital until 1968. German prisoners of war were held at camps in Kendall and Homestead.

Rationing, blackouts, dimouts, thousands of servicemen around town, and, above all, the ever-present submarine threat just offshore, made Miami feel very close to the war.

War-born prosperity tempted tourists back to Miami, and hoteliers clamored to get their facilities back for business. As early as 1942 the *Miami Herald* confidently predicted that "political, economic and geographical factors slowly are swinging Miami into a position that will make the Indian wars, the coming of the railroad, the land boom and even the present military cauldron look like a quiet Sunday afternoon on a Swiss alp."

The talk of Miami as the "coming metropo-

lis," back in 1896, was ringing true. After the war, thousands of soldiers returned to where they'd gotten "sand in their shoes." Rows of pastel-painted boxy GI houses sprang up in isolated, outlying areas. GIs swarmed to the University of Miami, breathing new life into a moribund institution. By 1947, the main campus, so long vacant, was the site of the Memorial Classroom Building. In 1949, the university's administration building, long abandoned, became the Merrick Building.

A record number of eight hurricanes hit Miami between 1945 and 1950. The two that made landfall just a month apart in the fall of 1947 were minimal but very wet. After the storm on October 11, 1947, more than four-fifths of Dade and Broward counties was under water. The Orange Bowl stadium was flooded knee-deep, and areas west of Red Road looked more like lakes full of houseboats than residential subdivisions. Residents and businesses clamored for action to protect the city against future floods.

The government obliged, sending the Army Corps of Engineers to build new canals, locks and levees that would dry up much of the eastern Everglades. The legacy of these projects, aside from the Florida favorite – large tracts of new land for development – was an ongoing threat to the ecology of the Everglades, and to South Florida's water supply.

Modern woes and wonders

Crime flourished once again in the late 1940s, as gangsters took control of casinos, and public officials studiously looked the other way. Influential citizens formed the "Secret Six," a group dedicated to stopping illegal gambling. Their efforts exposed corruption in high places including the governor's office, and culminated in a 1950 investigation by Senate crime fighter Estes Kefauver. Miami's door was no longer wide open to criminals.

In 1949, Miami joined the new world of media with the inaugural broadcast of WTVJ, Florida's first television station. Although at the time few homes possessed TV sets, it wasn't too long before tuning in to watch Miami newsman Ralph Renick had become a statewide nightly ritual. Arthur Godfrey, whose show was one of the most popular on television, broadcast from the Kennilworth Hotel in

Bal Harbour for many years. To express the city's appreciation for this wonderful coast-to-coast publicity, Miami Beach renamed 41st Street Arthur Godfrey Road.

Florida had a series of unpleasant incidents during the Communist scares and witch-hunts of the early 1950s. The 1950 Senate campaign between Miamian George Smathers and incumbent senator Claude Pepper turned nasty when Smathers said his opponent was soft on Communism and called him "Red Pepper." George Smathers won the election. Pepper, who had moved to Miami, later ran for the House of Representatives in 1962 and served the House until his death in 1989.

> ### LIBERAL LEADER
>
> In 1954 Florida's Leroy Collins was the first governor of a Southern state to declare racial segregation to be "morally wrong."

ever-swelling numbers. Farmland was diced into ever-smaller suburbs as the town turned itself into a major metropolis.

Major metropolis

Voters approved a metropolitan government for Dade County in a highly debated decision in 1957. By the end of the decade the population had swelled to nearly 1 million. Tourism

In 1951 racial violence erupted in Carver Village, a black housing project. The first Dade County Council for Human Relations was organized and, by the late 1950s, a number of schools had been desegregated. Remarkable for the place and time, and symbolically a herald for the awakening of civil rights, in 1952 the contralto Marian Anderson sang to an integrated audience in the Dade County auditorium.

Through the 1950s, tourists and newcomers were flocking to the South Florida area in

was encouraged by the coming of air-conditioning against the tropical climes, and by glamorous new hotels like the Fontainebleau, which welcomed guests to 1,206 rooms, and enticed them with crystal chandeliers and marble staircases. Movie stars and business moguls arrived in droves, eager to be seen in such lavish surroundings. The repulsive "Gentiles Only" and "Whites Only" signs that had haunted hotel entrances for years slunk away. The future looked prosperous and promising.

Miami's song had never been a soothing lullaby, though, and in the nearby Caribbean, a big surprise was tuning up, going by the name of Fidel Castro.   ❏

LEFT: an early Orange Bowl parade.
ABOVE: with glamorous hotels and wealthy tourists, the future in the 1950s looked prosperous and promising.

MODERN MIAMI

In the past 40 years Cuban exiles, flower children, sports supremos and glamorous newcomers have made their mark on the Magic City. Modern Miami is upbeat and booming, moving to a Latin rhythm

The most explosive, expansive, constructive and devastating phases of Miami's development took place in the last four decades of the 20th century. Kicked off by a loud political bang in the nearby Caribbean, South Florida's multi-cultural past sailed, swam and salsa-danced its way across the waters to form the tropical metropolis that continues to glisten in the sun.

The political bang was Cuba. Crowds around the world watched with interest in 1959 as extraordinary events began to unfold on the island, where a 32-year-old rebel named Fidel Castro had deposed dictator Fulgencio Batista. The United States government initially welcomed the revolutionary, but at that time, most Miamians paid little attention. It seemed just like another upheaval in a nearby island's rickety power structure, and only later proved to be more enduring. As disillusionment with the "conquering hero" set in, and Castro's Communist ambitions appeared, more and more Cubans fled their homeland. By the summer of 1960, six planes a day were departing Havana, most of them bound for Florida.

Initially, Miamians welcomed these exiles, sympathizing with their plight and admiring their hard-working ethics and strong family structure. Some resentment and hostility followed, however, as, seemingly overnight, schools and neighborhoods filled with people who spoke only Spanish.

The Bay of Pigs

The Miami Cubans weren't too happy either; most of them wanted to go home. Until 1961 many did, and many more believed they would – and soon. The CIA organized and trained a small exile brigade of 1,300 people to invade Cuba and depose Castro. On April 17, 1961, "Brigada 2506," as it was called, landed on Playa Giron, a beach on Cuba's southern coast near the Bay of Pigs. The men were counting on US air support, and the US was counting on support from a popular uprising, inspired by the invasion. Neither materialized, and the mission was doomed from the start. Nearly 100 men died and about 1,000 were taken prisoner.

LEFT: Art Deco sparked Miami's 1990s tourist boom.
RIGHT: President John F. Kennedy in 1962, honoring veterans of the ill-fated Bay of Pigs operation.

Fidel Castro

He is the most hated man in Miami. Spanish radio commentators refer to him as "the tyrant." Others curl their lips and spit his name in disdain. Even his sister Juanita, owner of a Little Havana pharmacy, despises her brother.

The longest reigning military leader in Latin America, Fidel Castro is still the controversial and charismatic leader he was when he first captured Cuba in 1959, but in Miami, his hardline, purist stance has earned him the title "Fossil Communist."

While much of the Communist world has crumbled away, Castro remains faithful to his "socialism or death" philosophy and continues to condemn Yankee imperialism. And his miraculous perseverance has given him an undeniable mystique.

After the Revolution, American mobster Meyer Lansky, who lost a fortune in the Communist take-over, offered a million-dollar bounty for Castro's head. Later, several CIA plots, including an invasion, exploding cigars and drops of poison, failed. Amid it all, in a country short of food, clothing and medicine, Castro has kept a chokehold on his island's own dissidents.

Castro may have contributed to Miami's history more than any other individual, and many concede that much of the best of modern Miami was influenced by Fidel. But for the more than 700,000 Cubans in Miami-Dade County, this influence has inspired a powerful anti-Castro feeling that is as much a personal vendetta against the man as a hatred for Communism. For exiles who still pine for the "good life" of their homeland, and for their children who feel deprived of their roots, Castro-bashing is a perennial pastime. The city often seems awash in the Honk-If-You-Hate-Fidel sentiment. Bumper stickers shout "No Castro, No Problem."

Some exile groups still dream of toppling him. During the 1970s and early 1980s, local "freedom fighters" turned into bomb-tossing terrorists, targeting Miami businesses and individuals who advocated peaceful dialogue with Cuba. Several Miamians were killed and many were injured.

The city has also been the center for heated airwave wars involving Radio Marti and TV Marti, two broadcasts of American programs and anti-Communist propaganda to Cuba. Many Miami Cubans see them as making the "dirty little worm squirm."

When Panamanian General Manuel Noriega was captured by the US government, a billboard was set up with the slogan: "Now Manuel, Next Fidel." Motorists honked in approval. When the Communist governments in East Germany and Nicaragua were given their last rites, Miami's anti-Castro factions were euphoric.

In 1996, Cuban MIG fighters shot down two planes, killing four Cuban-Americans. Castro said he was defending his air space. Three years later came the custody battle over Elián González. In 2006, when Castro went into the hospital for surgery and duties reverted to his brother, there was dancing in the streets of Miami.

More than four decades of dictatorial rule on the isolated tropical island have left their mark on the mainland. When Castro finally fades into history, it will take Miami many years to recover from the most passionate hate affair it has ever known. ❑

LEFT: Fidel Castro, a figure of hate in Miami.

Exiled leaders in Miami believed their valiant fighters had been betrayed by the United States.

In the fall of 1962, US spy planes discovered signs of a military build-up in Cuba. Soldiers swarmed into Miami once again, and President John F. Kennedy addressed the nation on October 22 to explain what became known as the Cuban Missile Crisis. War loomed. In the end, Soviet leader Nikita Khrushchev backed down and agreed to remove the Russian missiles from Cuba. In return, the US promised not to invade the island – or allow anyone else to. The exile community, now extending to about 100,000, had to face the realization that Miami was

VOTES FOR WOMEN

Florida was the last state in the country to grant women the right to vote. The new legislation was ratified only in 1969.

Freedom Flights ended in 1973. In order to process this wave of immigrants, the government took over the old *Miami News* tower, and renamed it the "Freedom Tower" *(see page 113)*.

Flower children

As the era of "Camelot" faded into the Vietnam protest years, Coconut Grove attracted flower children and hippies, who congregated

going to be more than a temporary home.

Kennedy honored the Bay of Pigs prisoners (freed in late 1962 in exchange for $62 million) at a ceremony in the Orange Bowl. The young president visited Miami once more, in November 1963, en route to his fatal stop in Dallas.

Beginning in 1965, twice-daily flights took off from Havana to bring refugees to Miami. By the end of the 1960s, a Cuban refugee was arriving every seven minutes. Miami's Cuban population doubled, reaching 300,000 – none of them friends of Castro – by the time the so-called

ABOVE: the first wave of Cubans arrived in Miami around 1960, where they were warmly greeted.

in Peacock Park and made long-time residents feel as if their town, too, was under siege. The hard-to-patrol coastline that made South Florida so inviting to rumrunners in the 1920s proved equally attractive to smugglers eager to supply America's growing appetite for illegal drugs. Huge amounts of drugs, and drug money, poured into Miami.

"Great Society" urban renewal brought bulldozers to Overtown as new housing projects and expressways took shape. Displaced residents poured into Liberty City, which had once been a model black community. Substandard housing became horribly overcrowded, and a civic time bomb began to tick.

Liberty City exploded into Miami's first race riot in August 1968, just as Richard Nixon, who had vacationed for years on Key Biscayne, was giving his acceptance speech to the Republican National Convention in Miami Beach.

The 1960s had their brighter moments, too. Miami-Dade Junior (later Community) College opened, as well as a new seaport at Dodge Island. A professional football team called the Dolphins came to town, and comedian Jackie Gleason broadcast weekly television shows from Miami Beach.

In 1964, a long-haired singing group, the Beatles, crossed the Atlantic. It was from Miami that they made their historic broadcast on the *Ed Sullivan Show*, which went out live from Miami Beach. Thousands of teenage girls went wild, and the Sixties had truly arrived. While the city continued to grow (the population reached 1 million in February 1962), people began to express concern about the environment. Their efforts led to the saving of the old Cape Florida Lighthouse and the establishment of John Pennekamp Coral Reef State Park (containing Florida's last living coral reef) and Biscayne National Park in the Florida Keys.

The Seventies

At the beginning of the 1970s, Miami seemed poised on the brink of a new boom. Community pride ran high as President Nixon's "vacation White House" on Key Biscayne, the Dolphins' perfect 1973 season, and Super Bowl victories kept Miami in the news. Florida International University, Miami's long-awaited state college, opened in 1972. Cubans, no longer refugees, were establishing a resident, rather than an exile, community, and running successful businesses. "Calle Ocho" (SW 8th Street in Little Havana) was thriving. Then a recession hit – the worst since the 1930s. Projects were abandoned and once again half-finished buildings loomed across the skyline. Unemployment was as high as 13 percent by 1975.

In spite of hard times and Watergate, the nation paused in 1976 to celebrate its Bicentennial. During the celebration in Miami, one of the official Bicentennial cities, 7,300 people, mainly Cuban refugees, became American citizens in a huge ceremony.

City leaders formed the Downtown Action Committee to spur revitalization for downtown Miami, and made big plans for the future. The city successfully turned itself into an international banking center; it seemed like a bank was going up on practically every corner. By the late 1970s, a rapid transit system was under construction and new government and cultural centers were springing up.

The 1980s got off to a poor start. The popular black Superintendent of Schools was charged with, and later convicted of, the theft of school property. In May 1980, after a Tampa jury acquitted a white policeman of the slaying of a black man, Arthur McDuffie, Liberty City and other areas again erupted in riots. The city despaired. Meanwhile, "Haitian boat people" were landing on the beaches daily, fleeing dictatorship and putting new pressure on the Miami infrastructure.

In 1980, events in Cuba once again took a hand in Miami's history. Fidel Castro announced that anyone who wished to leave the island could do so, and thousands did. Miami Cubans sailed to Mariel harbor to help their countrymen escape. Castro's government forced them to bring back to Miami unwanted passengers as well, including inmates from Cuba's jails and mental institutions. Miami struggled under the weight of 125,000 "Marielitos," many of them criminals. Tent cities sprang up to house them and the prison population swelled.

Things were looking bleak. Residents who were tired of crime and upheaval, and many who hadn't taken to Spanish, Creole and "Spanglish" culture, moved to quieter, calmer places. Cars sported bumper stickers that read: "Will the last American leaving Miami please bring the flag?"

The Magic City

Miami had had a bumpy year in 1980, but the city had been down before and it never lasted long. Soon the headlines were for news other than the frequent drug stories, when in 1982 the *Wall Street Journal* referred to its business as "bustling." The next year *House and Garden* magazine eulogized Miami as "magical" – one of the reasons for its nickname "The Magic City" – and a $3 billion building boom again transformed the Downtown skyline.

Ironically, though, it was an offshoot of the illegal drugs business that won back Miami's place in the nation's heart. The TV show *Miami Vice* bust onto the small screens on September 16, 1984. The hit show's slick style glamorized Miami life and the world flocked to the city to experience it for themselves. Miami passed a political milestone in 1985 when its citizens elected Xavier Suarez as its first Cuban-born mayor. The new open-air Bayside Marketplace attracted tourists and shoppers. Metrorail and Metromover facilitated transportation to, from and around Downtown. Even the Pope came to town, visiting for two days in September 1987 as part of his monumental tour of the United States.

Miami became a sports fan's paradise, as the new Miami Arena welcomed sell-out crowds for the professional basketball team, the Miami

Heat. Key Biscayne hosted tennis luminaries at the Lipton Tournament (now the NASDAQ-100 Open), and every spring downtown Miami reverberated with noise and excitement as Grand Prix race cars roared through the streets. The University of Miami basked in the limelight as its football team took the national championship three times in the decade: 1983, 1987 and 1989. Joe Robbie Stadium (now Dolphin Stadium) opened in the fall of 1987 and hosted the Super Bowl in January, 1989.

Miami entered the 1990s with a whole new sense of identity. The skyline had become beautiful, South Beach's Art Deco District was being renovated and was experiencing a

LEFT: 1984's *Miami Vice* enticed visitors to the city.
RIGHT: Gianni Versace's sister and brother attend his funeral after the designer was gunned down on Ocean Drive in 1997.

comeback. People were even coming back to Downtown – for sports, culture and fun. But most of all, for the first time in years – possibly the first time ever – all over Miami was the feeling that the city was coming into its own.

The city thrived thanks to an influx of Europeans, South Americans, Canadians, Japanese and others, who saw South Florida as one huge investment opportunity. In addition to winter homes, they invested in hotels, restaurants and businesses. Tourism continued to thrive and flourish.

Then, on August 24 1992, Hurricane Andrew paid a momentous visit, destroying thousands of homes and causing billions of dollars in

damage. It was then the costliest natural disaster the United States had ever endured. Andrew, though, brought Miamians together, peeling away layers of difference and leaving everyone in the same situation, with no water, electricity or air conditioning.

In 1994, another wave of Cuban rafters and Haitian refugees arrived in Miami, and the city struggled to cope with the influx as it faced financial trouble. Many of Miami's wealthier and non-Spanish speaking residents followed their predecessors and headed north. But Miami still hung on.

South Beach continued its renaissance and was making big waves in the tourism industry.

Fashion models, photographers, and trendsetters elbowed each other for space at Ocean Drive cafés and bars. Celebrities, from Madonna to Jack Nicholson and Cameron Diaz, were drawn to the excitement of South Beach. Limousines and convertibles competed for parking spaces. Gianni Versace bought a choice property on Ocean Drive, and lived there, until he was gunned down on the very same street in 1997. A serial killer, Andrew Cunanan, was said to have been the killer, and Cunanan himself was found dead shortly after, apparently by his own hand.

The music industry woke up to the local Latin sound, and hometown diva Gloria Estefan and her Miami Sound Machine made it big. Her marriage to Emilio Estefan created a Latin music giant that is now a major force for new talent in the business. Later – and spurred on by Art Basel – one of the world's foremost art events (*see pages 64 and 129*), a visual arts started to flourish in the sunshine. Word was out: Miami was a great place to be.

Cuban-American traumas

What Art Basel and the Estefans were doing in the arts, other Cuban-Americans were accomplishing in politics and business. Cuba, though, and what it represents, were still kept at arms length. Even after 40 years of exile the wounds were too raw, and performers from the island only 90 miles (145 km) south of Key West were not welcome in the city. Miami's Cubans lived by the motto, "never forget." They were ready to declare war when Castro's MIG fighters shot down four Cuban-American flyers in 1995. The young Miamians belonged to *Hermanos al Rescate* (Brothers to the Rescue), a group of pilots who scoured the Florida Straits for rafters fleeing Cuba's hardships. President Clinton reversed the loosening of the four-decade-old trade embargo.

Jorge Mas Canosa, a prominent Miami businessman predicted by many to restore Cuba as a capitalist paradise after Castro's demise, never saw that dream come true. In 1997, after an "American-dream" rise from refugee to power broker, he died aged 58. His funeral was a major event, attracting thousands. His legacy is the powerful Cuban-American National Foundation, which lobbies Congress for democratic changes in Cuba.

The success of his telecommunications company was a beacon for the progress that many first-generation Cubans were making in the booming city. In 1999, the CANF came to national prominence when a six-year-old Cuban boy named Elián González, whose mother died fleeing Cuba, was found at sea. Jorge Mas Santos, who had inherited the exile leadership from his father, Mas Canosa, was seen directing Elián's Miami relatives as they tried to keep the boy from returning to his father in Cuba.

Elián spent five months in a Little Havana home, which federal agents stormed in a fierce dawn raid to seize the boy. He was finally returned to Cuba in June, 2000. The fallout from

A YOUNG OUTLOOK

Miami's image has changed radically. No longer a haunt for senior citizens, it is now an outward-looking, very youthful city where the median age is 38.

tion brought by hurricanes Dennis, Katrina and Wilma. Forecasters expect the trend to continue (see pages 172–73).

A bright destination

In 2000, South Beach was named best urban beach in the US. Since September 11, 2001, when tourism overall took a terrible hit, Miami has made a better recovery in both vis-

the Elián affair was as destructive as a bomb. Cubans protested at the government's action, and whites and blacks counter-protested.

The hurricane season, always a grim mark on the Florida calendar, intensified enormously in 2004, with hurricanes Charley, Frances, Ivan and Jeanne lashing the state and causing 49 local deaths in the fiercest season on record. All weather records were shattered again the following year, with more devasta-

LEFT: Art Basel has energized Miami's art scene.
ABOVE: in 2004, Fisher Island (in foreground, with South Beach behind), was purchased by a real estate company headed by a 28-year-old French citizen.

itor numbers and tourist-dollar receipts than any other US city. Cruise ships fill the port and tourists fill the shops and restaurants. Lavish civic projects include the Miami Performing Arts Center – a $27 million project – with venues and homes for the Florida Grand Opera, the Miami City Ballet and the Concert Association of Florida, as well as being a principal venue for the New World Symphony Orchestra.

The colors of the downtown skyline reflect at night in Biscayne Bay and in the Miami River. The image shimmering in the waters is one of a city sparkling with tropical promise for the remaining part the 21st century. ❏

Decisive Dates

circa **8000 BC** Nomadic tribes reach Florida, probably having migrated from the North American northwest. The Tequesta people settle the verdant areas surrounding present-day Miami.

AD 1400s About 10,000 Native Americans are living on the peninsula when the Spanish arrive.

1492 Christopher Columbus arrives in the New World, landing first on Hispaniola.

1513 Spanish conquistador Juan Ponce de León "discovers" Florida and sails into Biscayne Bay.

1562 The French arrive in Florida to challenge the Spanish, who then strengthen their hold.

1566 Pedro Menéndez de Avilés, the first Spanish governor of Florida, visits the Tequesta people of the Miami area to set up trade links.

1580s–1760s Florida is disputed between Britain, France and Spain.

1763 The French and Indian War ends, with Florida becoming a British colony.

1784 Britain swaps with Spain, trading Florida for the Bahamas. Miami's first residents Pedro Fornells and John Egan are granted land.

1817–18 First Seminole War.

1821 The US gains control of Florida and hundreds of runaway slaves settle in the area.

1825 The Cape Florida Lighthouse, the first permanent structure in South Florida, lights up.

1835 Seminole Indians attack settlers and the bloody "Dade Massacre" occurs. This sparks off the Second Seminole War, which lasts for seven years. Many Seminoles are deported from Florida to Oklahoma.

1838 Fort Dallas is built to defend against Seminole attack.

1843 William English settles in Miami area. He is the first to use the name "Miami."

1845 Florida becomes the 27th state.

1850 Miami's first post office is in operation.

1855–8 The Third Seminole War makes the area unstable once more.

1861–5 As a major slave-holding state, Florida joins forces with the South in the American Civil War. However, the Miami area is barely affected.

1870s Developer William Brickell arrives in Miami and establishes a trading post.

1896 Julia Tuttle convinces Henry Flagler to bring his railroad to Miami. City status is conferred on Miami. The city's first newspaper, the *Miami Metropolis*, hits the streets.

1898 Miami's growth accelerates after being chosen as a military training base for the Spanish-American War.

1905–12 The final section of the East Coast Railway, from Miami to Key West, is built.

1906 Governor Broward begins to drain parts of the Everglades to open up the area around Miami to farming.

1914 Chicago millionaire James Deering starts work on Vizcaya, his grand Miami retreat.

1915 Collins Bridge, now the Venetian Causeway, is built to link Miami with present-day Miami Beach. The latter becomes a city, as casinos, cabanas and cafés blossom.

1917 World War I transforms Miami's Dinner Key into a US Navy air base.

1920 The city's population nears 30,000.

1920s The Roaring Twenties bring a huge real estate boom and grand buildings to the city, plus population growth and modernization. Prohibition fails to take hold in Miami, and it becomes a haven for "rumrunners."

1921 George Merrick begins work on the new suburb of Coral Gables.

1926 The University of Miami is founded. A brutal hurricane batters the city, leaving over 200 people dead.

1928 The Tamiami Trail opens – the first major road across the Everglades, linking Miami with Tampa. Gangster Al Capone moves to Miami.

1930s Miami Beach's Art Deco hotels are built and tourism thrives in South Florida.

1933 An attempt is made on the life of Franklin D. Roosevelt at Bayfront Park.

1935 A huge hurricane hits the Keys, killing more than 400 people.

1936 Miami hosts the Orange Festival, beginning the tradition of the Orange Bowl Parade.

1942 Hotels are transformed into barracks and hospitals during World War II.

1947 Everglades National Park is created.

1950s The tourism boom brings grand-scale hotels to Miami Beach, and the government cracks down on Miami's mobsters and illegal gambling halls.

1959 Fidel Castro leads a revolution in Cuba, and later embraces Communism.

1960s In the years following the Cuban Revolution, thousands of Cubans flee the island and settle in the Miami area. More emigrés from Central and South America follow.

1961 Cuban exiles unite with American agents in the foiled Bay of Pigs invasion of Cuba. Almost 100 people die.

1962 The Cuban Missile Crisis threatens war, and exiles realize that Miami is no longer just a temporary home. The city's population reaches 1 million people.

1970s US economic recession badly hurts Miami. President Nixon vacations on Key Biscayne as four Miamians break into a Washington DC office, triggering the Watergate scandal. Conditions on the island of Haiti worsen considerably, and thousands of Haitians sail rickety boats to Miami.

1973 The Miami Dolphins win the Superbowl and finish the first-ever unbeaten, no-tie season in the history of the National Football League.

1980 A race riot erupts in the neighborhood of Liberty City over the acquittal of a white police officer accused of murdering a black man. In the so-called Mariel Boatlift, President Castro allows 125,000 Cubans, many of them convicted criminals, to leave the island and come to Miami.

1980s The city becomes known as the principal east coast entry point for drug runners. The campaign to restore the Art Deco District of Miami Beach gathers pace and launches the area's renaissance as a resort.

1984 The television series *Miami Vice* premiers, vastly changing the public image of Miami.

1985 The city elects Xavier Suárez, its first Cuban mayor.

1990 Manuel Noriega, former chief of state of Panama, is tried in Miami on drugs charges.

1992 Hurricane Andrew makes a direct hit just south of Miami. The damage is estimated at around $25 billion.

1994 Economic collapse in Cuba brings another wave of refugees, scores of whom are plucked from the water by the US Coast Guard.

1995 Two American planes flown by members of the Miami-based Cuban group Brothers to the Rescue are shot down by the Cuban Air Force.

1997 Fashion designer Gianni Versace is murdered outside his South Beach mansion.

1999–2000 Elián González is plucked from the sea after his mother dies fleeing Cuba. Emotions run high when the government insists that Elián be returned to his father on the island.

2002 Art Basel Miami Beach transforms the art scene and contributes to the growth of the Wynwood Art District and the Design District.

2003 Marlins win the World Series (baseball).

2004–5 South Florida is hit by an unprecedented number of hurricanes, but damage is contained.

2006 The Miami Performing Arts Center opens. The Miami Heat win the NBA (National Basketball Association) title. ❑

LEFT: the Spanish land at Tequesta (Miami), 1500s.
RIGHT: skycrapers are part of the modern landscape.

THE MANY FACES OF MIAMI

The endless energy and Miami's spot in the sun are beacons for Cubans and Haitians, gays, Latin Americans, party-time clubbers and wealthy mavericks from all over the world

Miami is often called the most un-American American city, and it's true. Look in the local phone book and you'll find 10,000 listings for the name Rodriguez. Look up Smith and you'll find a mere 2,000. What is "foreign" here is commonplace, what is "native" is hard to find. Ethnicity defines Miami. It is its core, its essence. It is what gives the city its super-charged multicultural ambience and exotic kick.

According the US Census Bureau, Miami has more foreign-born residents (60 percent) than any other large city in America including New York, San Diego and Los Angeles. If it were a demographic pie chart, it would be cut into three pieces – 60 percent Hispanic, 20 percent African-American, and 20 percent non-Hispanic white. When at home, more than 68 percent of Miamians speak a language other than English.

Ethnic debates

Delving into Miami's ethnic dynamics is not about quaint foreign customs or immigrant subcultures at the margins of society. Rather, it is to reach into the soul of the city. Looking at the long history of immigration and ethnicity in the United States, Miami's ethnicity often proves puzzling. What is usually a struggling minority is the dominant and successful majority here. Old-fashioned demographic

PRECEDING PAGES: under the stars on a balmy night.
LEFT: multi-culturalism at the beach.
RIGHT: cheerleader for the Miami Dolphins football team performs during half-time.

patterns do not materialize, and the rules of the game are different.

In Miami, an ex-president of Panama sits in prison while newly rich Russian mobsters cut deals on global cell phones. In Miami, the daughter of a former Dominican Republic dictator shops at upscale boutiques while Fidel Castro's sister tallies up the sales at her Little Havana pharmacy. In Miami, retired Colombian drug dealers kick back at Key Biscayne condos while descendants of reggae star Bob Marley buy organic vegetables at the Coconut Grove farmer's market. And gay and lesbian couples from all ethnic backgrounds stroll down Lincoln Road, with their kids in tow.

Cubanismo

While Miami's ethnic makeup includes more than 100 nationalities, Cubans are the dominant group. Miami-Dade County has a population of about 2.4 million, and inside that figure are about 700,000 Cubans, almost one-third of the local population. The *Cubanismo* of contemporary Miami is evident not just in their overall numbers, but also in their economic, social and political clout.

Today, the mayors of the city and the county, the county state attorney, the president of the largest bank, the presidents of the two local state colleges, the owner of the largest real estate company, the publisher of the

Miami Herald, the managing partner of the largest law firm, and nearly half of Miami-Dade County's state legislature are either Cuban-born or of Cuban descent. They are a people who have put down deep roots, worked hard, and now enjoy the fruits of their labor. Polls show that fewer than 30 percent of them say they would return to Cuba when Fidel Castro is no longer in power.

The foundation for this powerful immigrant community was laid down by the first wave of Cuban exiles that arrived in the early 1960s, following Castro's take-over of the country. Most of these "first-wave" Cubans were of the entrepreneurial, managerial and professional class; people who had the advantages of education, assets and business know-how when they arrived, which made their adjustment to life here easier. Of all US cities, Miami today has the largest number, per capita, of Hispanic-owned businesses. Ranging from small, family-run operations to large corporations, a great number of these Hispanic businesses were founded by early Cuban immigrants. Within the Cuban community, a bustling ethnic network is well established in helping new arrivals with professional contacts and employment opportunities.

Starting in the early 1960s and continuing for about a decade, Cuban migration to Miami was substantial and steady. Then there was the Mariel boatlift in 1980 that brought over 125,000 Cubans to Miami. The exodus continues today, with almost weekly arrivals of Cubans landing on South Florida's shores. Because they come from a Communist country, and, because of the Cuban Adjustment Act of the 1966, Cubans are given special privileges that no other group enjoys. As soon as they set foot on US soil, they are given political asylum, work permits, and permanent resident status.

This disparity in immigration rights, often called the Wet-Foot-Dry-Foot policy, has led to a resentment of the Cubans by other groups, including immigrants from other Spanish-speaking countries.

Along with the Cubans, many other Caribbean, Central and South American immigrants have come to Miami during the past 20 years after fleeing political upheavals or economic hardships in their homelands. Among them are large numbers of Haitians, Nicaraguans, Salvadorans, Venezuelans, Jamaicans, Trinidadians, Colombians, Dominicans, Peruvians, and Hondurans. Many of these new immigrants are young, and their presence has drastically changed the average age of the local population. No longer a senior citizen's haven, Miami is now a youthful city with a median age of 38.

Black communities

With a population of more than 240,000, Haitians are the second largest immigrant group in Miami, but they have not been as fortunate as the Cubans or other Spanish-speaking immigrants. Often, they come here with few professional skills and resources, and have had to work exceptionally hard to get ahead.

Although they have been subjected to discrimination by the local community as well as by the US Immigration Service, Haitians have done relatively well here, forming their own network of self-employment and small business opportunities. While the neighborhood of Little Haiti is still where most newly arrived Haitian immigrants settle, and it continues to be the political and social backbone of the community, many other neighborhoods now serve as home to a rapidly growing group of middle-class professional Haitian-Americans. Haitians have also prospered in the local arts

LUXURY IN BLACK

The upscale oceanfront Royal Palm Resort, 1545 Collins Avenue in South Beach, opened in 2002. The African-American owned and managed hotel was the first of its kind in the United States.

Spanish-speaking majority when it comes to employment, politics, and professional advancement. They have also come up against diverging points of view when it comes to many social issues.

This was made painfully clear in 1990 when South African anti-Apartheid leader Nelson Mandela paid a visit to the city. Shortly after

scene, and have recently begun to play a more active role in local politics. Several Haitian-Americans have served as local mayors, council members, and in the state legislature.

What the Haitians – and other non-Hispanic black immigrants – have not done is build a consensus with native-born blacks. With only 20 percent of the population, Miami's African-Americans are among the most socially and economically segregated groups in Miami.

Because they usually don't speak Spanish, they have often felt disenfranchised by the

his arrival, a group of Cuban-American mayors refused to give Mandela an official welcome because he once shook hands with Fidel Castro and was seen as a Communist sympathizer. Along with great community embarrassment, what ensued was a nationwide boycott of Miami's tourism industry by African-Americans that cost the city over $50 million in revenues. The boycott ended three years later when Miami commissioners agreed to funnel local monies into a newly built African-American-owned and managed hotel. That hotel, the luxurious Royal Palm on South Beach, opened in 2002 and is the first of its kind in the United States.

LEFT: Cuban grandmother.
ABOVE: Easter Sunday in Little Haiti.

White flight

African-Americans have not been the only ethnic group that feels alienated by Miami's immigrant infusion. American-born, non-Hispanic whites – referred to here as Anglos – have showed their frustration with their feet. In the past 20 years, more than 200,000 of them have fled to other parts of South Florida and elsewhere in the US. According to recent census data, for almost every immigrant who has come to Miami-Dade County in recent years, a white non-Hispanic has left. This dramatic out-migration of whites has not hurt the local economy, but it has had a negative affect on cultural institutions such as symphony

Wealthy newcomers

Another factor added to the multi-cultural equation is the significant influx of wealthy Europeans in the past decade, the most prominent perhaps being the late Italian fashion designer, Gianni Versace. There have also been many others whose money has gained potency due to the weakness of the dollar, and who now see Miami as a real estate investment bargain. Among them is a 28-year-old French citizen who bought the exclusive 216-acre (87-hectare) residential enclave of Fisher Island in 2004.

A few years after the break-up of the Soviet Union, tens of thousands of newly rich Russians, Ukrainians, and Lithuanians started mak-

orchestras, ballet companies, and arts organizations that previously received substantial donations from them.

Included in this "white flight" has been the dramatic drop in the local Jewish community. Once home to the second largest Jewish population in the US, Miami-Dade County has seen that figure decrease from about 250,000 to barely 100,000 in the past 15 years. Although some of that drop has been due to attrition – many elderly Jews have died – many have simply moved northward to Broward and Palm Beach counties where the Jewish population has doubled in the same timeframe and is now far larger than that of Miami.

ing Miami their home, and they now have a fairly strong community. So many are arriving that a Russian owned airline inaugurated non-stop flights from Moscow to Miami in 2006.

And then there are the many, many upperclass South Americans who keep second homes in Miami, and come here regularly to shop and visit doctors. These wealthy South Americans have more or less replaced the former "snowbirds" who used to come to down to Miami each winter from the cold, American Northeast.

This newer wealthy population base has been a boon to the local economy by creating a market for luxury condos that sell for $1 million each. But it has also led to the dwindling of the middle-class. Teachers, firefighters and nurses can barely afford to live here and the gap between rich and poor is widening. This glaring fact was made public in 2003 when Miami was given the dubious honor of being the "poorest large city in America" with over 30 percent of residents living below the poverty line.

There is one American-born middle-class demographic group, however, that has consistently grown in recent years and that is the gay community. Largely responsible for the Art Deco revitalization of the early 1990s as well as the lucrative art and design scene, the gay population has established a powerful base in Miami and is now one of the most vibrant gay communities in the US. It is also politically active – the City of Miami Beach recently extended domestic partnership benefits to all gay city employees.

Gay men and women are made to feel welcome in Miami, and the city's tourism board was one of the first in the country to designate an office that marketed strictly to gays and their much sought after double-income-no-kids buying power. Today, Miami hosts an annual Gay and Lesbian Film Festival, along with the White Party and Winter Party, two nationally acclaimed gay fundraising events. Miami doesn't celebrate an annual Gay Pride Day as do many other cities in the US because it doesn't need to; every day is gay pride day in Miami.

The face of the future

While Miami's multi-ethnic character is at times conflictive and gives the appearance of a city divided along racial and ethnic lines, it in fact serves as a living, breathing testing ground for the demographic transformations that will likely occur across the US in the next 20 years. Hispanics are the fastest growing ethnic group in the US, and based on current trends, the US

Census Bureau predicts a 75 percent increase in their population by the year 2015, and an overall Hispanic population of 96 million by the year 2050. Many sociologists are taking a serious look at Miami today, because they see it as a harbinger of what's to come.

While there are many people who still look at Miami and say, "This is not America," they are wrong. While giving a reading in Miami recently, former US Poet Laureate Robert Pinsky told his audience, "Miami is a more intense version of the United States itself." Pinsky is right. Miami is indeed an intense version of America, and the modern, multi-cultural face of the country's future. ❑

LEFT: Miami Beach now has fewer Jewish people and more young Europeans and South Americans.
ABOVE: sailing past celebrity homes on Biscayne Bay.

BODY CULTURE

The South Florida climate provides a perfect backdrop to a buff body. Those who've got it, flaunt it. Those who haven't can easily buy it in this nip and tuck Nirvana

The year-round sunshine, the hot breezes and the miles of golden beach make Miami a sparkling and languid altar for the universal religion, the cult of the body. Not just anybody's body, of course. One's own body. One's own – and perhaps the other bodies one may arrange around it. The peculiar craze for 90-minute nose-jobs, and cosmetic surgery generally, is such a feverish enthusiasm that unlicensed and foreign practitioners do a blazing, though illegal, trade at private parties. These have the atmosphere of Tupperware parties, but with more dramatic products for a more personal form of preservation.

Rollerbladers by land, windsurfers by sea, all are members of Miami's Sweat Set, and the spas and health clubs are cathedrals of calisthenics raised in the subtropical heat. Cruise ships at the Port of Miami may be chosen for the quality of their on-board spa.

Look at me

Like the convertibles whisking tourists from Miami International Airport to the closest beach, this is a top-down, look-at-me, full-tilt metropolis. Look at the ice-blue glass towers along Brickell Avenue, each bank with its own sky-high logo as corporate ego. "It's Miami," went one catchy booster jingle, "It's my Miami. And Miami's for me."

As far back as Ponce de León's search for the fabled "fountain of youth," people have come to Florida to defy the aging process, to

pretend they'll never die. It's small wonder that narcissism, that anaesthesia for mortality, comes so naturally to Miamians. Maybe it's in the water. Then again, the town does sit on the youngest piece of land mass in all of America.

Carl Fisher may have realized this when he called Miami Beach a place "where the old could grow young and the young never grow old." Fisher arrived in 1913, with deep pockets and the prototype of the modern Miami man: part visionary, part exile, part huckster. He had the money and vision to suck the muck up from Biscayne Bay and create a perfect platform for self-promotion, Miami Beach. This end of the Florida peninsula made dreams into

---

LEFT: sex and South Beach.
RIGHT: tanned and taut, Miamians hit the beaches.

---

a cash crop, many of them too good to be true. "The whole creation of the beach was to appeal to escape," publicist Hank Meyer once said. "You were dealing with subliminal suggestion – moods, desires, dreams, fantasies."

Like the great seasonal storms that whip through the Caribbean each summer, Miami lives in the eye of its own hurricane, the winds blowing in the curious from all points

of the compass. Dreamers in New York and Bogota alike feel the city's drum beat of bronzed display. A red-hot mix of Cubans and Haitians, American blacks, Central American refugees, and wealthy young European newcomers all heed the call.

The *crème de la crème* of the world's plastic surgeons make annual pilgrimage to the mecca of Miami. For more than 30 years, the annual Cosmetic Surgery Symposium has convened at this nip and tuck Nirvana. Face lifts are auctioned at film festival benefits, and cosmetic procedures are given as prizes in competitions, often for beauty contests, and with no discernable irony. Wrinkle-filling and bottom-

boosts are such big business that it inspired the hit TV show, *Nip/Tuck*, and in true Miami style, they have spawned their own underworld.

Private parties in hotel suites swirl around Colombian, Venezuelan or Peruvian practitioners, who give fat-gobbling injections and botox jabs on the spot. Prices are keen and trade is brisk. Practitioners are announced as assistants or juniors to famous surgeons in their home countries, in town for a short visit. Of course, there is no comeback if something goes wrong, and quite often it does. In a 2006 *New York Times* article, Miami dermatologist Dr Mayoral said that he was often seeing five patients a day with deformities caused by illegal cosmetic procedures. "It's an epidemic," he said. In 1999, Reinaldo Silvestre's treatments, some carried out in an office he shared with a realtor and some in parking lots, earned him the name of the "Butcher of South Beach." Describing a Mexican body-builder, Spencer Aronfeld, attorney for three of Silvestre's victims, said his client awoke from surgery, "expecting to look like Tarzan. Instead, he looks like Pamela Anderson."

Bronze is beautiful

Miami shares with California the North American patent on the fine art of Flaunting It. Since the climate requires so few clothes here, skin is a visible status symbol. People also come here just to talk about it: Miami hosted the first International Congress of Esthetics, a meeting of beauticians who specialize in skin care. The state having one of the highest cancer rates in America doesn't seem to deter anyone: people keep on baring and bronzing.

To ensure this tan attracts the right kind of attention, a firm body is in order, and some sporty exertion makes for a good display. A jog along most Miami city blocks will pass a tennis court, health-food store, martial arts school, yoga club, diet center, dance studio or workout gym. Bicycle and jogging paths line grand winding routes like Old Cutler Road and the causeway to Key Biscayne.

Tanned and taut, Miamians take to the streets. And beaches. And clubs. Topless bathing on Miami Beach, if not officially sanc-

LEFT: open-air massage at the Doral Golf Resort.
RIGHT: South Beach, a model society.

tioned, has become *la mode*. Dressed to kill, party-goers descend 5,000-strong on South Beach, Coconut Grove and Downtown nightclubs. They dance all night in over-the-top, up-to-the-minute premises or in old Art Deco palaces, where intermissions include lingerie and swimsuit shows.

Looking good

One club owner is renowned for his 60 pairs of shorts, often worn with a tuxedo jacket and no socks. It's ego-dressing: the women don low-cut tops, hot pants, skirts slit to the thigh or stopping just above the breeze. Leopard skin and leather is tighter on the women than it

was on the animals who donated it. Fashion models stalk the town, and it's not that uncommon to see Miamians with parrots, or even boa constrictors, adorning their shoulders.

They should have called it Me-ami. On one tiny stretch of Coconut Grove, 18 sidewalk cafés offer 721 seats from which to see everyone else. "We thought about getting entertainment," says one owner. "But we don't need it. People have people."

So it goes. Non-stop entertainment. With a backdrop of fruit-salad sunsets and palm-tree props, tongues firmly in cheek – the show-off of American cities admiring itself in a full-length mirror. Me-ami, indeed.   ❑

FASHION SHOOT CENTRAL

We've come a long way since the 1890s, when South Florida's founding mothers, undeterred by heat, humidity, insects and Native Americans, took to the beach in thick black stockings and closed-toed bathing shoes.

Now, models bare as much as possible for the annual swimsuit edition of *Sports Illustrated* or *Ocean Drive Magazine*. Staying in one of the upmarket South Beach hotels, sometimes it seems as though all the other guests are supermodels. And sometimes they are.

From all over the world, models cluster on South Beach and Coconut Grove, where the rich natural light perfectly reflects youth and beauty. They do it for European catalogues, South American stores, magazines and perfume ads. It's hard to spend a day on the beach without seeing at least one fashion shoot, especially in wintertime. Portfolios under their arms, models vamp up and down Ocean Drive and Collins Avenue between castings, taking calls from modeling agencies such as Elite, Ford and others.

A typical shoot can start at 7am and last until sunset, with much of the day spent waiting around, or having endless, minute adjustments to perfect hair and make-up. During a good week in the peak winter season a young model, who may still be in school, can earn as much as her teachers do in a year.

SHOPPING IN THE SUNSHINE

South Americans flock to shop in their thousands, eager for tech treasures and the bargains of bling

Bling and bliss. Glamour and great bargains. Outdoor malls with waterfalls, or indoor specialty shops with fashions that show up in films. This is retail reality, Miami style. In an open-air city, cool clothes are second only to naked skin in the "look-at me" sweepstakes. If money is no object, try Miracle Mile or the Village of Merrick Park in Coral Gables. Alternatively, visit the elegant Bal Harbour Shops, where restaurants will even feed your poodle. If design is your thing, head to the Wynwood Art District or the Design District, and overindulge in the attitude.

For knick-knacks and bargains, there is the Flagler Flea Market on SW 7th Street, an open-air bazaar where you can find everything from jeans to plastic toys. Bird Road, the continuation of SW 40th Street, is gaining a reputation for vintage clothes, while the funky streets of North Beach are the place to head for used vinyl and CDs.

Downtown's Flagler Street remains the mecca for export-ready electronics and jewelry. Be prepared to haggle, though, and always check that the merchandise you bought ends up in your bag. *A complete list of malls can be found on pages 230–31.*

ABOVE: CocoWalk is one of Miami's hangouts for young people, who come to shop for music and clothes, see a movie, grab a bite and sip on a salty margarita.

RIGHT: Shop for vintage va-va-voom – Pucci, purses and all things nice – at the department store Miami Twice. It's open every day at 6562 SW 40th Street, tel: 305-666-0127.

ABOVE: Need spiritual help? You can find lotions, potions and statues to aid your prayers at *botánicas* in Little Havana and Little Haiti *(see page 132).*

THE BEST OF MIAMI'S MALLS

● **Lincoln Road Mall:** *(right).* South Beach's pedestrian retail center has outdoor restaurants and great opportunities for people-watching.
● **Aventura Mall:** the locals' favorite, with a 24-screen theater and a branch of almost every chain store.
● **Bal Harbour Shops:** high-end boutiques and charming cafés in a luxurious setting.
● **Bayside Marketplace:** more than 120 stores, bars and restaurants that stay open late in downtown Miami.
● **Village of Merrick Park:** stores for the ladies who lunch in Coral Gables.
● **The Falls:** open-air mall with waterfalls and more than 100 stores.
● **Prime Outlets at Florida City:** 60 factory outlets with prices below regular retail.

ABOVE: Beyond Miami, opportunities can be upscale and elegant. Worth Avenue in chic Palm Beach is Florida's answer to Beverly Hills' Rodeo Drive.

LEFT: In Little Havana is a factory that recalls old Cuba, where cigar aficionados can see their stogies being rolled and come away with a souvenir box.

LEFT: Tiffany and Co. is just one of the upscale emporia at beautiful Bal Harbour Shops. Others include Prada, Chanel, Dolce and Gabbana, Lalique, Versace and Armani.

MIAMI IN FILM AND FICTION

The Magic City is a modern-day frontier town, painted with tropical colors and air-brushed with urban grit. It's a steamy location for tales of lawbreakers, jet-setters and cross-dressers

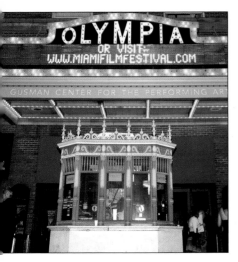

The edgy tropical exuberance of the Latino community, shady land-deals as endless and impenetrable as the Everglades, the shimmering modern skyline, and the glitz and glamour of the beach have all made the Magic City a tasty and tempting backdrop for film and fiction. Ever since Betty Grable, Don Ameche, Dana Landis, and Robert Cummings starred in the 1941 movie *Moon Over Miami*, this international playground within the United States has provided inspiration for writers and filmmakers.

An undercurrent of infinite mischief sets up glamorous and intriguing possibilities for books, movies and television shows among the city's palm fronds and blue, blue ocean. A Mariel refugee fought and clawed his way to become a cocaine boss, ravaged by drugs, heat and hubris in Al Pacino's 1983 move *Scarface*. The following year, while cocaine cowboys in Maserattis were ripping up the Miami highways and trading in coolers (ice-boxes containing a million dollars' cash), two television detectives managed to stay undercover without socks or ties, and fought the bad guys with coat sleeves pushed up to their elbows. The city fathers didn't seem to mind.

The opening credits for TV's pacy *Miami Vice* (1984) flashed by fluttering flamingoes at Hialeah Racetrack, audacious high-rises on

Brickell Avenue and speeding cigarette boats on the glittering bay, and it did the tourist business no harm at all.

Tinseltown, Florida

As early as 1919, D.W. Griffith saw the appeal of filming in South Florida. The pioneer director of *The Birth of a Nation* set up cameras on Fort Lauderdale's New River to film his South Seas-themed *The Idol Dancer*. Half a century later Connie Francis sang *Where the Boys Are* just blocks away at the Elbo Room in Fort Lauderdale, helping to make the area's Spring Break reputation for college students.

Today, you're likely to be in striking distance of a movie location almost anywhere in Miami. Strolling down Ocean Drive, you're on the set of *The Birdcage* or Cindy Crawford's jogging path in *Fair Game*. Driving across the MacArthur Causeway takes you on a location from numerous Miami movie hits including Will Smith and Martin Lawrence's *Bad Boys*. Take a drink at the Wreck Bar in the Sheraton Yankee Clipper in Fort Laud-

erdale to see the giant aquarium, a set for Billy Crystal and Robert De Niro's *Analyze This*. Or stroll down the Broadwalk to the Hollywood Beach Theatre up the coast in Hollywood, Florida. Seeing that bandstand and evocative building may stir steamy recollections of the charged encounter between sultry Kathleen Turner and lustful William Hurt in *Body Heat*.

You can try your hand driving golf balls into the water as Cameron Diaz did in *There's Something About Mary* at the Aqua Golf Driving Range by Pembroke Park. You probably won't see Diaz or co-star Matt Dillon, but the range's golf pro can tell you tales of the filming. The

building used for Diaz's apartment is just a block off Biscayne Boulevard in downtown Miami, and looks out over Biscayne Bay.

Arnold Schwarzenegger and Jamie Lee Curtis's *True Lies* features a Harrier fighter jet protruding from a Downtown office building. *Caddyshack*, the crude golf movie with Bill Murray and a gopher was filmed at the Grand Oaks Golf Club in Davie, just north of Miami. *Miami Rhapsody* with Sarah Jessica Parker features a scene in the Bal Harbour Shops.

The Marx Brothers' *The Cocoanuts*, *Key Largo*, *Ace Ventura: Pet Detective* and three James Bond movies – *Dr No*, *Live and Let Die* and *Goldfinger* all used Miami locations.

FAR LEFT: the Gusman Center is a site for the Miami International Film Festival. **LEFT:** poster for South Beach-based movie *The Birdcage*.
ABOVE: John Travolta and director Barry Sonnenfeld on the set of *Get Shorty*.

Crime between the covers

Crime statistics have been going steadily down in recent years, but Miami's reputation as a city of sin, where the bizarre and exotic are commonplace, continues to provide a wealth of inspiration for tough and wry writers like Edna Buchanan, Carolina Garcia-Aguilera, Carl Hiaasen, Dave Barry and Elmore Leonard, as well as many others.

Although "Dutch" Leonard lives in Detroit, Miami Beach is a regular setting for his tough yarns. He says that he loves the edginess South Florida gives to his tales. Leonard has set many of his best-selling novels here, including *Get Shorty, Rum Punch, Maximum Bob, Swag, Gold Coast, Stick* and *The Switch*.

Carl Hiaasen, a columnist for the *Miami Herald*, made an international name with satirical, funny and off-beat tales of eccentric characters under stress. Themes take in Hurricane Andrew, former Florida governor Lawton Chiles crossing the state on foot, greedy developers, wacky environmentalists and the state lottery. Hiaasen's *Stormy Weather, Skin Tight, Native Tongue, Strip Tease, Lucky You* and *Skinny Dip* have joined the local literary mythology.

Buchanan, the Pulitzer Prize-winning former *Miami Herald* police reporter, summed up Miami's image in the title of one of her books,

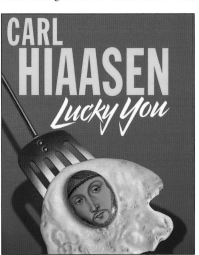

Miami, It's Murder. Her first book – and her best according to many fans – *The Corpse Had a Familiar Face*, was based on her hardcore beat. Calvin Trillin wrote in a *New Yorker* magazine profile of Buchanan, "In Miami, a few figures are regularly discussed by first name among people they have never actually met. One of them is Fidel. Another is Edna." She once showed up at the Miami Book Fair wearing a pair of gold pistol earrings.

Hollywood has raided South Florida literary creativity with successful screenplays including Leonard's *Get Shorty* and *Out of Sight*, and Hiaasen's *Strip Tease,* filmed by Paul Verhoeven as *Striptease,* starring Demi Moore.

People, and some of the old *Miami Vice* glamour is updated by the Miami branch of the *CSI* franchise, *CSI Miami*.

In the 1990s, a Latin American Hollywood began to emerge here, a production center for Spanish-language television shows aimed at Florida's Central and South American neighbors. But South Florida still hasn't caught on

Small screen sparkle

South Florida's TV history stretches over four decades, from Jackie Gleason's *Honeymooners* and Ivan Tors' *Flipper* and *Gentle Ben*, to *Miami Vice*. The unlikely comic potential of cosmetic surgery produced a hit show – *Nip/Tuck*. Another show, *The Golden Girls*, featured the tales of four retired women in South Florida. MTV also found Miami perfect for the chemistry of their "reality" show *Real*

as a major film and TV player in the way that New York, Las Vegas and LA have. Some cite stifling red-tape of the many municipalities; others say the pool of talent isn't as deep as in Tinseltown. Making *Jackie Brown* from Elmore Leonard's *Rum Punch,* Quentin Tarrantino moved the setting from Miami to LA, saying, "Miami is very hot. You don't want to shoot there."

For the 1996 film of *Romeo and Juliet*, Baz Luhrmann updated Verona to a comic-strip evocation of Miami Beach, although he actually shot the film in Mexico. For all that, no stand-in can really fill the role of the beaches and natural beauty of the real Miami. ❏

FAR LEFT: Elmore Leonard sets many of his crime novels in Miami. **LEFT:** local writer Carl Hiaasen's books are popular around the world.
ABOVE: the cast of *CSI Miami* pose with the city.

A TASTE OF MIAMI

Celebrity chefs and down-home diners conjure the cuisine of Cuban, Caribbean and South American cooking, or combine tropical tastes with fresh Florida flavors in a "Floribbean " mix. It all tastes even better outdoors or under the stars

Dining out in South Florida is like choosing a vacation destination. Think of a country, conjure its cuisine: French, Spanish, Caribbean, Southern, Asian, you'll find it here. Celebrity restaurants and chefs arrive to regular fanfare, as befits its cosmopolitan status. Gloria Estefan has a Cuban eatery called Casa Larios, and Emeril Lagasse's name is a beacon for New Orleans-style fish and seafood.

Cutting-edge styles like New American, a more informal cuisine emphasizing fresh fusion dishes with local ingredients, and Pan-Asian, spicy combinations drawing on everything from Japanese to Vietnamese, are among the Miami gourmet adventures. "Floribbean" is a local blend of Florida, Caribbean and Latin flavors; mangos mingled with snapper and lemon grass; cilantro merged with curry, coconut and citrus are mouth-watering treats found at spots like Chef Allen's, Norman's and Nemo. Being such a melting-pot city, the cuisines often intermarry, so you may well find grits on a Cuban breakfast menu, or mozzarella and prosciutto may show up in your otherwise French sandwiches.

Latin spices

A popular Miami flavor is that most humble of vegetable staples, the bean. Not just any bean, though, but the earthy Cuban black bean. Poor man's food, beans and rice make a nearly perfect protein, the equal of red meat but without

CUBAN ESSENTIALS

- *boniato:* a tasty tuber not unlike sweet potato.
- *carne asada:* roasted pork.
- *flan:* a dessert similar to creme caramel.
- *mojo:* a sauce made of oil, garlic, herbs and lime juice, often used as a meat marinade.
- *palomilla:* a thin steak with fried onions.
- *piccadillo:* minced beef with peppers and olives.
- *plátanos:* plantains – cooking bananas – sliced and fried as a side dish. Some prefer the sweeter *maduros.*
- *ropa vieja:* "old clothes" – shredded beef in tomatoes.
- *yuca:* the essential Cuban tuber, boiled or fried as a vegetable, or cut in chunks for stews.

LEFT: smoothies with a smile.
RIGHT: Cuban paella at the Calle Ocho Festival.

the fats, and called *moros y cristianos,* after the famous encounter of Charles Martel and the Arabs in AD 732.

Beans also fetch up in soups, in stews, served cold in salads, or simmered with an onion and a bay leaf to be poured over rice as a side dish. Cooked black beans are mashed into a paste, flattened and fried into black bean cakes to serve with salsa and a dot of sour cream. *Bolichemechado* is a beef dish stuffed with rice and beans.

Nationally and culturally identified dishes often become clichéd, but in Miami young cooks improvise with themes and staples to produce gourmet Cuban food. This can be found at

of meats hot off the grill – steak, chorizo, blood sausage, sweetbreads. With sexy samba beating in the background, try the Brazilian national dish, *feijoada*. It's a slow-cooked black bean stew full of juicy pork loin and smoked sausage, and accompanied by *farofa*, which is sauteed ground *yuca*. One restaurant that's a favorite with Brazilians is Porcao off Brickell Avenue.

One of Miami's little secrets is its authentic Mexican food, best sampled in the Homestead area. Even less known, but just as tasty, is the Colombian fare, like delicious plantains cut in thick slices, fried and used to hold combinations of meats, shrimps and sauces.

a few pricey spots such as Yuca on Lincoln Road; elsewhere, simpler recipes are dished up.

Hispanic Miami is not only Cuban cooking. The city's large Nicaraguan population has opened numerous restaurants. In the heart of Little Havana is Guayacan. The specialty of the house here is steak, grilled and served with a pungent *chimichurri* sauce, made from parsley and garlic. Another dish is *pescado a la Tipitapa*, worth trying if only to say the name. It's a deep-fried red snapper drenched in an onion and pepper sauce.

Several North Beach Argentinian and South American restaurants also satisfy the beef-lover's palate. The *parrillada* is a treasure trove

Island eats

The nearby Caribbean islands have all contributed to the local cuisine. Upscale Haitian, at Tap Tap in South Beach, for instance, is a feast of vibrant color. Jamaican food is hot and spicy. Try jerk chicken, curried goat, oxtail stew or the famous patties, filled with meat and hot sauce.

Bahamian restaurants serve butterfly fish with Johnny cake, the island's version of corn bread. Then there's lots of conch – the queen of the mollusks that inhabits a large spiral-shaped shell. Conch meat needs tenderizing, usually with a severe beating, and often soaked in lime juice, but the result is delicious. It's firm, and with a flavor unlike any other seafood. Cracked conch, a sort of conch cutlet, is breaded, quick-fried and served sizzling with a wedge of lime. Conch also makes great chowder or fritters.

Haitian food in Miami is a treat. Little Haiti has storefront restaurants where just a couple of dollars will get you a plate of beans and rice, fried plantains and *griot* – fried pork chunks – to fill you up for the rest of the day.

Unlike Cubans, Haitians prepare their rice with red beans, not black. Cooks from northern Haiti spice the bean sauce with cloves. Some put more peppers in their version of *legume* – the vegetable stew. Whole red snapper is fried, or cooked in a light tomato sauce with onions.

Simmering seafood

Fabulous bounty comes from the Atlantic and the Gulf of Mexico to grace Miami's tables. Look out for fresh yellowtail, a smallish snapper with moist, elegant meat. A *ceviche* – raw fish marinated in fresh lime juice and cilantro – is wonderful if it is made with local yellowtail. Ceviche is often offered in large servings, and in varieties including shrimp, octopus, squid or a combination. It's particularly good in the city's Peruvian restaurants.

Dolphin, or *mahi-mahi*, is no relative of the smiling, people-friendly mammal. It is a lean, succulent, blunt-headed fish. Lobster in Florida is really a clawless crawfish, a seasonal food that is legally caught from August to March. It is not as rich as Maine lobster, and is firmer. A great way to enjoy Miami seafood is to watch the barges go by on the Miami River while dining at Garcia's Seafood Grille.

All this is just appetizers to the main course, stone crab, most often had at Miami's famous restaurant, Joe's Stone Crab in South Beach. The fat claws are plump with firm, pure white meat. The meat is lightly flavored, much of the taste coming from the mustard sauce or the melted butter dip, but no one minds; stone crabs are an exotic Miami essential, and only available mid-October to mid-May.

If modern Miami dining is an international buffet, old Miami is distinctly more Dixie. For the real roots, look toward the Everglades. Of the indigenous creatures found in early Miami, the alligator was the only plausibly edible inhabitant. Millions were killed for their hides, and by the 1960s the alligator's survival was threatened, so hunting was prohibited. In a couple of decades, the alligator was back, and by 1988, it was legal again to hunt them. Alligator became a menu item, especially the tail, all lean white meat, and often described as tasting like chicken. In fact, Florida alligator tastes the way it is cooked. Often it is breaded and fried, presented as an appetizer with a red tomato sauce like fried clam strips. It is also served stewed, like conch, or made into sausage.

HOW TO MAKE KEY LIME PIE

● Mix together 2 cups of cracker (or sweet biscuit) crumbs, 8oz (225g) of melted butter and half a cup of granulated sugar and press into a buttered pie dish. Preheat the oven to 350°F (180°C) and bake for 10 minutes.

● Beat 5 egg yolks until smooth. Add 15oz (425g) of sweetened condensed milk and beat until smooth. Then stir in half a cup of fresh Key lime (or ordinary lime) juice and 2 tbsp of grated lime peel.

● Fill the pie crust with the mixture and chill for at least one hour. Garnish with a slice of lime or lemon and serve chilled.

FAR LEFT: Argentinian bakery in North Beach.
LEFT: black beans are a Cuban staple.
RIGHT: Key Lime Pie: serve it chilled.

Venturing into the swamps, the fires of Miami native Americans – the Miccosukee Indians – can sometimes be seen. Many Miccosukee ceremonies remain secret but the cooking is an open book. Worth the trek (go with a guide and search carefully), are Everglades frogs' legs: delicate, alabaster meat that gently pulls away from tiny bones. The Indians' fried bread – a dough dropped in hot oil and fried to a golden puff – is another delicacy.

Soul food

Another Southern culinary root comes from Miami's African-American community. Grouped under the term "soul food," fried

Florida, and nowhere else in the US. While the rest of the country is in cold, gray winter, Miami grows strawberries, tomatoes, beans and squash. Citrus were once the coveted crops, the country in awe of the January oranges, tangerines and grapefruit, but most early citrus is now limited to backyard growers.

Virtually the whole US crop of the plump little twist of green in a gin and tonic, the Persian lime, still flourishes in South Florida. The sour orange is another tiny little fruit that plays a key role in one of Miami's most flamboyant dishes, whole roast pig. Hours are spent squeezing the baby oranges to make a marinade for the pig, called *lechon*.

fish, collard greens, black eyed peas, and, best of all, barbecue are well worth seeking out. Oil drums are cut in half as grills and set up on street corners in Liberty City or Overtown, and the aromatic smoke entices from afar.

Miami also dishes up a healthy share of East Coast traditions. Jewish food like bagels and lox, matzo ball soup and New York delistyle corned-beef sandwiches are found in different neighborhoods, most notably at Wolfie Cohen's Rascal House and Jerry's Famous Deli, both on Collins Avenue.

While Miami is sea and swamp, it is also a bountiful garden. Exotic fruits, none of them Florida natives, grow on the southern tip of

The biggest exotic cash crop in Miami now is the sacred fruit of India, the mango. Also known as the apple of the tropics, the mango comes in red, orange, yellow and purple, the sweet flesh ranging from yellow to golden orange. Once an exotic import, it is now a thriving export and has been adopted as part of the flavor of Miami. In India, they sing songs of love to the mango; in Miami, mango trees line streets and show up in side yards, the ripe, heavy fruit a part of the lazy, languid tropical landscape of this city of infinite variety. ❏

ABOVE: people with different outlooks and outfits gather in South Beach cafés.

Café Cubano

At Cafeteria El Pub on Miami's Calle Ocho, a dark-eyed waitress slides a thimble-sized paper cup across the shining counter. Sweet and heavy, the arrival of the dark brew begins a local ritual. Soon, the caffeine and sugar infusion sharpens the mind and awakens the tongue. The steamy antithesis to a soothing shot of bourbon, Miami's favorite drink transforms a 10-second sip into a cerebral celebration that winds you up instead of down.

Café Cubano is served from lace tablecloth restaurants to beauty parlors, dress shops, Art Deco hotels, hospitals to funeral homes. Take-out windows sell it in large plastic containers with a supply of tiny paper cups. Even the McDonald's restaurant in Little Havana offers café Cubano to go with the Huevo McMuffins. While the decor varies, the coffee is a constant.

Taken alone as a pick-me-up, or with a guava-filled Cuban pastry, café Cubano is sipped throughout the city from morning till night. Bite-size pieces of bread dipped in sugar are dunked in the coffee. After meals, it is served in the company of a hand-rolled cigar. While *café con leche* – Cuban coffee with warm milk in a regular-size cup – is often served and frequently given to children, in true café Cubano, cream is a sacrilege, a social taboo.

During the early 1900s, cafés along the elegant boulevards of old Havana sold the local drink from enormous machines that clamored and chimed with each freshly brewed batch. Later, cafés improvised their own Pavlovian call by ringing a bell on the streets to entice people in.

Café Cubano came to Miami in the 1960s with the first wave of Cuban immigrants. Café Pilon, a major Miami supplier, services over 1,500 restaurants and supplies beans, grinders and machines to almost 5,000 Miami businesses. Imported from Latin America, the beans for Cuban coffee are roasted at a slightly higher temperature and for longer than for American coffee. Red-and-white espresso machines force an ounce of steaming water through three scoops of tightly packed coffee, and a foamy, molasses-thick nectar drops into a tiny metal pitcher below. Two teaspoons of sugar are stirred in and the liquid is poured into a tiny paper, plastic, or china *demi-tasse*.

At home, some older Miami Cubans brew coffee the old-fashioned way – in a cheesecloth funnel filled with coffee and boiling water. For the foam, a drop of coffee is added to two spoonfuls of sugar and mashed into a paste, then fluffed up. Grounds are saved for the flower garden.

Coffee and sugar have been two of the

main ingredients of the Cuban economy for the past 200 years. The coffee bean was cultivated by European settlers as early as the 1500s. By the 1800s, *cafetals* – coffee plantations – flourished throughout the fertile mountainous land.

Today, the potent aroma of Cuban coffee scents the city, from the chrome-and-glass Downtown skyscrapers to the ham-and-cheese lunch counters of Little Havana. While across the country many Americans have become caffeine conscious and sugar phobic, for Miamians coffee is as much a local staple as sweet Florida sunshine and salty sea air. ❑

RIGHT: Miamians get a fix from Cuban coffee.

CELEBRATE IN THE SUN

Miami is the perfect party town, and the calendar
is crammed with celebrations. Slip into your
brightest clothes and conga, strut, pose
and preen in the sunshine

Miami is a town that likes to celebrate – publicly, visibly, loudly and, mostly, outdoors, whether in the rarefied sophistication of high-art events like Art Basel, the aquatic festival of the Columbus Day Regatta or Calle Ocho, the carnival that salsas over 23 blocks. In a recent year 119,986 people in Miami's Little Havana followed compelling drum beats and squeezed, shoved and sweated onto the longest Conga line on record. Why? Because, in Miami, especially in winter, it's a civic duty to party.

The guaranteed good weather, the innate sensuality, and the general vibe of "fun in the sun" is an irresistible draw for college kids on Spring Break, northerners outlasting winter's wrath and the gorgeous people topping up their tans in sight of each other: it all encourages a street-party culture. As early as 1915, cars bedecked with plants rolled through the Magic Knight of Dade's Mid-Winter Festival parade, advertising arrowroot starch as the locally supplied ingredient.

When Miamians conga-ed into the *Guinness Book of World Records*, they turned a neighborhood block party into an *event*. America's biggest Hispanic party, the week-long Carnaval Miami/Calle Ocho, shows off the city's Latin pride and hospitality, with scents, sounds, color and chaos. At its inception in 1978, the festival spilled over 15 blocks. Now covering eight blocks more, the all-day (and into the night) party offers "dance 'til you die" on Calle Ocho

(SW 8th Street) between 4th and 27th avenues, with Carnaval salsa in venues across the city; beauty pageants; a masquerade ball and Latin performers from Arturo Sandoval and Voltio to Queen Ivy. Calle Ocho's organizers, the civic-minded Kiwanis Club, twice banned entertainers who had performed in Cuba. The music won out on *Calle Ocho* albums that included – surprise! – the blacklisted stars.

Goombay

Billed as the largest black heritage festival in the United States, the Miami/Bahamas Goombay Festival celebrates Bahamian slaves' independence and the old ties between Miami and

LEFT: Coconut Grove Goombay Festival.
RIGHT: all set to do the King Mango Strut.

FUN FOR FOODIES

The South Beach Wine and Food Festival is in February; the Biltmore Food and Wine Weekend is in May. August is Miami Spice Restaurant month.

the Bahamas, transforming Grand Avenue into Nassau's Bay Street.

The weekend romp in early June, dating from 1977, captures the joy of *junkanoo* – dancers in gaudy crêpe-paper costumes sway to the clamor of whistles, washboards and cowbells. On the street and on stage, rappers compete with steel bands. In noon parades, the Royal Bahamian Police Marching Band con-

TOP EVENTS

ducts precision drills in starched white uniforms. More than 400 vendors of arts, crafts, and food line Grand Avenue, culinary highlights being the conch fritters and Bahama Mama's salads. Just a few short blocks bring thousands of real or would-be Bahamians together, and a little closer to home.

Sports spectacles

The Orange Bowl college football classic frequently decides national championships. Since 1935, the annual King Orange Jamboree Parade on New Year's Eve has mated with the Orange Bowl on New Year's Day, to launch football fans into ecstasy for the coming year. The jamboree seats 80,000 fans in bleachers along the Downtown route. Bands play Sousa marches, and school fight songs stir onlookers. The King Jamboree takes physical form in a huge smiling balloon face, while Coconut Grove's King Mango Strut *(see page 150)* spoofs the parade and everything else besides.

When Miamians leave the streets, they party on the water, as in the Columbus Day Regatta, which runs in mid-October from Coconut Grove to Elliott Key and back. Early on Saturday, boats lurch to a start through Biscayne Bay. TV and radio stations announce the number of beers drunk and topless bathers spotted. The cruising regatta logs up to 650 participant and 2,000 spectator boats, with regular confusion over who's who. With moonlight skinny dips and a fireworks display, the weekend event has been one of camaraderie more than competition since its inception in the early 1950s.

Other major sports events punctuate the early spring. February sees the massive Miami International Boat Show and the Homestead Championship Rodeo. In March are the Key Biscayne NASDAQ-100 Open Tennis Championship and the Miami Grand Prix, held at the Homestead-Miami Speedway.

Art for art's sake

The world's most important art fair, Art Basel from Switzerland, has a sister festival in Miami Beach Convention Center. Every December since 2002, the 20th and 21st century works of more than 2,000 artists have been represented by 195 international dealers and galleries.

Although the week is primarily a prestigious trade fair, galleries and spaces in the Art Deco

District host shows and exhibitions that are open to the public. Complimentary events, sometimes known as "Alt. Basel," take place in the Wynwood Art District and the Design District. Miami also has street festivities centered around the arts, with the mid-February open-air Coconut Grove Arts Festival the oldest in the state. In 1963, a few dozen local artists chatted with a few hundred neighbors. Exhibitors and art lovers still talk one on one, but over the hum of a crowd that can build to 100,000 people.

In mid-January, South Beach is washed with pastel colors for design lovers' Art Deco Weekend. This is when the elite "Moon Over Miami" Art Deco preservation fundraiser tumbles into

fans from around the world to the downtown Gusman Center for the Performing Arts and art theaters across the city. In 2000, organizers broke ranks with Cuban exiles and dared to screen a movie made in Cuba.

Though the film was critical of Castro, just showing it was provocative, and flouted Miami-Dade's own foreign policy. The His-

the street, closing Collins Avenue between 10th and 11th streets. Dancing to Big Band revival tunes, tuxedos brush up to Art Deco T-shirts. Crowds partying in the mile-square, Deco District sway to rhythm and blues, reggae and *lambada*, and easily top half a million revelers.

Cultural highlights

Even normally indoor events, like book and film festivals, hit the streets in Miami. The Miami International Film Festival in February *(see page 55)*, brings film stars, directors and

panic Film Festival and the Gay and Lesbian Film Festival, are also popular events held here, in early May and July, respectively.

In 1984, local booksellers, a community college and the public library started the eight-day annual Miami Book Fair International *(see page 54),* which attracts more than 300 exhibitors and half a million browsers to town every November.

The Magic City was made for festivals and partying. The weather and the location are perfect, and the town is a perfect stage. Most of all though, the up-for-it Miami mood makes an irresistible lure for visitors to come, join in and celebrate every kind of culture. ❏

LEFT: Calle Ocho Festival in Little Havana.
ABOVE: Art Deco Weekend brings out lovers of design.

HEDONISM IN THE HEAT

From the clamoring club scene to sophisticated
night spots with jazz or sexy salsa, there's always
a great night out to be enjoyed right here, right now

Miami is a city made for nightlife. Dazzling people, clothes and jewelry, musical influences from the Caribbean and
South America, and tropical ocean breezes
make it a perfect party town. Romantic dining
tables in tropical gardens, sidewalk seating with
first-class people watching, top-floor bars with
ocean views and cocktails of seismic sophistication all guarantee unforgettable evenings and
early-morning memories.

If the club scene's your thing, start at South
Beach and follow the music – house, progres-
sive, trance, tribal or garage – that thumps
from the darkened halls out to the sidewalks
along Ocean Drive or Washington and Collins
avenues on weekend evenings. Or just watch
for the lines of young things in full bling who
tumble out of the clubs and jam the streets.

On the wild side

In all great clubs, the first thrill is just from
getting in, and that means a large crowd is left
on the sidewalk. For elite events like the Nikki
Beach Club Sunday afternoon party, if you're
on the list at the door, you'll be ushered past
the line and red velvet ropes will part. If not,
your fate hangs on your style and charm. Arriving in an eye-popping ride can help. Many
South Beach hotels have connections with the
clubs, and whispering the right words into the
ear of the concierge can smooth your entry.

A number of websites offer routes on to
club guest lists via e-mail subscription, and

one, www.miamibarsclubs.com, has a link to a
VIP-pass South Beach tour. If you're ready to
brave the crowds without a connection, the
advice from seasoned clubbers is to be
extremely well dressed. For men, a razor-
sharp suit and tie is a good start. Dressing
crazy can get you noticed, but without style it
won't get you in. Once past the door, try not
to appear shocked by the cover charge or the
prices of drinks.

If you have the time, you won't be short of
clubs to check out in a 20-block area on South
Beach, with names like Angel, Liquid, Glass,
Opium Garden, Amnesia, Tides and the super-
exclusive Mansion, to name but a few. Some

LEFT: a typical night out on South Beach.
RIGHT: Miami has a great gay scene.

are live-music venues; others feature celebrity DJs. Tantra on Española Way is a sensuous restaurant earlier in the evening – dishes fused with aphrodisiacs – before turning into a sexy late-night club, with chandeliers, a waterwall and fiber-optic ceiling.

If you can't be bothered to get out of bed, have the food served as you lie recumbent, in the appropriately named B.E.D. on Washington Avenue. For special occasions, DJs and traveling bands take over hotel ballrooms and throw their own parties. To find out what's happening while you're in town, check out the *Miami Herald* or the free *New Times* newspaper that hits the racks on Thursdays.

Away from the frenetic South Beach scene – weekend traffic along Ocean Drive or Washington Avenue stretches as far as the eye can see – more and more clubs are opening up across the causeway in downtown Miami, including the massive Club Space, in the Park West district and 42 Below on 2nd Avenue. The dance-club scene has swelled to such a crescendo that it has spawned the high-profile Miami Winter Music Conference, an Ibiza-style festival of dance events and parties, held every year in March.

The climate and atmosphere of Florida has drawn a terrific gay and lesbian scene. The freedom to live and play without inhibitions

GALLERY WALKS

On the second Saturday of every month throughout the year, many of the Design District and Wynwood Art District venues are open to the public from 7 to 10pm. A walk is conducted around local events and exhibitions in the neighborhoods, which includes gallery and studio visits, trips to alternative spaces for performance and video arts, in addition to special viewings of selected private collections. Similar walks are conducted on certain Friday nights in Coral Gables, Little Havana and North Miami (NoMi).

Maps and details of these evening art events are available on the internet at www.artcircuits.com

here has bred a great selection of clubs and bars. Check out Twist, a club with an outdoor lounge and dance floor on Washington Avenue, and Pump, also on Washington, with partying that goes on until breakfast-time.

After midnight

If clubs aren't for you, or before clubbing, or even afterwards if you flex that kind of stamina, South Beach has great lounges and bars. Lola Bar at 23rd and Collins, for example, has a cool interior and is more laid back than a typical club. In Coconut Grove, CocoWalk is a popular late-nite spot, with bars, restaurants, stores and movie theaters. Live music has been played at Tobacco Road by the Miami River since Al Capone was a regular; blues greats like KoKo Taylor, Albert King, and B.B. King grace the two stages.

Churchill's Hideaway, an incongruous British pub in Little Haiti, draws crowds for the rock bands on stage seven nights a week. A down-home, funky rock 'n' roll venue with goood local acts, the drinks are great, the food not so great, and the neighborhood one to be alert to late at night. Haitian music is played at Tap Tap in South Beach, while jazz clubs are scattered across the landscape, from the Van Dyke Café on Lincoln Road to Jazid on Washington Avenue.

GLAD TO BE GAY

Gay events include the Winter Party, a wild fling in South Beach in March, and the November White Party, which raises money for Aids.

The rhythms of Latin-influenced jazz abound and are always high-octane. Cuban maestro Arturo Sandoval and Puerto Rican Tito Puente created a musical stir in Miami, although the local politics of the city have been know to chase some Cuban artists away. Arturo has recreated the Rat Pack ambience with his own club in the 1950s Deauville Hotel in North Beach.

How about experiencing the raw passion of flamenco? Casa Panza in Little Havana has live flamenco on certain nights of the week. It's a tiny place, and very popular, so arrive early and dine first on a few plates of spicy Spanish *tapas*.

Ocean Drive is also lined by restaurants with outdoor seating, many featuring live jazz or Latin-American music. The salsa lessons at Starfish on West Avenue have a slinky enough allure to have enticed movie star Will Smith for tuition.

LEFT: there's no need to get out of bed at B.E.D.
ABOVE: Ocean Drive in after-midnight mode.

The smooth side

There is more to Miami's nightlife than music, dining and dancing. Live theater offers a variety of choices from Spanish-language plays to off-beat productions in small venues throughout the county. The Coconut Grove Playhouse and the Jackie Gleason Theater stage traditional Broadway-style shows.

The city also offers opera productions, a ballet company and the New World Symphony orchestra to please lovers of the classics. There are two terrific theater venues for orchestral concerts, the ballet and the Florida Grand Opera in the lavish Miami Performing Arts Center, which opened in 2006. ❑

PLACES

A detailed guide to Miami and the surrounding area with the principal sites clearly cross-referenced by number to the maps

At dawn, a red-headed rooster crows his morning call through Little Haiti. Across the bay, the pastel-painted Deco world of South Beach is waking up – or just going to sleep – to another glorious day beside the hippest stretch of sand in the US. Miami's cityscape is incongruous – part American dream, part Caribbean countryside.

The Places section that follows is designed to evoke a sense of place. It's a portrait of Miami's neighborhoods – from the high-powered offices of downtown Miami to the simple solitude of Key Biscayne.

The city can be confusing to get around. There are 31 municipalities spread over 500 sq. miles (1,300 sq. km), and areas with similar names. For instance, there's North Miami and separately, North Miami Beach. There's South Miami (a city), and south of Miami (mainly berry fields). City officials claim that public transportation is integrated, with buses and trains linking up, but in fact it's rarely a smooth journey. To do any kind of sightseeing, a car is essential or, for that sun-in-your-face, bugs-in-your-teeth experience, a motorcycle. If you don't want to fuss with a car, make do with staying in South Beach or Coconut Grove, and you'll make do very nicely.

Understanding the street numbering system helps. There are four quadrants on the mainland: NW, NE, SW, and SE. In downtown Miami is an intersection of two thoroughfares: Flagler Street and Miami Avenue. Flagler divides the city from north to south, and Miami Avenue divides the city from east to west. Street and avenue numbers start from here (1st Street, 1st Avenue) and increase as you head farther out. Avenues generally run north to south, and streets east to west. The golden strip of land that is Miami Beach follows a similar layout, but begins at the southern tip of South Beach. If you get lost, just get on Collins Avenue, which makes the entire beach journey from sandy tip to rocky toe.

The best way to enjoy the Magic City, though, is to slip into light, gauzy clothes and move to the local Latin beat. Let things flow; the food is good and the weather is flawless. Bask in the simple secrets of the city, wherever you find them, like stone crabs with mustard sauce, or a *salsa*-filled nightclub. In other words, the things that make a place a place. ❑

PRECEDING PAGES: commuting, Coral Gables style; grabbing a bite in Little Havana.
LEFT: swimming in solitude at the Raleigh Hotel, South Beach.

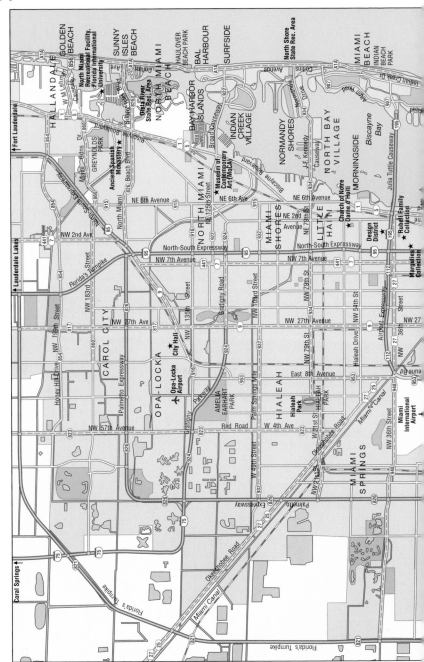

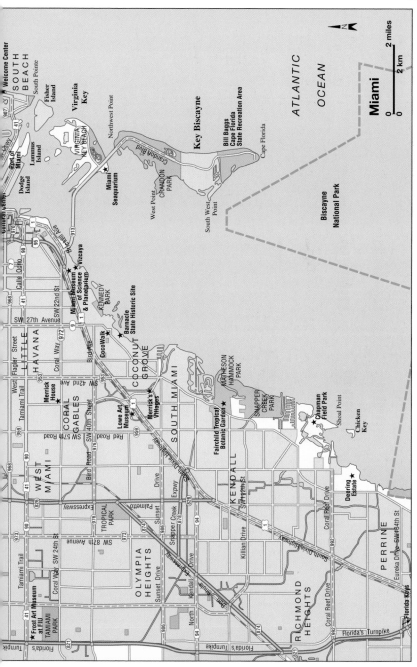

Miami

ATLANTIC OCEAN

SOUTH BEACH

South Pointe

Fisher Island

Lummus Island

Port of Miami

Dodge Island

Welcome Center

Virginia Key

VIRGINIA KEY BEACH

Northwest Point

Miami Seaquarium

Virginia Key

Key Biscayne

CRANDON PARK

Crandon Blvd

West Point

South West Point

Bill Baggs Cape Florida State Recreation Area

Cape Florida

Biscayne National Park

Cultural Center

Calle Ocho

LITTLE HAVANA

Flagler Street

West Flagler Street

Tamiami Trail

Coral Way

SW 22nd St

Miami Museum of Science & Planetarium

Vizcaya

KENNEDY PARK

Barnacle State Historic Site

CocoWalk

COCONUT GROVE

SW 27th Avenue

Bird Ave

Coral Way

Merrick House

CORAL GABLES

SW 42nd Street

SW 57th Road

Red Road

Lowe Art Museum

Merrick's Villages

SOUTH MIAMI

Fairchild Tropical/ Botanic Garden

MATHESON HAMMOCK PARK

SNAPPER CREEK PARK

Chapman Field Park

Shoal Point

Chicken Key

WEST MIAMI

Bird Road

Sunset Drive

South Dixie Highway

KENDALL

SW 112th St

Killian Drive

Coral Reef Drive

Deering Estate

Expressway

Palmetto

TROPICAL PARK

Snapper Creek

Sunset

OLYMPIA HEIGHTS

SW 87th Avenue

Coral Way

SW 24th St

Tamiami Trail

Frost Art Museum at FIU

TAMIAMI PARK

Florida's Turnpike

North Kendall Drive

Kendall Drive

Bird Drive

Sunset Drive

RICHMOND HEIGHTS

Coral Reef Drive

Florida's Turnpike

PERRINE

Eureka Drive · SW 184th St

Florida Keys

N

0   2 miles

0   2 km

SOUTH BEACH

South Beach is an eye-candy sugar rush, from the ice-cream pastels of the Art Deco District to the great outdoor cafés, to the beautiful people the beautiful people come to watch

South Beach, or SoBe, is quintessential Miami. Sparkling 24 hours a day with a cosmopolitan congregation of beautiful people, it's where stunning girls and sleek hunks cruise from chic hotel to café to club to bar. International bright young things forage for trinkets and threads at boutiques in the Deco district, or the bird-song landscape of car-free Lincoln Road mall, then lunch and laze at shaded tables. Buff, bronzed bodies play and display on the soft sands of one of the world's most glamorous beaches.

Petite pastels

In the 1970s, SoBe was just called South Beach, a sorry and faded seaside dame, past her prime and perilously unpredictable after dark. But the history of Miami has been a story of regular, phoenix-like regeneration. Energy for South Beach's rebirth, shiny and stylish and painted pastel, came from the Miami Design Preservation League.

The City of Miami Beach (of which South Beach is a part), is separated from the mainland by the broad expanse of Biscayne Bay; South Beach extends from the south of the island to 23rd Street. Arrival is usually by a drive across the MacArthur Causeway, a great way to snatch views of the Port of Miami, the bay and the mansion-studded islands *(see pages 98–9)*. MacArthur Causeway leads right into 5th Street, the southern border of the Art Deco District.

A good way to explore South Beach is to start here, among the much-admired Deco delights, then head for the southern tip, which has yet to play a central role in SoBe's glitter. Its main attraction is as a place to have a memorable lunch, on highly sought-after stone crabs at Miami's most famous restaurant. The northern part of the area, above 15th Street, has

Map on page 80

LEFT: Ocean Drive ambience.
BELOW: rollerblading by the beach, with friend, in Lummus Park.

South Beach and Biscayne Bay

| 0 | | 400 yds |
| 0 | | 400 m |

some of the loveliest hotels, many with glamorous swimming pools and with private access to the beach. North SoBe is also where the Miami Beach Visitors Center is situated, so tucked away it remains undiscovered by many *(see page 91)*.

Deco delights and more

South Beach's Art Deco architecture began in 1930. One hotel in 1931 was followed by four more in 1932. Thirteen hotels were built in 1936; 23 more in 1939 and another 10 by 1940. The pastel palaces had arrived. But by the 1960s and early '70s, the streamlined sirens were in a sad state, and the area had become dangerous. After a rigorous preservation campaign, South Beach was transformed, and right now North Beach is following *(see page 104)*.

In 1973, as preservationist Denise Scott Brown noted, "From south to north along Miami Beach is a progression through recent American architectural history from the 1930s… through the 40s… into the famous hotels of the '50s and '60s."

Committed campaigners peti-tioned, lobbied and fought with politicians, state and federal agencies. In 1979 this part of Miami Beach, containing more than 500 pastel, playful buildings, became the youngest historic district in the United States. Its official name: the **Miami Beach Art Deco National Historic District**.

For the most dramatic architectural introduction to the SoBe revival, head up **Ocean Drive ❶**. To the west are restored hotels and apartment houses, outdoor cafés, stores, and restaurants. The sidewalks have been enlarged and painted. Painted pink, naturally.

To the east is **Lummus Park**, a glorious beach with white sand that stretches 300 ft (90 meters) to the Atlantic Ocean. Here sun worshippers sprawl in barely perceptible bathing suits. Beach-goers play huge sound systems, rollerblade or jog on the undulating, tree-lined promenade, **Beach Walk**.

Sections of the beach are colonized by different groups of people: athletes crowd the volleyball courts (6th Street); a young, local crowd

The Breakwater at 940 Ocean Drive was designed in 1939 by Anton Skislewicz.

BELOW: happy to be in a Deco hotel.

On South Beach even the lifeguard stations are eye-catching and colorfully whimsical.

hangs out around 9th street; gays greet and gather from 12th to 14th streets, and the sleek domain of sophisticated hotel guests is from 16th to 20th streets.

Ocean Drive is very popular at night, and traffic is a slow procession. Parking is difficult, and over-zealous meter maids prowl mercilessly for victims. Adding to the congestion – and to the view – is an endless parade of Jeeps, BMWs, SUVs, convertibles, Harley-Davidsons, and all manner of other fashionable vehicles, cruising along the street. Drivers peer into restaurants and onto porches, and people in the restaurants and porches gaze back – a ritual that has been known to yield dates.

SoBe is also a place to walk, a rarity in car-addicted South Florida. Even the police ride around on bicycles. Locals – like Haydee and Sahara Scull, buxom Cuban twins known for their campy Carmen Miranda-style outfits as much as for their brightly colored street-scene collages – blend with half-naked rollerbladers and the equally lightly-attired tourists on the beach.

On Ocean Drive between 6th and 8th streets are rows of 3- and 4-story Deco hotels, culminating in the **Colony Hotel** (tel: 305-673-0088), its blue neon sign a SoBe landmark. Just beyond, the sea of green umbrellas on the corner of 8th Street is the **News Café**. Since it opened in 1988, the News has been jam-packed day and night. Jazz in the background, and the selection of foreign magazines and newspapers satisfies a local and European clientele. Italian designer Gianni Versace was an habitué, and this was his last stop before being gunned down on the steps of his mansion farther along Ocean Drive.

Model society

The modeling business is a multi-million dollar industry for Miami Beach, and creates almost perpetual beautiful-people alerts. Some trendier cafés seem to employ only models, each waiter and waitress more stunning than the last. They provide a pretty tableau, but their attention often seems more given to mirrors than to their hungry customers.

Deco Walking Tours

The beauty of the Art Deco buildings is in their details – flamingo and pelican motifs, windows shaped as portholes, stucco stylized friezes in geometric designs, tropical pastel shades of pink, aqua, and yellow. So put on comfortable shoes, grab the camera and head to the Art Deco Welcome Center at 1001 Ocean Drive.

Tours led by a member of the Miami Design Preservation League (MDPL) – a local historian or an architect – take place several times a week, usually at 10.30am or 6.30pm. The 90-minute tours (charge), depart from the Welcome Center and take in the history of South Beach, from its earlier days when the hotels were built, to the fight in the 1970s and '80s to save the decaying structures, to the present day. Reservations are not necessary, just show up about 15 minutes in advance. Self-guided audio tours in five languages are also available every day from 10am–4pm.

Books and other items relating to Miami and Art Deco can be bought at the MDPL's gift shop at the Welcome Center. This is a particularly good place to shop for souvenirs, as a portion of the money from each sale goes toward preserving the historic buildings. For more information call 305-531-3484 or go to www.mdpl.org.

During the winter months, photographers rise early for the bright morning light. Reflectors in hand, they call out directions in Spanish, French, Italian, and English, to models striking poses and tossing their hair. Vast, air-conditioned motor homes line the streets, providing changing rooms and rest spots for the models and photographers.

Heading up Ocean Drive, more Art Deco treats compete for attention; the yellow and white **Waldorf Towers Hotel** (tel: 305-531-7684); the blue and white stripes of **The Breakwater**, at 940 Ocean Drive; and the **Clevelander Hotel** (tel: 305-531-3485) where the sprawling outdoor bar is *de riguer* for party-goers all night long – and sometimes all day, too.

Ocean Drive attractions

Directly on the beach at 10th Street is the **Miami Beach Ocean Front Auditorium**, where beach residents throng for the enjoyable music, lectures, and lunches.

On the ocean side of the auditorium is the sand-colored, pleasingly curvy **Beach Patrol Headquarters**, designed in 1934 by Robert Taylor.

Next door, the busy **Art Deco Welcome Center** ❷ (open daily; tel: 305-531-3484), is operated by the Miami Design Preservation League, the non-profit group responsible for the preservation of the Art Deco properties, and for listing them on the National Register of Historic Places. The Welcome Center has a wealth of information, and provides books, postcards and souvenirs.

The spectacular success of South Beach has been at a cost, however. At certain times of the year, and especially in March – during college Spring Break – Ocean Drive can be more tacky than tempting.

The small, less expensive Deco hotels pack in guests, several to a room. Girls in string bikinis chug considerably more beer than they are able to hold. Boys in baggy tee-shirts and even baggier pants bar hop, then hip hop until they drop, partying all night long. These tourists are loud, and the music even louder. For the under 25s who come for raucous abandon, it's a blast. Anyone who

Map on page 80

TIP

The pastel-painted, air-conditioned South Beach Local bus stops at 20 different places, from one end of the district to the other. The service runs every 10–15 minutes until 1am and it only costs 25¢.

BELOW: the News Café, an Ocean Drive institution.

BELOW: if you're over
25, it's an idea to avoid
Ocean Drive during
Spring Break (March).

prefers a less turbo-charged visit should choose a quieter time, during February's Food and Wine Festival, for instance, or check into a hotel farther north than Ocean Drive for a more relaxing retreat.

Casa Casuarina ❸ is a magnificent Mediterranean Revival-style mansion behind huge gates you can peek through. It was modeled on Christopher Columbus' home in the Dominican Republic, with 15-ft (5-meter) high antique wooden doors. Designer Gianni Versace bought it in 1992 for $2.9 million.

At the time, the building was a huddle of low-rent apartments, and about to be condemned. A year later, Gianni bought the neighboring Revere Hotel for $3.7 million, and tore it down to make room for a private courtyard and pool. Ocean Drive had truly arrived on the international jet-set scene.

After the designer's death in 1997 *(see page 34)*, the Versace family put the mansion up for sale. It now houses a members-only club, where stylish functions are held.

Adjacent to the Versace mansion is the **Hotel Victor** (tel: 305-428-1234). Built in 1934, its interior has been remodeled by Parisian designer Jacques Garcia. Attracting a hip crowd *(see page 95)*, the Victor is a Hyatt hotel, although not one your parents would recognize.

The **Tides** (tel: 305-604-5070) has a quietly understated elegance unmatched on Ocean Drive. The original terrazzo floor in the calm white lobby is polished to perfection, and each luxurious suite contains a telescope, for peering out to sea. At the front is a spacious verandah to survey, or to escape from, the high-pitched happenings on Ocean Drive.

SoBe stories

On the next few blocks of Ocean Drive are more petite pastel buildings, which were among the first to be refurbished in the early 1990s. On the corner of 13th Street, the **Carlyle** has appeared as a backdrop for movies and modeling sessions, as have many of the Ocean Drive gems.

On either side of the Carlyle are the **Leslie** and the Cardozo; beyond the Cardozo is the **Cavalier**. The

pretty **Cardozo ❹** (tel: 305-535-6500) still accepts guests, but most of the others have gone the modern way of being developed into condominiums; just the facades remain from their 1990s hotel heyday.

Much of the Art Deco District's gentrification has sprung from the energy of the gay community; the *Miami Herald* once estimated that one-third of the apartments in the area had gay tenants.

In the late 1980s and '90s, the gay population was large enough for city commissioners to campaign for votes in gay bars. Officers of the Miami Beach Police Department attended gay sensitivity programs, and a gay chamber of commerce and support groups were established, which remain active today. The scene has quietened down and may be moving on, but South Beach is still a popular gay vacation spot, and the Winter Party in March and the White Party in November are key calendar dates.

Collins and Washington avenues are also part of the South Beach scene. Running parallel to Ocean Drive, **Collins Avenue** is the beach's longest thoroughfare, continuing north out of SoBe, through Miami Beach and all the way to Bal Harbour and beyond. Around 6th to 8th streets on Collins are high-end boutiques, and above 15th Street are high-end hotels.

Away from the beach

A block west of Collins Avenue (so just two blocks from the beach), **Washington Avenue** is a frenetic, clamoring thoroughfare that feels more New York than Miami Beach. A walking street, Washington has both new and old. Nightclubs and chic restaurants are neighbors with fruit markets and tattoo and body-piercing parlors. On weekend nights, kids converge on Washington for a slow parade of shining cars – with weapons-grade sound systems.

At 801 Collins is **The Hotel ❺** (tel: 305-531-2222) built as the Tiffany in 1939. An icon of Tropical Deco, the slim sign on the roof was designed to evoke the Empire State Building in New York. The hotel was compelled to change its name in

Map on page 80

Dancing the night away in a SoBe pleasure palace.

BELOW: the center of all open-air action: the Clevelander.

1998, after renovation by fashion designer Todd Oldham, when the famous jewelry establishment of the same name took exception. The sign, however, still says "Tiffany."

Popular with fashionistas, the rooftop pool and alluring restaurant, Wish *(see page 95)*, please the tastes of sophisticates. Order a cocktail under the full moon for a memorable Miami experience – the cocktails have ice cubes that glow.

The **Wolfsonian Foundation** ❻ (1001 Washington Avenue; open daily except Wed; Sun pm only; charge; tel: 305-531-1001), is housed in the pretty, Mediterranean-Revival-style former Washington Storage Company building, at the intersection with 10th Street.

In the 1920s, seasonal beach residents stored their possessions here – everything from curtains to cars – before heading back north. One client was Mitchell Wolfson Sr, the founder of the Wometco movie theater chain. His son and heir bought the building in 1984 and established an art foundation two years later.

For more than three decades,

Mitchell Wolfson Jr, traveled the world collecting objets d'art, concentrating particularly on propaganda art of the 19th and early 20th centuries. His eccentric collection of more than 70,000 pieces includes oddities like Hitler propaganda posters and bronze busts of Mussolini, along with furniture designed by architect Frank Lloyd Wright; industrial and domestic products; trains and comic books, in addition to ceramics and paintings.

Old City Hall

A block north of the Wolfsonian, a handsome 1920s Mediterranean Revival-style landmark towers over the neighborhood. **Old City Hall** was the place for everything from an auspicious marriage to a fishing license, and was the first building to receive historic designation in this part of SoBe.

Behind Old City Hall is the **Miami Beach Police Station** with a glass brick front, aqua and white, in Streamline Moderne style. Another kind of diversion altogether is provided by the erotic sculptures, paint-

In 1944, Benjamin Green, a Miami Beach pharmacist, put cocoa butter in a coffee pot and heated it up in his kitchen at home. The result? America's very first suntan cream.

BELOW:
Casa Casuarina, the mansion owned by the late Gianni Versace, is now a private club.

ings, tapestries and other artifacts at the **World Erotic Art Museum** (1205 Washington Avenue; open daily 11am–midnight; charge; tel: 305-532-9336).

The 12 classy suites of the winsome **Marlin Hotel** (1200 Collins Avenue; tel: 305-604-3595) are housed in another Streamline Moderne gem, mostly inhabited by beautiful people. The previous owner's music-biz background lured South Beach Recording Studios to the basement. The place literally hops, especially during the Miami Winter Music Conference in March. Lending glamour to the sounds, the Elite Model agency has offices upstairs.

On the corner of Washington and 13th Street are the pale, sun-kissed contours of the **Miami Beach Post Office**. Built in 1937, the curved, building is crowned by a marble and stained-glass lantern. Inside, murals and bronze grillwork decorate a vast rotunda.

Farther along Washington Avenue is the old **Cameo Theater**, which opened as a premier movie theater in 1936. After years of refurbishment, the 980-seat theater is now a club called **crobar**, with Latin and reggae concerts, and dance nights with hip-hop, trance, and techno.

Española Way

Española Way ❼, between 14th and 15th streets, is a charming little artists' enclave designed by Robert Taylor in 1925. One of the finest examples of Mediterranean-Revival architecture with awnings, wrought-iron balconies, and hand-painted tiles, the upper floors of the flamingo-pink structures are still inhabited by artists and artsy types.

At street level are intriguing clothes and furniture stores, coffee houses, restaurants, and art galleries. About halfway down the street (lined with gas lamps) is the **Miami Beach Cinematheque** (tel: 305-673-4567), a gallery and bookstore, the home of the Miami Film Society, and an intimate screening room showcasing arthouse movies.

At the top of Española Way, and also in Mediterranean-Revival style, the **Clay Hotel and International Youth Hostel** (1438 Washington

Map on page 80

The Scull sisters are Cuban-born twins and painters who maintain a high profile at Miami social events.

BELOW: Española Way has Mediterranean-Revival buildings.

*Exhibit from the
Wolfsonian museum.*

BELOW: the Jewish
Museum of Florida is
housed in an Art Deco
synagogue.

Avenue; tel: 305-534-2988), is one of the best bargains by the beach. The hostel is the old Village Tavern. Cuban bandleader and husband of TV star Lucille Ball, Desi Arnaz, played here, and Al Capone and his cronies were said to hang out here.

What has to be one of the prettiest delicatessens anywhere is the former Hoffman's Cafeteria at 1450 Collins Avenue. This is where, in what is now **Jerry's Famous Deli**, pastrami and lox are dished up in a spectacular Deco building, designed by an uber-architect of the style, Henry Hohauser, in 1940.

South of 5th Street

The area between the southern tip of the island and 5th Street, less blessed with Deco delights, has lagged behind South Beach's rise to gentrification, but is slowly catching up. Until the 1970s, this part of the island was home to some of the oldest and poorest in the city.

In the early 1970s, the City of Miami Beach put a moratorium on building and planned a Venice-like community, complete with canals and gondolas. That idea did not succeed. The neighborhood, formerly an enclave of Jewish retirees, many from 1930s Eastern Europe, is now transforming into a livable urban quarter with townhouses, skyscrapers and restaurants.

Between Jefferson and Meridian on 5th is **Tap Tap** *(see page 95)*, a Haitian restaurant, art gallery, and popular hangout for artists, journalists, and film-makers. Decorated with bold, primitive floor-to-ceiling murals, Tap Tap hosts some of the best live Haitian music this side of Port-au-Prince.

The next block to the east is the site of the former 5th Street Gym; boxing greats Muhammad Ali, Sonny Liston, Joe Louis, and Roberto Duran trained here. At 301 Washington Avenue is the **Jewish Museum of Florida 8** (open Tues–Sun; charge; tel: 305-672-5044), in a handsome 1936 synagogue with Art Deco features. The museum has a permanent exhibition, "Mosaic: Jewish Life in Florida," and nearly 80 stained-glass windows, one of them commemorating gangster Meyer Lansky.

On the southern tip of the island is **South Pointe Park ❾**, 17-acres (7-hectares) of meandering sidewalks, grassy walkways, a fitness course, and a beach, though this isn't the park's best feature.

The 150-ft (45-meter) South Pointe Pier joins the long jetty at the mouth of Government Cut, providing a prime spot for fishing and watching the cruise ships as they head out to deep water. The park also has benches, an observation tower, charcoal grills, picnic pavilions, and a children's playground.

Joe's Stone Crab ❿ has been a South Beach institution since 1913 *(see page 93)*. At Joe's, pride gives way to pleasure. Diners have huge paper bibs tied around their necks by tuxedoed waiters in preparation for the stone crabs dressed in delectable mustard sauce. The wait for a table can be long, but there's a bright, modern take-out section with a sit-down lunch-counter just next door. Joe's also ship crabs all over the United States.

On the beach at 1st Street, a relaxed, waterfront complex has several bars and restaurants. This is one of the few places in South Beach that is actually on the beach itself, where you can walk from café directly onto sand without having to cross the street.

North of 15th Street

Heading back north, either by cab from Joe's, or on the South Beach Local bus, the scale of architecture shifts. Above 15th Street, oceanfront mansions of the 1920s became palatial hotels in the 1930s, and began to draw contemporary visitors later than the smaller, 4-story hotels along Ocean Drive.

First to be renovated was the **Delano Hotel ⓫** (1685 Collins, tel: 305-672-2000). Built in 1947 and crowned by a modernistic finned tower, the Delano was remodeled by French designer Philippe Starck and his partner Ian Schrager. The Delano is cool in all senses. Entering from the bright sunlight into calm darkness, the eyes need a minute to adjust. A dark, echoing corridor highlights a shaft of light at the end of the "tunnel" that leads to the ter-

South Beach is about to get a WiFi network; just sit with your laptop and surf away. If you need to use a terminal, one of the best internet cafés is Kafka's Café, 1464 Washington Avenue, tel: 305-673-9669.

BELOW: Tap Tap: the best Haitian food and music this side of Port-au-Prince.

The Holocaust Memorial on Meridian Avenue.

race and swimming pool. Almost next door is the **National Hotel** (tel: 305-532-2311), built in 1940. Its wonderful infinity pool seems to stretch all the way to the beach. A backstroke swim gives a marvelous view of the silver and pink Deco dome, now a South Beach icon.

The sensuous **Raleigh Hotel** (1775 Collins Avenue; tel: 305-534-6300) is a favorite for fashion shoots and fashionistas alike. The interior of the Deco building has been sympathetically reinterpreted by André Balazs, retaining the style of the past while including post-millennium embellishments.

Secluded gardens with hammocks and cabanas in the sand make the Raleigh a coveted South Beach hideaway. What attracts photographers most is the swimming pool *(see page 74)*. Its fabulous, 1940s emblematic curves may be a reference to Sir Walter Raleigh's shield, although no one really knows.

At the top of Collins Avenue, bordered by 21st and 23rd streets, is **Collins Park Cultural Campus**. The highlight of the campus is the respected **Bass Museum of Art** (2121 Park Avenue; open Tues–Sun; charge; tel: 305-673-7530), with European art including major works from the 15th to the 20th centuries. Paintings, tapestries, ecclesiastical artifacts, and sculpture are displayed. Notable are a Peter Paul Rubens painting, *The Holy Family*, and a 16th-century Flemish tapestry called *The Tournament*.

The 1930 Art Deco building was enlarged in 2002 by the Japanese architect Arata Isozaki. The extension includes an excellent gift shop, and a café with an outdoor terrace

Also on the campus is the **Miami City Ballet** in a curvy building by local architects Arquitectonica, and the **Miami Beach Regional Library**. The library (open until 9pm on weekdays), has internet access, US and foreign (mostly Spanish) newspapers and a tranquil reading garden lined by palm trees.

Convention Center area

In Miami Beach, streets are named, not for presidents or war heroes, but for entertainers and publicists.

Hank Meyer Boulevard, *aka* 17th Street, commemorates the publicist who brought comedian Jackie Gleason's TV show to Miami. The wide thoroughfare ends with an uplifting view of the soaring Deco towers of the National and Delano hotels.

A performing arts center is named for Gleason, who immortalized Miami Beach as the "sun and fun capital of the world." Concerts and productions are staged in the **Jackie Gleason Theater of the Performing Arts** (1700 Washington Avenue; tel: 305-673-7330), the tropical-blue, Deco building where the show was made. On the sidewalk along the south side is a **Walk of Stars**, where handprints of well-known inductees include Muhammad Ali and comedienne Joan Rivers. In front of the theater is *The Mermaid*, a sculpture by Roy Lichtenstein.

On the other side of the Gleason is the **Miami Beach Convention Center**, home to trade fairs, and more glamorously, December's Art Basel. The streets around here are glaring and hot, with few trees or places to rest, and chewing gum on the sidewalks gets sticky in the hot sun. Fortunately, by Convention Center Drive is a pocket-sized oasis, the **Miami Beach Botanical Garden** (open 9am–5pm, free). The small, irregularly shaped garden has sweet-smelling orchids and native Florida flowers. Picnic tables under the palms make a shady spot to enjoy a take-out lunch.

Holocaust memorial

The **Holocaust Memorial** , on Meridian Avenue, is a testament to the tragedies of World War II, built at a time when Miami Beach still had many Jewish residents. Designed by Kenneth Treister, the 42-ft (13-meter) sculpture is of a hand reaching to the heavens. Set against images of Nazi death camps and the names of victims, the sculpture depicts tormented souls, struggling upward.

Nearby is the good-looking **Miami Beach Visitors Center** , on the corner of Meridian Avenue and Dade Boulevard. The modern building has a wall of curved windows looking on to a green park. The

Map on page 80

TIP

The attractive Miami Beach Visitors Center, 1920 Meridian Avenue, tel: 305-672-1270, is open from Mon–Fri 9am–6pm; Sat, Sun 10am–4pm. The South Beach Local bus stops nearby.

BELOW: lazing the day away in a South Beach hotel.

Map on page 80

Deco towers of the Delano (left) and the National hotels.

BELOW: twilight dining on Lincoln Road.

center is a good source of maps and brochures, and a number of SoBe tours depart from here.

Lincoln Road

The playground for north SoBe is the mall at **Lincoln Road** , a pedestrian-only thoroughfare, known in its 1930s heyday as "the Fifth Avenue of the South." Morris Lapidus, the "father of MiMo" architecture *(see page 104)*, brought an ambitious concept to the road around 1960. Laupidus' vision was for stores to be set on either side of rectangular lawns under swooping awnings, with gardens and gurgling fountains. Strolling was the only way to get around, Lapidus' dictum being, "a car never bought anything."

Window shopping in the upscale chain stores or lounging at one of the scores of outdoor restaurants and bars (some with sofas), visitors do, in fact, stroll, with the happy burble of running water from the fountains never far away. Lincoln Road is delightful and low-key, except on Friday nights and at Halloween.

At No. 541 Lincoln Road is the **Lincoln Theatre** (tel: 305-673-3330), a stylish example of Tropical Deco and now a venue for the New World Symphony. The New World is America's only national training orchestra for musicians age 21 to 30. The traveling orchestra has received acclaim in Paris and at New York 's Carnegie Hall.

At No. 800 is the **South Florida Art Center**, three storefronts transformed into galleries and studios for more than 100 artists, who can be seen at work. Farther down at No. 1040 is the **Colony Theater** (tel: 305-674-1026), a former movie house and now a city-owned performing arts center. The mixed architectural elements display both Tropical Deco and Mediterranean-Revival styles.

A number of stores are also housed in notable structures (like Banana Republic, in a 1947 former bank building), making the architecture as much fun as the fashion. The most appealing time to visit is at dusk, when chattering birds in the trees and the changing tropical colors of the sky conjure a little touch of Miami magic. ❑

RESTAURANTS, BARS & LOUNGES

Restaurants

A La Folie
516 Española Way (at Drexel Ave). Tel: 305-538-4484. Open: B, L & D daily (til midnight). **$$**
A romantic outdoor setting with the atmosphere of a Left Bank café, where handsome young waiters serve French crepes with good-value wine to accompany.

Balans
1022 Lincoln Rd (at Lenox and Michigan aves). Tel: 305-534-9191. Open: B, L & D daily, BR Sun. **$$**
Sibling to the excellent London café of the same name, this sidewalk favorite offers breakfast, lunch, and dinner with equal panache. Great people-watching and moderate prices soothe the occasional attitude lapses by the servers.

Café at Books & Books
933 Lincoln Rd (at Jefferson Ave). Tel: 305-695-8898. Open: B, L & D daily, BR Sat–Sun. **$$**
Fresh, well-composed lunches and dinners make this bookstore's New American café one of the best on Lincoln Road. Outdoor seating and sassy servers add to the literary allure.

El Chalan
1580 Washington Ave (at 16th St). Tel: 305-532-8880. Open L & D daily. **$$.**
A cheerful Peruvian *ceviche* bar with a wide range of authentic specialties. Helpful, mostly Spanish-speaking staff, serve up big portions with small prices.

Eleventh Street Diner
1065 Washington Ave (at 11th St). Tel: 305-534-6373. Open: B, L & D daily. **$$**
This classic diner in an aluminum trailer smack dab in the middle of South Beach clubland is a perfect spot for the "morning after" cure. Greasy grill fare, with a full bar. Best of all, the diner is open 24/7.

Emeril's Miami Beach
The Loews Resort, 1601 Collins Ave. Tel: 305-695-4550. Open: L & D daily. **$$$**
Grand TV chef Emeril Lagasse may not actually be here, but his specialties like blackened pecan redfish and gumbo sure are. Quality can vary, but the star power is definitely in abundance. Make a reservation early and ask for an outdoor table.

Escopazzo
1311 Washington Ave. Tel: 305-674-9450. Open: D daily. **$$$$**
Northern Italian dishes are made with lots of local produce, accompanied by a fine, all-Italian wine list and served by knowledgeable, helpful staff. A better choice than many of the flashy South Beach eateries that cost as much but don't deliver the quality.

Ice Box Café
1657 Michigan Ave. Tel: 305-538-8448. Open: L, D daily, BR Sat & Sun. **$$**
This Ice Box is worth a raid at any time of day or night for homestyle cooking like pot roast and fine broiled seafood. The incredible home-made cakes are irresistible.

Joe's Stone Crab
11 Washington Ave. Tel: 305-673-0365. Open: Tues–Sat L & D daily (closed mid-May through mid-Oct. but open June–July Wed–Sun for summer menu, dinner only) **$$$$**
The oldest and most talked about restaurant on the beach, some might even call it a tourist trap. But Joe's is still great *if* you can nab a seat (reservations are not accepted). Service is brusque but worth it for the nationally-known stone crabs in season mid-Oct to mid-May.

La Provence
French Bakery
1627 Collins Avenue (at Lincoln Rd). Tel: 305 538-2406. Open: B, L & D daily. **$**
The beach's finest French bakery has a

PRICE CATEGORIES
Prices for a three-course dinner per person with a glass of house wine:
$ = under $25
$$ = $25–$40
$$$ = $40–$60
$$$$ = over $60

constant carb-hungry line for baguettes and croissants. Big salads are on offer, as are yummy sandwiches with prosciutto or mozzarella, quiches, and temptingly pretty pastries.

La Sandwicherie
229 14th St (at Collins and Washington aves). Tel: 305-532-8934. Open: B, L & D daily, late night til 3am. **$**
Unrivaled French bread sandwiches, perfect before or after a day at the beach, complemented by baby cornichons and a vinaigrette to knock your socks off. All washed down with sweet smoothies, frothy espressos or freshly squeezed juices.

Lime Fresh Mexican Grill
1439 Alton Rd (at 15th St). Tel: 305-532-5463. Open: L & D daily. **$**
Miami is not known for great Mexican cuisine, but this California-style burrito bazaar is one of the best. The toppings and stuffings make this a popular stop among the discerning, southward-looking diners.

Mr Chu' Hong Kong Cuisine
890 Washington Ave (at 9th St). Tel: 305-538-8424. Open: D daily. **$$$**
The signature duck and handmade snow tofu, or dim sum offered on weekends, are served in an opulent setting complete with overstuffed red-and-gold banquettes. A great place for a special occasion.

Nemo
100 Collins Ave (at 1st St). Tel: 305-532-4550. Open: L & D, Sun BR. **$$$$**
A veteran on the fine-dining scene, this sexy, casual New American is still great. Sunday brunch is a popular treat with smoked salmon, great salads and outstanding pastries. Very professional, good-looking staff, and a raw bar add to the distinctions.

OLA on Ocean
The Savoy Hotel, 455 Ocean Drive (at 4th and 5th sts). Tel: 305-695-9125. Open: L & D daily. **$$$$**
Celebrity chef Douglas Rodriguez prepares legendary *ceviche* and other exotic Nuevo Latino creations, all served up in a sleek Ocean Drive setting. A hit, particularly among adventurous diners.

Osteria del Teatro
1443 Washington Ave (at Española Way). Tel: 305-538-7850. Open: D Mon–Sat. **$$$**
This pocket-sized corner gem is a perennial favorite with the cognoscenti for the fine pasta and other homemade Italian specialties. Prices are high and the space is uncomfortably tight, but that doesn't deter the lines of fans. After 10pm, a special menu (little known) gets a bargain price on pasta, soup, or salad, served with a glass of wine.

Pacific Time
915 Lincoln Rd (at Jefferson and Michigan aves). Tel: 305-534-5979. Open: Mon–Fri L (in season) & D daily. **$$$$**
Dine outside for a real plunge into South Beach chic at this Pan-Asian veteran. You'll pay dearly for the ticket, but the exceptional food and first-class cocktails are worth it. The servers are some of the most experienced in Miami.

Prime 112
112 Ocean Drive (at 1st St). Tel: 305-532-8112. Open: Mon–Fri L & D daily. **$$$$**
Call well in advance and then still expect to wait for a seat at this five-star steakhouse, because this is South Beach's biggest success story in about a decade. This posh and prodigiously pricey gathering spot serves excellent meat, fish, and lobsters.

Shoji
100 Collins Ave (at 1st St). Tel: 305-532-4245. Open: L & D daily. **$$$**
Sushi like you won't find elsewhere. Shoji impresses even Japanese expats with huge slabs of jewel-like fish and shellfish, as well as cooked dishes like oyster miso and grilled skirt steak with enoki mushrooms. The sexy interior attracts a great-looking crowd, so dress up.

Spris
731 Lincoln Rd (at Euclid and Meridian aves). Tel: 673-2020. Open: L & D daily. **$**
Roman-style pizzas with paper-thin crusts charred on the edges and nearly see-through in the middle are all the rage at this busy Lincoln Road pizzeria. The good news is that you can also order from the menus of the eateries on either side of Spris, so try the mussels from le Bon, or

the pasta from Tiramisu; all are owned by restaurateur Graziano Sbroggi.

Tap Tap
819 Fifth St (at Jefferson and Meridian aves). Tel: 305-672-2898. Open: D daily. **$$**
The beach's only Haitian eatery, this Caribbean restaurant is decorated with brightly colored murals, and attended by equally colorful patrons. The food, including fried pork tidbits and curried goat stew, recalls the taste of the islands. Live music on weekends completes the exotic scene.

Taverna Opa
36 Ocean Drive (at 1st St). Tel: 305-673-6730. Open: D daily. **$$**
Opa is like a souped up Greek frat party, replete with raucous plate-smashing. The lamb, squid and moussaka make the inevitable wait worthwhile.

Toni's Sushi Bar
1208 Washington Ave (at 12th St). Tel: 305-673-9368. Open: D daily. **$$$**
A veteran on South Beach, this Japanese pearl still pleases finicky raw fish lovers with pristine sushi served in cozy curtained booths. It's usually crowded with regulars on weekends, but always worth the wait.

Wish at The Hotel
801 Collins Ave (at 8th St). Tel: 305-674-9474. Open: B & L daily, D Tues–Sun. **$$$$**

Delightful and totally tropical, the romantic setting is enchanting in this Todd Oldham-designed restaurant. The inner garden is exotic, but the outside tables among palms and twinkling lights are truly magical, while the classic American and contemporary Asian cuisine is a perfect match for the setting. Be sure to enjoy a pre-dinner drink at the upstairs terrace bar.

Bars & Lounges

Buck 15
707 Lincoln Lane. Tel: 305-538-3815. Open: Mon–Sat 8pm–5am
A hip, upstairs hideaway hangout where you can find the coolest DJs and club kids, gathering here for drinks before hitting the South Beach scene. It's also a good after-hours haunt. Retro art hangs among the rec-room décor.

Clarke's
840 1st St. Tel: 305-538-9885. Open: D Mon–Sat
An Irish pub and bar that serves remarkably good food way beyond shepherd's pie and fish and chips. There's a killer wine list, and of course, a great range of beers and ales on tap.

Kafka
1464 Washington Ave. Tel: 305-672-4526. Open: Daily 8:30am–midnight
A bookstore, cyber café

and all around excellent place to loiter. This corner spot appeals to the literary crowd as well as to their smart friends.

Mac's Club Deuce
222 14th St. Tel: 305-531-6200. Open: 8am–5am daily.
An all-day and all-night institution on South Beach, this hard-drinking Deco bar across the street from a tattoo parlor is a place not to be missed while you're in town. Everyone from bikers to bankers are made to feel welcome.

Segafreddo Café
1040 Lincoln Rd. Tel: 305-673-0047. Open: daily for appetizers and drinks
Luxurious sofas with lounging Europeans line this Lincoln Road location. They come here for cocktails and even better coffees, *carpaccio*, and huge sandwiches, served at all hours.

VIX and VUE at the Hotel Victor
1144 Ocean Drive. Tel: 305-779-8888. Open L & D daily
With glowing jellyfish tanks, thumping DJs and an open-air lounge, the Victor plays host to one of the hottest scenes on the beach. On offer is not only the unbeatable view over South Beach's sexy oceanfront, but also the pretty young things lounging under the stars on canopied orbit beds – all the while nibbling on tasty tapas and sipping from the latest luscious liquid libations.

PRICE CATEGORIES

Prices for a three-course dinner per person with a glass of house wine:
$ = under $25
$$ = $25–$40
$$$ = $40–$60
$$$$ = over $60

LEFT: stone crabs are a South Florida specialty.
RIGHT: savor the mood and food of Haiti at Tap Tap.

ART DECO: SOUTH BEACH STYLE

Streamline Moderne and Tropical Deco buildings have been painstakingly preserved and put to excellent use

The Art Deco buildings in South Beach were built to raise the spirits of Americans during the Great Depression. The roots of Deco go back to 1901, when the Société des Artistes Décorateurs was formed in Paris with the goal of merging the mass production of industrial technology with the decorative arts. It was introduced to the world in 1925 at the Paris Exposition Internationale des Arts Décoratifs et Industriels Modernes, but the name "Art Deco" came about only in 1966, when it was used for a retrospective of the 1925 Paris show.

The Art Deco style was evocative of the new Machine Age, inspired in part by the aerodynamic designs of airplanes and cars. But the style combined many influences, from the swirls of Art Nouveau to the hard lines of Cubism. In the 1930s and '40s, hundreds of Deco structures were built in South Beach. Art Deco's stark, white exteriors were already well suited to the climate, but architects soon developed their own style, called "Tropical Deco". Many features, from the design of the windows to the choice of colors, were inspired by Florida's weather and seaside location. The more futuristic Deco style, Streamline Moderne, which replaced some of the detail characteristic of traditional Deco with smoother lines and sweeping curves, was particularly popular in Miami. Several elements, such as "porthole" windows and tube railings, were borrowed from the design of sleek, ocean-going liners.

ABOVE: Long bands of windows, often continuing around the corner of a building (as seen here, on the Park Central Hotel on Ocean Drive), allowed in plenty of natural sunlight and soft, cooling sea breezes.

BELOW: The Marlin Hotel on Collins Avenue is a classic Streamline building. Notice the rounded corners and "eyebrows" – canopies that shade the windows against the sun. Deco roofs were generally flat but often broken by a raised central parapet or pointed finial.

THE FIGHT TO SAVE SOUTH BEACH

The Art Deco hotels of South Beach had provided a refuge for visiting northerners, but by the 1960s they had begun to decay. Several of the area's once-glamorous hotels became low-rent housing for the elderly, and much of the district became run-down and crime-ridden.

In 1976, Barbara Capitman (1920–90) set up the Miami Design Preservation League to stop the demolition of the Art Deco buildings and to encourage their restoration. In 1979, one square mile of South Beach was listed on the National Registry of Historic Places. It was the first 20th-century district to receive such recognition.

In the 1980s, a designer named Leonard Horowitz endowed South Beach with a new color palette, nicknamed the Deco Dazzle, by painting many of the old buildings in bright colors; originally most would have been white with just the trim picked out in color.

Media interest in Miami's Art Deco enclave gradually increased, and then rocketed after South Beach became one of the favorite backdrops in the hit TV series, *Miami Vice*. Fashion photographers were drawn south to Florida too, Bruce Weber being one of the first to be lured both by the stylish and colorful location and by the ever-sunny climate. In the late 1980s, developers and other entrepreneurs moved in, opening nightclubs and model agencies and creating a cool mystique. By the turn of the millennium, most of the hotels in South Beach had been renovated.

ABOVE: Ocean Drive's Breakwater Hotel, illustrated here on a Deco-style postcard, has a tower like a ship's funnel and horizontal, colored "racing stripes" that give a feeling of movement.

RIGHT: The Ritz Plaza was built in the 1940s, when design was influenced by the science-fiction fantasies of Buck Rogers and Flash Gordon. Note the tower.

RIGHT: Art Deco architects in Miami tried out all kinds of new materials, including chrome, glass blocks and terrazzo – a cheap, imitation marble. Neon lighting was used for the first time and is one of the most distinctive features of South Beach. The dazzling neon means that the architecture can be enjoyed day or night.

BISCAYNE BAY

The stretch of water separating South Beach and Miami Beach from the rest of the city is punctuated by exclusive residential islands and is home to one of the world's largest cruise ports

Driving over Biscayne Bay, tourists and even some locals become transfixed by the yachts, sailboats and condominium-size cruise ships plying the waters below. Either that or they gaze at the panorama of Miami's glittering downtown skyline.

A good view of all this can be had from the **MacArthur Causeway** ⑱. Coming from South Beach, the first thing you'll notice is the **US Coast Guard Station**, a launching point for cutters patrolling the seas. To the south is **Fisher Island** ⑲, one of the highest priced pieces of real estate in South Florida. Founded by the Vanderbilts, some of its exclusivity comes from being linked to the causeway by helicopter or ferry only. Celebrities like Oprah Winfrey and Boris Becker have been drawn to the island, which was sold in 2004 to a real estate company headed by a 28-year-old French citizen.

Farther along, on the north side of the MacArthur Causeway are bridges to **Star**, **Palm** and **Hibiscus** islands. These islands, dotted with mansions, yachts moored in the backyards, have had their share of famous and infamous residents. Al Capone, the gangster who terrorized Chicago in the 1920s, lived at 93 Palm Island. Novelist and journalist Damon Runyon lived at 271 Hibiscus Island. Now Gloria Estefan and Miami Heat basketball stars call these islands home.

Isolated on a speck of land north of Star Island is the **Flagler Memorial Monument**, an obelisk honoring developer Henry Flagler.

The Port of Miami

On the south side of MacArthur Causeway are **Lummus** and **Dodge** islands, which together make up the **Port of Miami** ⑳. The port has secured a huge chunk of the cruise market, with over 3 million passen-

BELOW: the MacArthur Causeway over busy Biscayne Bay connects South Beach to downtown Miami via a series of islands.

gers traveling each year. Visitors choose between a short cruise lasting just three days, through a range of options that culminates in an 11-day voyage. Most ships set sail from Miami for the Bahamas. The port also handles cargo that generates $12 billion annually.

The closest bay island to downtown Miami is **Watson Island ㉑**, and there are few better spots to watch the massive liners making their way out to sea. At night the view is spectacular. Lights in the cabins and lamps on the decks glow on the liners moored in a row. Thursdays and Fridays are the best days to catch a glimpse of these floating hotels, as they load up for weekend sailings.

Parrot Jungle

On the northeast side of Watson Island is the popular children's attraction **Parrot Jungle** (open daily; charge; tel: 305-400-7200). The site has lush foliage and is a pleasant enough place, although the sound of squawking parrots can be deafening. The birds perform tricks at the commands of their trainers. The "jungle"

has animals other than just parrots; the orangutans are favorites.

The **Children's Museum of Miami** (open daily, charge; tel: 305-373-5437) is the place where visitors get a chance for hands-on education and discovery about the environment in general, and Florida in particular. The museum also sponsors a Miami Children's Museum film festival.

Beyond these attractions, Watson Island remains a cavalcade of sounds, from the echoing horns of the cruise ships plying the waters in and out of the port, to the roar of jet airplanes overhead as they climb in and out of Miami International Airport, to the rumble of causeway traffic heading back and forth to the island.

Seeing the bay from a car is a sight for sure, but a much closer view of it all is available from the waterline. Boats like the *Island Queen* (tel: 305-379-5119) leave regularly from Bayside Marketplace in downtown Miami, Watson Island or the Port of Miami. Day trips also leave for the Bahamas or cruise beyond the US borders, providing opportunities for gambling in international waters. ❑

Map on page 80

When the upscale residents of Fisher Island catch the car ferry to the mainland, workers at the ferry station hose down their cars as they arrive, in case they got splashed with sea water during the 10-minute crossing.

BELOW: a cruise ship sails Biscayne Bay between South Pointe, at the tip of South Beach, and exclusive Fisher Island.

MIAMI BEACH

Mile after mile of golden sands, upscale
communities and the eye-catching architecture
of Miami Modernism, known locally as MiMo,
mean that Miami Beach is back on the scene

The artist known as Christo may have shown foresight with his Miami Beach installation. After more than a year of battles with environmentalists, politicians and tourism honchos, Christo obtained permission to use gleaming Biscayne Bay as a canvas for his art.

In the pink

On May 7, 1983, when Miami Beach was passé as a resort, Christo and a band of loyal workers completed the wrapping of 11 islands in Biscayne Bay with 6½ million sq. ft (600,000 sq. meters) of flamingo-pink plastic. For two weeks, the shiny fabric floated around the islands, and the grumbles gave way to swells of civic pride. After decades of gloom, Miami Beach was again in the pink.

Miami Beach has reinvented itself many times over the years; golden days have come, gone and returned again. For the last two decades, this northern part of the beach has been eclipsed by the dazzling popularity of its pastel-painted neighbor, South Beach. Miami Beach, by comparison, was dowdy and drab – OK for grandparents, but uncool for anyone under the age of 50.

Now, hipsters by the hundreds are packing their stylish luggage and heading to the beach – this beach, the "other" beach. They're checking into

weird and wonderful hotels, marvels of modern architecture with floating staircases, glass-curtained walls and flying roofs. This exuberant, post-World War II architecture is called MiMo, short for **Mi**ami **Mo**dernism *(see page 104)*.

Miami Beach – a 15-mile (24-km) spit of sandy land connected to the mainland by causeways – is divided into four "neighborhoods." There's South Beach, of course, followed by the area directly north, unofficially called "Middle Beach" or "Central

Map on page 102

LEFT: Miami Beach.
BELOW: *Surrounded Islands*, Christo's 1983 "wrapped" installation.

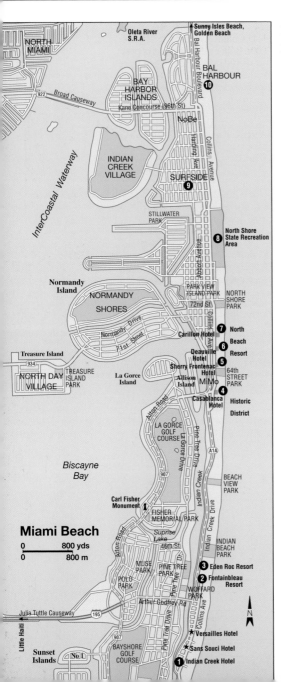

Miami Beach

| 0 | 800 yds |
| 0 | 800 m |

Beach." Then comes North Beach, and, finally, a few northern beach-towns. Middle Beach stretches from 23rd to 47th streets, and is defined by white sands and huge hotels. **North Beach** is the cool kid on the block, with MiMo architecture and a funky attitude; befitting its newfound status is a newly-minted moniker: **NoBe**. At the top end are Surfside, Bal Harbour, Sunny Isles Beach and Golden Beach – technically outside the incorporated city of Miami Beach, but only officials and taxpayers care.

These neighborhoods are effectively islands off the city of Miami, the Atlantic on one side and **Indian Creek** and the **IntraCoastal Waterway** on the other. They share the same characteristics of sun-drenched shores, towering palms, heavenly white sands and sweeping ocean views that go on forever.

North of South Beach

The main attraction is, of course, the beach. Miami Beach's total water frontage is 63 miles (101 km), and the average temperature is a balmy 75°F (24°C). There's public assess to the sand at 21st Street, 46th Street, 53rd Street, 64th Street, 72 Street, and at North Shore State Recreational Park. Ocean Rescue, a division of the fire department, guards them, providing a regular view of fit, bronzed personnel patrolling on the sand or in four-wheel drive vehicles.

One pretty perk north of Middle Beach is a **public boardwalk**, which stretches 1¾ miles (3 km) along the ocean from 21st to 46th streets. Families stroll, couples jog, teenagers hold hands and gaze at the water and each other. With the ocean on one side and fancy hotels on the other, it's a fine scene. Though well-lit, parts of the boardwalk have been known to be hazardous at night, so take care.

A lovely, off the beaten track hostelry around 28th Street is the Deco-era **Indian Creek Hotel** ➊

(2727 Indian Creek Drive; tel: 305-531-2727). Style on a budget is the keynote here; it's within walking distance of South Beach, but has the ambiance of a Key West guesthouse.

On the mainland behind Indian Creek, stately mansions with kidney-shaped pools have boats moored on private docks. For one week every February, hundreds of expensive yachts bob on the creek across from the grand hotels, up for sale in the Yacht and Brokerage Show.

March of MiMo

The march of MiMo architecture begins on 29th Street, with the **Seville Hotel** (1955); the **Sans Souci Hotel** (1949); the **Saxony Hotel** (1948) and the **Versailles Hotel** (1941) all in a row. Some of these hotels are open; some are awaiting preservation status, others are sleeping princesses poised to awake at the kiss of a sympathetic developer. These are followed by the two MiMo "grand dames" of Miami Beach.

Architect Morris Lapidus was the doyen of this style, and his most celebrated example was the lavish, enormous **Fontainebleau Resort** ❷ (4441 Collins Avenue; tel: 305-538-2000). Built in 1954, it reeks of postwar confidence, a time when large families drove to Florida in huge gas-guzzling cars for indulgent sojourns of sun and fun, retreats from the frozen, gray north. Everyone who was anyone in the 1950s and '60s performed or stayed here, including Frank Sinatra and Bob Hope.

The two curving 14-story edifices face out to the Atlantic, bedecked with marble staircases, crystal chandeliers and two pools (one is a two-story lagoon with a floating bar). The hotel has been heavy-handedly remodeled, and a tower added.

The restoration of the **Eden Roc Resort** ❸ (4525 Collins Avenue; tel: 305-531-0000) is more successful. From the lobby's curvy contours and carved columns of marble, to the highly polished terrazzo floors, classic elegance flirts with whimsy in a way that some of the Eden's original guests – like Bogie and Bacall – might enjoy. Approving of the restoration, Morris Lapidus said, "I did elaborate, not gaudy."

Map on page 102

Miami Beach police officers patrol in a variety of vehicles.

BELOW: Miami home, with dock, along the IntraCoastal Waterway.

TIP

The Miami Design
Preservation League
offers MiMo tours led
by local historians and
architects. Call 305-
531-3484 for an
appointment. Tours are
also arranged by the
North Beach Develop-
ment Corporation:
gonorthbeach.com

BELOW: caryatids
galore support the
Casablanca Hotel.

MiMo in NoBe

Morris Lapidus was the father of the MiMo style; his curving flamboyance defined the Miami Beach resort hotel – the blueprint for many Miami Modern buildings. "MiMo" (pronounced My-Moe) describes architectural features characteristic of the jet-set futurism of the 1950s and early '60s: back-lit floating ceilings, staircases to nowhere, stylized caryatids; anodized aluminum; painters' palette shapes; walls with circular holes like cement Swiss cheeses. Lapidus said, "You're selling a good time."

The architectural playfulness was also practical. Glass-block walls allowed in sunlight, but kept out strong winds. Before central air conditioning, curving walls caught sea breezes. Cheese-hole walls did the same, and at the same time protected guests from prying eyes.

In the 1980s and '90s, the style fell out of favor, seen as vulgar, old-fashioned and overblown, compared to the graceful Deco delights down the beach. Lapidus was lampooned, and many examples were – or are being – demolished. But after the

millennium came a reappraisal, led in part by a handsome book, *MiMo: Miami Modern Revealed* (Chronicle Books, 2004) by Eric P. Nash and Randall C. Robinson, Jr.

Robinson is now executive director of the North Beach Development Corporation, and a keen campaigner. The movement is gaining strength *(see page 135)*, and began with the establishment of the **North Beach Resort Historic District** along 12 blocks of Collins Avenue between 60th and 72nd streets.

A tour is the best way to explore MiMo as, unlike the Art Deco District, sites are spread between the drab buildings of a style Robinson calls "NoMo" (standing for no more). Highlights include the **Casablanca Hotel ❹** (6345 Collins Avenue; tel: 305-868-0010) built in 1950 by architect Roy France and the **Sherry Frontenac Hotel ❺** (6541 Collins Avenue; tel: 305-866-2122), designed by Henry Hohauser in 1947.

Frank, Sammy and Dean partied at the **Deauville Hotel ❻** (Radisson Deauville, 6701 Collins Avenue; tel: 305-865-8511), and then later, the

Hello MiMo

The 1950s and '60s architecture MiMo (Miami Modern, or Modernism) is seen mostly around North Miami Beach, but examples are all over town. Some of the best include:

- **Lincoln Road**, South Beach (1960) architect Morris Lapidus' retail glory
- **Archway**, Sunshine State International Park, NW 13th Avenue (1964)
- **Bicardi Building**, 2100 Biscayne Boulevard (1963)
- **Foremost Building**, 14 NE 1st Avenue (1952)
- **Miami Herald Building**, 1 Herald Plaza (1957)
- **Vagabond Hotel**, 7301 Biscayne Boulevard (1953)

Beatles recorded a performance for the *Ed Sullivan Show* in the Napoleon Ballroom. The Deauville (1957; architect: Melvin Grossman) revives the Rat Pack ambiance in a sophisticated supper club called the **Arturo Sandoval Jazz Club**. Musicians play and swap tales late into the night.

The area's recent historic designation also brought a well-deserved reprieve to the **Carillon Hotel ❼** (6801 Collins Avenue), designed by Norman Giller in 1957 with a glass-curtain wall. A condo complex is being built around the hotel.

Beyond MiMo

The pace settles down west of Collins Avenue. Around 71st Street and Normandy Drive is a neighborhood popular with Brazilians and Argentinians, with plenty of restaurants and bakeries to prove it *(see page 107)*.

From 79th to 87th streets is the popular, attractive **North Shore State Recreation Area ❽**, a good choice for a day out if you have a family. Picnic tables and grills, a fitness trail and meandering boardwalks all provide outdoor fun.

The City of Miami Beach ends around 88th Street, which is where Surfside begins. **Surfside ❾** was a 1930s winter destination resort for French Canadians; for decades it threw a bash, Canada Week, to honor its transplanted population.

Today, Surfside is a comfortable, low-key neighborhood where young and old, established and still-striving, mingle, although yuppification is fast setting in. The **Surfside Community Center**, at 9301 Collins Avenue, interlaced with vegetation, has a zig-zag colonnade framing the town seal, which is suspended above the passage to the pool and the beach.

Harding Avenue is Surfside's main commercial street. One morning after eating eggs and bagels at Sheldon's Drug Store (now gone) on Harding, the late Isaac Bashevis Singer learned that he had won the Nobel Prize for Literature *(see pages 108–9)*. Singer lived for about 20 years in Surfside; 95th Street is known as Isaac B. Singer Boulevard.

In Bay Harbor Islands and **Indian Creek Village**, grand, Mediterranean Revival-style homes were built,

Map on page 102

Architect Morris Lapidus (1902-2001) on MiMo: "You're selling a good time."

BELOW: the lobby of the Eden Roc is pure MiMo.

Map on page 102

Bal Harbour Shops is Miami's most upscale mall; J-Lo indulges in retail therapy here.

BELOW: shades of summertime.
RIGHT: shop for souvenirs.

mainly in 1925, a year before the disastrous land bust (which also affected Coral Gables). An impressive array of these mansions ranges along NE 96th Street. **Bay Harbor Islands** itself is a tiny town resting over two islands on the IntraCoastal Waterway.

Bal Harbour and beyond

Just north is **Bal Harbour** ⑩, a 250-acre (100-hectare) flashy enclave of condominiums and landscaped medians. Elegant stores like Tiffany & Co, Prada, Versace and Valentino nestle around ponds and foliage at the upscale **Bal Harbour Shops**. Prince Dimitri of Yugoslavia launched a range of jewelry here; when national style magazines want Miami opinions, this is where they canvas.

North of Bal Harbour is **Haulover Park**. Just over the bridge, the sky swarms with colorful kites of all shapes and sizes, and all available to buy. Kayaks can be rented from **Haulover Marina**, and provide an exhilarating way to explore the mangroves lining Dumbfoundling Bay. The northern part of Haulover Park has become the unofficial preserve

for nude sunbathers, the only nude beach in the county. Although park officials are uncomfortable with the bounty of exposed body parts, they allow the practice to continue, as they say without apparent irony, "at least it is contained." Shielded from the highway by sea-grape trees, nudists happily flock to enjoy the beach, the sun and the sand *au naturel*.

Sunny Isles Beach, about 2 miles (3 km) long, is covered in rocky sand. The winds and rough surf here lure surfers and sailors, while the **Newport Beach Pier**, built in 1936 and three times destroyed by hurricanes, is a great fishing spot. Sunny Isles, like many of the beaches here, once had several cute MiMo motels, some of which have been torn down in the past few years.

Golden Beach, like its name, is a wealthy coastal community, and the beach is private. Palatial, Venetian-style homes occupy 2 miles (3 km) of Atlantic shoreline. The most famous is 461 Ocean Boulevard. This is where rock star Eric Clapton stayed, and he gave his 1974 album the same name as his address. ❏

RESTAURANTS

Arnie & Richie's

525 41st St (at Prairie & Royal Palm Aves). Tel: 305-531-7691. Open: B, L daily. **$**
Still Miami Beach's best deli after six decades, this is a temple to New York-style bagels, pastrami, corned beef and rye. A recent revamp has not detracted from the authentic fare, or the brusque service.

Café Prima Pasta

414 71st St (at Collins Ave). Tel: 305-867-0106. Open: L & D Mon–Sat, D only on Sun. **$$**
A real neighborhood pasta joint that offers seating inside or out on a cozy terrace. Service is friendly, but can be slow. Moderate prices and decent Italian fare – including the fine gnocchi – keep locals and tourists coming.

Café Ragazzi

9500 Harding Ave (at 95th St). Tel: 305-866-4495. Open: L & D Mon–Sat, D only Sun. **$$**
You'll feel like one of the *familigia* at this crowded but charming Italian ristorante. Waits are common, but compensated by a glass of house wine outside to pass the time.

Carpaccio

Shops of Bal Harbour, 9700 Collins Ave (at 96th St). Tel: 305-867-7777. Open: L & D daily. **$$$**
Armani, Fendi and Gucci parade in this posh Italian restaurant standby for ladies who lunch. The signature *carpaccio* is recommended as are the delicate, handmade pastas, the fresh salads and extensive wine list. Prices soar, but this is Bal Harbour, after all.

Creek 28

At the Indian Creek Hotel, 2727 Indian Creek Dr (at 28th St). Tel: 305-531-2727. Open: L & D daily. **$$**
Tucked away in a hotel on a one-way street, Mediterranean and North African flavors make this place perfect for a romantic tryst, especially in the glow of the low-level lighting at the poolside tables.

The Forge

432 Arthur Godfrey Rd (at Royal Palm Ave). Tel: 305-538-8533. Open: D daily. **$$$$**
An institution in Miami Beach for four decades, this gilded icon is a magnet for celebrities and celeb-spotters. Tuxedoed servers give tours of the historic and well-stocked wine cellar.

Las Vacas Gordas

933 Normandy Dr (at Bay Dr). Tel: 305-867-1717. Open: L & D daily. **$$$**
The cows sure are chubby at this rocking Argentine *paradilla* but the waitresses are not. In fact, a beautiful young crowd congregates for the superior beef and deafening music.

Talula

210 23rd St (at Collins Ave & Pine Tree Drive). Tel: 305-672-0778. Open: Tues–Sat L & D, Sun BR and D. **$$$**
Husband and wife duo, Andrea and Frank Randazzo delight their local regulars with impressive Tartare of Ahi Tuna dotted with serrano chiles, cucumber, and crisped rice and conch ceviche. The rustic brick interior is romantic and cozy, while the enchanting courtyard is a dream in the cool months.

Tamarind

946 Normandy Dr (at 71st St). Tel: 305-861-6222. Open: L & D Tues–Sun. **$$**
An little-known Thai delight, almost lost in an area dominated by Argentinian eateries, this authentic, good-looking and moderately-priced spot is well worth a detour. Specialty dishes include tamarind duck, shrimp and sweet corn cake, or you could opt for the fantastic pad Thai. The award-winning chef, Vatcharin Bhumichitr, never fails to deliver a delightful evening with his superb cuisine.

PRICE CATEGORIES

Prices for a three-course dinner per person with a glass of house wine:
$ = under $25
$$ = $25–$40
$$$ = $40–$60
$$$$ = over $60

RIGHT: hot dog on the beach.

My Love Affair with Miami Beach

Before his death, Isaac Bashevis Singer, winner of the Nobel Prize for Literature, recalled his early days on the beach.

In 1948 when my wife, Alma, and I visited Florida for the first time, the face of Miami Beach resembled a small Israel. From the cafeterias to the streets, Yiddish resounded around us in accents as thick as those you would hear in Tel Aviv. It was remarkable: Jewishness had survived every atrocity of Hitler and the Nazis. Here, the sound of the Old World was as alive as ever.

Alma and I had not had a vacation since 1940, when we were married. (I was lucky to have a wife who did not resent being married to a poor writer.) But it was a particularly cold winter in New York in 1948, so we decided to buy two train tickets to Miami.

All night we traveled, sitting up in our seats, until the early morning, when the conductor told us to step out of the train at Deerfield Beach for a glass of fresh orange juice. That first sip was nothing less than ambrosia. In my native Poland, orange juice was considered a most healthful drink. Even today, Alma carries home oranges from the grocery and squeezes fresh juice for breakfast. When we arrived at the train station in Miami, a taxi took us to Miami Beach.

Indescribable glow

As we rode over the causeway, I could hardly believe my eyes. To me, being at a summer place in winter was a great event. It was almost unimaginable that in Miami it was 80°F while in New York it was 20°. Everything – the buildings, water – had an indescribable glow and brightness to it. The palm trees especially made a great impression on me. The driver let us off at the Pierre Motel. Owned by the brothers Gottlieb, it was a modern place but still had its own charm and good clientele. We were given a nice room with a balcony, where I worked every day. It was in those years that I wrote chapters of *The Family Moskat*, my first big novel, which ran as a serial in the *Jewish Daily Forward*.

In the 1940s and 1950s, Miami Beach was in its so-called heyday. During the day, planes with long streamers flew over the beach advertising dinners with seven courses for $1.50. Rather than eat in the hotel, we often had dinner with acquaintances and old friends at one of the cafeterias. We ate heartily: borscht, salad, bread, coffee and dessert.

The cafeterias were nostalgic places for me, and I loved going to them. They reminded me of the Yiddish Writers Club of Warsaw, where I had rubbed elbows with not only some of the great Yiddish writers and poets but English and German writers as well. The same food was served and the same conversations took place. I noticed that people met here again accidentally after a long separation during the Hitler era and a lot of tears were shed.

For some reason we stopped coming to Miami Beach in the 1960s. Then, in 1973, I was invited to give a lecture in downtown Miami. A former neighbor of Alma's in Munich happened to come to my lecture. Afterward, she invited us to her apartment on Collins Avenue. By then, we had fallen in love with Miami Beach all over again, and we considered buying an apartment. For five days, we struggled with the decision: Should we, could we, afford to buy an apartment? In the end, we bought one with a splendid view of the ocean where we live all year round today.

Ecstactic moment

One morning in 1978, I went to Sheldon's Drugstore to have eggs and bagels. Earlier, a friend had called to tell me she had heard on *Good Morning America* that I had won the Nobel Prize, but I had dismissed it as just a nomination and not the real thing. When I returned after breakfast, Alma was calling out to me excitedly. My editor at the *Forward* was on the telephone. He told me that he had heard on the transatlantic wire that I had won the Nobel. My hands grew cold and Alma says I turned as white as a sheet. Two months later, after hectic shopping trips to buy clothes for the big event, we flew to Stockholm. It was an ecstatic moment for me when the King of Sweden handed me the prize.

But just because someone has won the Nobel Prize does not mean that life changes dramatically. After the ceremonies had ended and the rush of interviews was over, life went on as before. Alma and I returned to our apartment and I continued to write each day.

From this oasis of comfort, I have pondered the many changes that have taken place on the beach since 1948, not all of them for the best. Nevertheless, for me, Miami Beach is still one of the most beautiful places in the world. Nothing can equal the splendor of nature. Every day, as I look out at the ocean, each palm tree, each wave, each sea gull is still a revelation to me. After all these years, Miami Beach feels like home. ❑

LEFT: early Miami map; Issac Bashevis Singer.
BELOW: Miami Beach in the 1950s.

Lummus Park, a Public Bathing Beach, Miami Beach, Florida

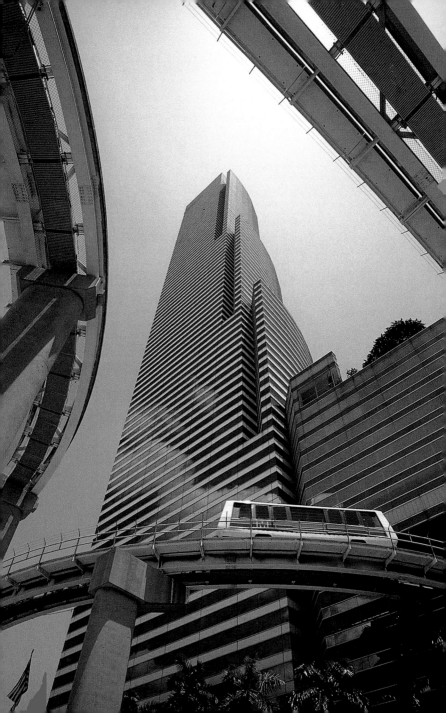

DOWNTOWN MIAMI

Beneath a building boom of soaring skyscrapers with signature details and architecture from Miami's past, street vendors cater to customers from all corners of the globe

Map on page 112

An infant in the family of America's Atlantic seaboard cities, most of downtown Miami's buildings are younger than the folks who migrate to Florida for their retirement. Since April 15, 1896, when Henry Flagler brought his East Coast Railway into the baby town that became Miami, literally putting the town on the map, this little devil has turned into a spunky, scrappy city. The excitable Latin edge of Downtown feels more like the northern tip of the southern hemisphere than vice-versa.

But since 2004, the influx of new money and newcomers from Central America, South America, and the frozen north of the US has brought downtown Miami into a major boom. Although a few skyscrapers still showed the scars from Hurricane Wilma up to six months after the storm, new buildings are going up at an astounding rate. Like metal giraffes, cranes silhouette the skyline – at a recent count, there were 65 of these symbols of new wealth and boom-time construction.

LEFT: the Metromover moving above Downtown's streets.
BELOW: architectural details at the Miami Performing Arts Center.

Magic skyline

From a distance, especially at night, downtown Miami looks like a throbbing megalopolis, with banks of skyscrapers floodlit and twinkling in colored neon, creating a magic-show skyline. Yet, for visitors walking along Biscayne Boulevard, through the central grid of streets, across the Miami River and into the gleaming Brickell Avenue quarter, Miami is really on a human scale.

There are cops walking beats along wide sidewalks; hawkers selling juices from pushcarts on corners; hotdog vendors and shoeshine men on the steps of the Dade County Courthouse. Here, the city feels more like a street fair than the nerve center of a sprawling metropolis.

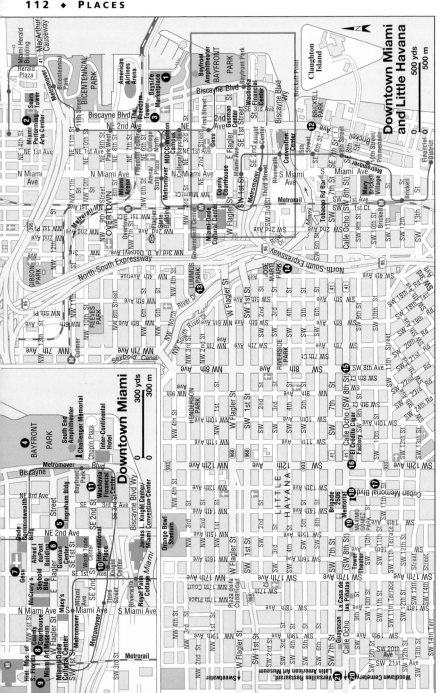

Downtown playgrounds

Just off Biscayne Boulevard – the main thoroughfare that runs parallel to Miami's waterfront – is **Bayside Marketplace ❶**, a 16-acre (6-hectare) extravaganza of more than 120 shops, restaurants and attractions. Since its development, Bayside has been the life of Downtown, attracting tourists and residents at all hours of the day and night. At the water's edge, boats dock for lunch and dinner, and bands, mime artists and jugglers entertain the crowds.

The huge neon guitar in the background marks the entrance to the Hard Rock Café Miami, this branch featuring memorabilia from the city's Latin superstars, like Gloria Estefan and John Secada.

Just north is the well-regarded **American Airlines Arena**, home of the white-hot Miami Heat basketball team and the venue for the city's biggest music and sports events.

Beyond the Arena, **Bicentennial Park** is the former site of the Miami Grand Prix; its Torch of Freedom often the backdrop for demonstrations. North of the park, at Biscayne

Boulevard and 13th Street, is the oldest Art Deco structure in Miami. The Sears Building, dating from 1929, is now gone save for the **Sears Tower**, standing proud in the bright white Florida sun. The tower is a linchpin for the **Miami Performing Arts Center ❷** (1350 Biscayne Boulevard, tel: 305-949-6722), a multi-million-dollar facility on both sides of Biscayne Boulevard, with a connecting walkway over the street.

The 570,000-sq.-ft (53-sq.-meter) project is home to the Concert Association of Florida; the Florida Grand Opera; the Miami City Ballet and the New World Symphony. The Cesar Pelli-designed venue includes Carnival Concert Hall, the Sanford & Dolores Ziff Ballet Opera House, the Studio Theater, the Plaza for the Arts, and a café.

The Freedom Tower

Opposite the American Airlines Arena, the **Freedom Tower ❸** rises on the west side of Biscayne Boulevard. Built in 1925 as the headquarters of the now-defunct *Miami News*, the tower served in the 1960s as a

Map on page 112

The Freedom Tower is a monument to the Cuban community.

BELOW:
Bayside Marketplace.

Metromover

Look up and you can see the Metromover whisking passengers between skyscrapers, unhindered by the traffic below. This driverless, rubber-wheeled train runs along an elevated 4½-mile (7-km) track through most of the downtown area. The route is an inner, central loop and two branches, serving Bicentennial Park and Omni Mall to the north, and Brickell Avenue to the south. Maps of the system can be found at the main station, Government Center (at 111 NW 1st Street), or at other visitor information centers. With 21 stations and a train every 90 seconds at rush hour, the Metromover is a convenient way to hop from place to place.

From pretty Bayside Marketplace (above), visitors can board the Island Queen *and take a cruise around the bay, day or night. Tel: 305-379-5119.*

processing center for Cuban immigrants, hence its name. It was abandoned for years, until Saudi Arabian investors in the late 1980s sank money back into the 17-story gem, once called "Miami's Statue of Liberty," and restored its former grandeur.

Since then, the site has often caught the eye of property developers, but Freedom Tower is presently in the care of Miami-Dade College, who plan to use it as a monument to the Cuban community.

Beyond Bayside Marketplace is **Bayfront Park ❹**, a large green space of earth dredged from Biscayne Bay in the early 1920s. At its southern end, a memorial by the late Japanese sculptor Isamu Noguchi is dedicated to the crew of the ill-fated *Challenger* space shuttle. This is also where, in 1933, an assassin attempted to kill President-elect Franklin D. Roosevelt. He missed Roosevelt, but mortally wounded Chicago's mayor, Anton Cermak *(see page 25)*.

The park underwent a $30-million facelift a few years ago and now features a 10,000-seat amphitheater for concerts and festivals. It's fun to

attend a gig here, sitting on the lawn in the sunshine, your back to the Miami skyline and with glittering Biscayne Bay just beyond the stage. At the eastern edge of Bayside Park is a statue of Christopher Columbus, presented to the city by the people of Italy on Columbus Day in 1953. In the evenings, horse-drawn buggies take sightseers through the park from Bayside Marketplace.

A walker's delight

For the true heart of Downtown, head west on Flagler Street to the city's geographical center at the intersection of Flagler and Miami Avenue. The two streets divide Miami-Dade County into the four quadrants of the compass, and it's from here that Miami gets its bearings: this is the eye of Miami's urban storm.

Two blocks east of the crossroads, at the intersection of Flagler and NE 2nd Avenue, is the best place to begin a walking tour of Downtown landmarks. The Streamline Moderne architectural gem on the southeast corner, now a Sports Authority athletic goods store, has a curved facade,

Many Miami addresses are given according to their location relative to Miami Avenue and Flagler Street: e.g. 1200 NW 26th Street is 12 blocks west of Miami Avenue and 26 blocks north of Flagler Street.

and a three-story atrium. A flagship branch of Walgreens until 1995, it opened in 1936 as one of the chain's most attractive shops.

Just south on 2nd Avenue is the classy **Ingraham Building ⑤**, a mock Florentine Renaissance beauty that opened in 1926. Its lobby, crowned by an ornate ceiling, has many original features, including light fixtures, the mailbox and the office directory. Scenes of South Florida wildlife play out in the gold of the elevator.

Movie palace

West on Flagler Street, at No. 174, is the Spanish-Moorish-style Olympia Building, now home to the **Gusman Center for the Performing Arts**. Built as a Paramount Pictures movie theater in the mid-1920s, the glorious auditorium is a romantic evocation of an Andalusian patio at night, with billowing clouds painted overhead and stars a-twinkling. The tall organ pipes tower in the cool cavern near to the left of the stage. This is the perfect venue for lovers of movies, as directors' talks and great

films are shown during the annual Miami International Film Festival. Elvis played here, too.

Opposite, the severe lines of the **Alfred I. duPont Building ⑥** define Miami's ode to New York's Rockefeller Center. An Art Deco jewel built between 1937 and 1939, the duPont served as the southeastern seat of the Florida National Bank and Trust system, and was a regional headquarters for the US Navy during World War II, whose mission here was to patrol the shorelines for Nazi submarines.

The duPont building's appearance has remained relatively unchanged. The lobby, the Deco-styled café and the directory recall a Miami that flared, then faded, more than half a century ago. At the foot of the escalator, near the front door, is an upward view of murals beautifully inspired by the Floridian landscape and history.

Back on the street is the buzz and hum of modern Miami. The electronic hardware outlets everywhere are the first things that come to many people's minds as essential components of "Downtown."

Map on page 112

TIP

In the Downtown electronics outlets, be wary of deals that seem too good to be true. For example, when store owners wrap up purchases for the trip home, tourists are occasionally surprised to unwrap a different item from the one they bought.

BELOW:
street scene, downtown Miami.

The stores, shoulder to shoulder throughout the downtown area, are magnets for shoppers from across the Caribbean and Latin America. They swarm and buy stereos, TV sets and DVD recorders by the carload, many bringing extra suitcases that they fill with tech toys to haul home.

A few doors down on Flagler is the **Capital Mall**, a short cut through to NE 1st Street. This corridor is one of Downtown's better-kept secrets, with architectural details dating from the 1920s. Look up to appreciate the structural and sculptural flourishes on the buildings, mostly obscured at street level by shop signs.

Majestic eagles

Exiting the mall, there's a view of the **Dade Commonwealth Building** across the street, with majestic eagles atop neoclassical columns. Born of the (first) boom era, the Commonwealth Building is an abbreviated version of itself; the killer hurricane of 1926 took off its top 10 stories.

West, on the south side of 1st Street, is the **Shoreland Arcade**. The arcade once housed the Shoreland

The top floors of the Miami-Dade County Courthouse used to be the city's jail.

BELOW: Mosaico is one of Miami's better restaurants.

Company, a huge boom-era developer. The structure dates to the mid-1920s. The highly ornate, classical design remains intact, its huge arched entranceways retaining the elaborately painted friezes. The original chandeliers, decorative terrazzo floors and mailbox also remain.

Carefully cross 1st Avenue – Miami drivers are notoriously reckless – and turn northeast. A French-inspired mansard roof, rare for Miami, tops off the slim, imposing **Capital Building**, at 117 NE 1st Avenue, which has now been converted into loft apartments. It was constructed in 1926 and was known as the Security Building.

Next door is the pretty and pink **Gesu Catholic Church ❼**, the oldest Catholic site in Miami. The Mediterranean-Revival structure was built in the mid-1920s on the site of its 1890s predecessor. Covering the ceiling is a mural, restored in its entirety by a Nicaraguan refugee in the late 1980s.

One block north on 1st Avenue is Miami-Dade College's **Wolfson Campus**. The largest community college in the US, Wolfson has given downtown Miami an extra boost of energy; the campus has hosted huge paella cook-off parties, and each November the massive Miami Book Fair International sets out lots of stalls here, with a great street fair open to the public *(see page 54).*

Directly west of the campus is the **United States Post Office and Federal Courthouse**. A 1931 neoclassical edifice, designed in part by Marion Manley, Florida's first licensed female architect, there is a mural on the second floor depicting Miami's growth from tropical backwater to booming city.

It also houses the small jail cell that was the unluxurious 1990 home-away-from-home for Panamanian dictator Manuel Noriega, detained for trial on drug charges.

Jewelry center

Returning to 1st Street, and heading west again, you pass by the rear of the old Jackson Byron's Pharmacy. A couple of doors farther on is the 10-story **Seybold Building**. Built in the 1920s, this is the heart of Downtown's booming jewelry business, one of the busiest in the country.

Next door is a building that once housed a Five & Dime store called **McCrory's**. This is one of the oldest buildings in Downtown, parts dating to 1906. An historic moment in the American Civil Rights movement occurred here in 1960 when black demonstrators staged a lunch-counter sit-in at the cafeteria.

One block south along the city's oldest thoroughfare, Miami Avenue, the Burdines Department Store was for years Downtown's flagship shop. Burdines began near this spot in the late 1800s and today, as **Macy's**, is popular with office workers. Note the footbridge crossing Miami Avenue, and tying the old Burdines to its younger counterpart. On the south facade, the mural is the work of seascape artist Wyland.

West on Flagler is the **Miami-Dade County Courthouse** ❽, the unofficial hub of Downtown. Built between 1925 and 1928 in the neo-classical style, the building once housed both the city and county jails, which were stacked safely on the top 10 floors. Earlier, along the building's north side, gallows for executions were erected when the occasion demanded. Each fall, turkey buzzards migrating from Ohio take over the courthouse's roof as their haven for the winter.

To the northwest is the **Miami-Dade Government Center**, headquarters of the county government. Wander around the lobby shops and cafés, then hop an elevator to the higher floors for a sweeping view of the curling Miami River, turquoise Biscayne Bay and the bay's port and many islands.

Across NW 1st Street is the **Miami-Dade Cultural Center** ❾, designed by architect Philip Johnson. The center is home to the Miami-Dade **Public Library**, the **Historical Museum of Southern Florida** (open daily; Sun pm only; charge;

Map on page 112

TIP

For almost two decades, Dr George, an historian at the Historical Museum of Southern Florida, has guided fascinating, often off-beat, tours of Miami. For more details, call 305-375-1621 Mon to Fri or go to: www.historical-museum.org

BELOW: Miami-Dade Cultural Center.

tel: 305-375-1492) and the **Miami Art Museum** (open Tues–Sun; Sat–Sun pm only; charge; tel: 305-375-3000). Costs are minimal and use of the library, of course, is free.

The plaza connecting the center's components is an architectural delight, a quiet world reminiscent of the piazzas of Italian hill towns. This urban oasis is a great place to bring a take-out lunch and relax in the sun. It is best approached around the corner from its southeast entrance.

South of Flagler

South of Flagler Street are two of Miami's more striking skyscrapers. On the corner of SE 1st Avenue and 2nd Street is the 48-story **Bank of America Tower** at **International Place** , which opened in the late 1980s and was designed by the internationally renowned architect I.M. Pei. At night, the tower is often floodlit in a display of colors – red, white and blue for the Fourth of July, emerald green on St Patrick's Day.

To the south is the last sloping bend of the **Miami River** before it spills into Biscayne Bay at Brickell

Point. Near the river is the **Royal Palm Cottage**, a yellow-framed house built in 1897. The cottage is the last of 30 houses that Henry Flagler built along SE 1st and 2nd streets, and was moved to this location in 1979. Today it sits next to a waterfront restaurant at the Riverwalk Metromover station.

Closer to the bay is the **Wachovia Financial Center** . Part of the Wachovia complex rests on the site of an ancient Indian burial mound. For years, the 55-story building stood as the tallest in Florida, but the explosion of condo high-rises, both in Miami and elsewhere, has long since whisked away that title.

SE 2nd Avenue crosses the river on the Brickell Avenue Bridge, adorned with a bronze statue of a Tequesta Indian warrior (by Cuban-born sculptor Manuel Carbonell), and continues south as **Brickell Avenue** , also known as "bankers row." Before the banks moved in, Brickell Avenue was the corridor for some of Miami's most beautiful mansions, a veritable millionaires' row. Now, international banks line

The Spring Garden Historic District, between NW 11th Street and the Miami River near the Seybold Canal, has lovely single-family homes. The most impressive is called the "Hindu Temple," based on a Hollywood movie filmed on the site in 1919. The house is at 870 NW 11th Street.

BELOW: downtown Miami has the city's best cultural venues.

the street, signalling the city's strong connections with the South American and Caribbean economies.

Eccentric buildings

Rounding the turn at 15th Street, the banks give way to an area with two famous high-rise residential buildings. **The Palace**, at No. 1541, is distinguished by two tall structures embracing each other, and (at No. 2025) the **Atlantis Apartments** is a glass building with a square punched through the middle. The Atlantis featured in the opening sequence of TV's *Miami Vice*.

Both were designed by Arquitectonica, a local architectural firm that made its mark in the 1970s. Arquitectonica has been responsible for some of Miami's most recognizable structures, including the American Airlines Arena.

One of the most interesting spots is back toward the river. **Tobacco Road** (626 S Miami Avenue; tel: 305-374-1198), a bar and restaurant, holds the city's oldest liquor license (1912) and operated as a speakeasy. Dark but no longer smoky, with walls papered with newspaper clippings about the club, Tobacco Road cranks out live blues or jazz most nights, as well as hosting occasional open-mike poetry readings.

Not far away, at 10 Street and 1st Avenue, is **Mary Brickell Village**, a shopping and entertainment enclave surrounded by beautiful trees.

Lummus Park

For a taste of Miami history, head west to **Lummus Park** ❸. The **William English Slave Plantation House**, a limestone fortress locally known as **Fort Dallas**, was built just down the river in the 1840s and moved here in 1925. A decade later, the **Wagner Homestead House** was crafted from Dade County pine by a 19th-century homesteader.

Lummus Park, named for Miami's second mayor, is a lovely place to wander around (though somewhat less so at night). One of Miami's best addresses in the early 20th century, structural reminders include a striking Scottish Rite Temple and handsome residential buildings along NW 3rd and NW 4th streets. ❑

Map on page 112

The Bank of America Tower at International Place changes color according to the occasion.

RESTAURANTS

Acqua at the Four Seasons Miami
1435 Brickell Ave SE. Tel: 305-358-3535. Open: B & L Mon–Sat, D daily, BR Sun. **$$$$**
An elegance unmatched in Miami, this international find in the Four Seasons Hotel is reason enough to book a room. The European-trained servers are a treat for diners, and the chef, Patrick Duff, previously cooked in the splendid Sukothai in Bangkok.

Caribbean Delight
236 NE 1st Ave (at 2nd & 3rd sts). Tel: 305-381-9254. Open: B, L & early D daily (closes at 6pm most nights). **$**
Maybe the best Jamaican food this side of Kingston; jerk chicken, rundown and saltfish and ackee are served in this cheery little dive.

Duo Restaurant & Bar
1421 S Miami Ave (at 14th St). Tel: 786-497-4386. Open: L Mon–Fri, D Mon–Sat. **$$$**

Owner Maria Frumkin excels at simple dishes and exceptional desserts in this welcome respite from the hot, busy streets of Downtown. The bargain wine list is a dream come true.

Garcia's Seafood Grille
398 NW North River Dr (at NW 5th St Bridge). Tel: 305-375-0765. Open: L & D daily. **$$**
A real locals' seafood shack on the Miami River, great for grilled mahi mahi, fried fish sandwiches or stone crabs in season (mid Oct–mid May).

Mosaico/Salero
1000 S Miami Ave (at 10th St). Tel: 305-371-3473. Open: Salero L & D Mon–Sat; Mosaico: D Mon–Sat. **$$–$$$$**
The stunning refit of a 1920s firehouse, chic Spanish fare and romantic outdoor terrace distinguish this restaurant. Downstairs is casual *tapas*; upstairs is experimental cuisine with an emphasis on fresh fish.

● ● ● ● ● ● ● ● ● ● ● ● ● ●
Prices for a three-course dinner per person with a glass of wine:
$ under $25, $$ $25–$40, $$$ $40–$60, $$$$ over $60

LITTLE HAVANA

In Little Havana, Latin traditions linger longest, a neighborhood where not only Cubans but immigrants from the Caribbean and Central America have made Miami their home

A flame leaps day and night as a beacon for the veterans of the ill-fated Bay of Pigs invasion. Schoolchildren march proudly for a homeland they've never visited or seen. Fast-food restaurants serve café Cubano – to go – alongside hamburgers and French fries.

At the core of Little Havana beats a rebellious exile's heart, scarred with sadness for a lost homeland, swelled with pride in its past. From pharmacies and restaurants to car washes and grocery stores, the names here speak of the land far away and long ago: Farmacia Camaguey, Frutería Los Pinareños, Managua Medical Center.

Havana, Cuba, never looked like this jamboree of car dealerships, strip malls, furniture stores, flower shops, run-down 1950s motels and bright, Mediterranean-style houses. This is Havana, Miami, an immigrants' enclave, a constantly changing assertion of new beginnings and hope.

Latin flavors

Little Havana's influence stretches wide across Miami, even if the Cuban flavor now mixes with Central American and other Latin cultures; you can dance salsa in Key Biscayne or sip *ajiaco* in Kendall. But this neighborhood remains the symbolic center for the Cuban community, a place to savor a good meal or a good memory.

Very roughly, Little Havana is bounded by the Miami River to the east, 37th Avenue to the west, State Road 836 to the north and Coral Way to the south. It sprawls over Miami neighborhoods settled after the turn of the 20th century with the names Shenandoah and Riverside.

Cuban exiles first came here *en masse* after their country's biter revolution; between 1959 and 1973, approximately 300,000 of them landed in Miami *(see pages 29–31)*. They reopened boarded-up stores

Map on page 112

LEFT: surrounded by colorful friends.
BELOW: Calle Ocho is the largest Hispanic festival in the US.

Playing for pennies on Calle Ocho.

BELOW:
the Brigade 2506 (Bay of Pigs) Memorial is lit by an eternal flame.

and filled vacant apartments. As Cubans moved up economically, they moved out to more affluent areas of the city, making space for new waves of migrants to reinvigorate the mix.

Since the late 1970s, city officials and local merchants have wanted to develop the tourist potential of the area west of 17th Avenue, with San Francisco's Chinatown or New Orleans' French Quarter as models. The idea is for hotels and specialty shops to fuel the urban, ethnic ambiance. Commerce *is* moving west, but the Latin Quarter is still only a modest success; brick sidewalks lined with trees and shops with white stucco walls and red-tiled roofs are the main indications of its existence.

River scenes

Little Havana is reached from Downtown Miami by crossing the **Miami River**. Once a waterway to the Everglades, which the Tequesta Indians plied in cypress canoes, today, Miami River is a busy shipping center. Boatyards, marinas, terminals and fisheries line the banks.

A boat isn't necessary to appreciate the river; public parks stretch along the banks. The most attractive is **José Martí Park** on the eastern edge of Little Havana, where pink stucco buildings and red-brick walks are sprawled along the river's south bank. Built on the site of a Tequesta Indian settlement, in 1980 the area was used as a tent city, a temporary refugee shelter.

In 1985, the space became a park dedicated to Cuban writer and philosopher José Martí, the leader of Cuba's independence struggle with Spain. The park has a pool, a fountain, a bust of José Martí, and a statue of the late South Florida Congressman, Claude Pepper.

The pulsing hub of Little Havana is **Calle Ocho (SW 8th Street)** , which heads west out of town, where it joins up with the Tamiami Trail and leads toward the Everglades. In January, Calle Ocho hosts the Three Kings Day Parade, as well as the schoolchildren's march in honor of José Martí. But the big annual event is the Calle Ocho festival in March, a mammoth street party and the largest

José Martí (1853–95)

A man of action and of letters and instrumental in the liberation of Cuba from Spain, José Martí is an inspiration for Cubans on both sides of the Florida Straits. In Miami, a park, streets and even the anti-Castro radio and TV stations are named after him.

Born in 1853 in Havana, Martí was frail as a young man. At 16, though, he founded an anti-colonial newspaper, *The Free Fatherland*, to campaign for Cuban independence from Spain. After a spell in jail for denouncing a fellow student who marched in a Spanish procession, Martí was sent into exile.

He settled with his wife and son in New York in 1881, and for 15 years he organized, lectured and wrote speeches, articles and poetry. In the 1960s, his *Versos Sencillos* became the unofficial Cuban national anthem, paired with the song *Guajira Guantanamero*.

In 1895, he and Máximo Gómez landed in Cuba intending to take the island from the Spanish by force. They were joined by hundreds of supporters but a month later, at the Battle of Dos Ríos, Martí was shot charging the enemy. Independence was achieved seven years after his death.

Hispanic celebration in the US. As many as 30 stages are erected for performances, where there is salsa, Latin and Caribbean music, and foodstalls for spicy treats *(see page 63).*

At 1106 Calle Ocho is the biggest producer of Miami handmade cigars, **El Crédito Cigar Factory** (open Mon–Sat; free, but call to schedule a tour; tel: 305-858-4162). Wreathed in the smoky-sweet aroma of tobacco, two dozen men and women nimbly cut the leaves, roll them into cigars and squeeze them into wooden presses. Apprentices learn the art under the watchful eye of owner Ernesto Perez Carillo, whose father had a tobacco business in Cuba. The factory turns out four brands: the star buy is the cigar La Gloria Cubana.

West of El Crédito is tree-lined **Cuban Memorial Boulevard** ⑰, the southern extension of SW 13th Avenue. At the boulevard's junction with Calle Ocho is the **Brigade 2506 Memorial** ⑱, the Bay of Pigs Monument to the ill-fated invasion. On April 17, 1961, 1,300 volunteers, trained and sponsored by the US Central Intelligence Agency, landed at the Bay of Pigs. The expected popular uprising against Fidel Castro did not occur, and after three days of fighting, nearly 100 men died, almost 1,000 were taken prisoner, and the remainder beaten to retreat to Miami. The memorial flame is surrounded by half a dozen missiles pointing upward. Plaques bear the names of the Cubans who lost their lives.

Also along Cuban Memorial Boulevard is **Plaza de Los Periodistas Cubanos**, a memorial to journalists who devoted their writing and their lives to speaking out against the Castro regime.

Music and magicians

A short distance east of the Brigade 2506 Memorial, **Casino Records** (1208 Calle Ocho) offers a huge range of music on CD, tape and vinyl. Choose from early 20th-century Cuban *danzons,* salsa by Cuban exile Celia Cruz or mambos and *cha-cha-cha* from the Cuban bandleader Damaso Perez Prado. The Latin mix includes Dominican *merengues*, Colombian *cumbias*, Brazilian sam-

Miami-Dade County is bilingual. Signs are often in both English and Spanish, and the Miami Herald (the state's most widely-read daily) has a Spanish edition, El Nuevo Herald.

BELOW:
best souvenir: a Gloria Cubana from El Crédito Cigar Factory.

TIP

Free tours of Miami's Hispanic sites, including several in Little Havana, are conducted every Saturday in October to coincide with Hispanic Heritage Month. For info, go to www.miamidade.gov/transit/hispanic.asp

BELOW: the domino effect in Máximo Gómez Park.

bas and sexy Argentinian tangos.

Another Cuban institution transplanted from Havana to Little Havana after the revolution is **La Casa de los Trucos** (1343 Calle Ocho). This House of Tricks carries strange hats, Uzi machine guns that spit water, magic tricks, maracas and a variety of masks, including some of Castro. The owners are known to demonstrate occasional sleights of hand.

Close by is **Pinareños Market**, a fruit stand – half indoors, half outdoors – with displays of tropical delicacies. Depending on the season, you might shop for papaya, *platanos manzanos* (apple bananas), *boniato* (the Cuban sweet potato) and *malanga*, a white-flesh root usually boiled or used in soups.

Items of Cuban nostalgia are worth the trek to **Sentir Cubano** (3100 Calle Ocho; tel: 305-644-8870). Shop for a *guayabera* (traditional embroidered shirt); T-shirts emblazoned with Cuban baseball heroes; dominoes; music and cookbooks in both Spanish and English.

On the sidewalk outside the Calle Ocho branch of McDonald's is Little Havana's **Walk of Fame**, a local version of the commemorative walk on Hollywood Boulevard. Gloria Estefan and the Miami Sound Machine were the first to have their names embedded in stars on the sidewalk.

Domino therapy

To the west, the rattle of dominoes and the smell of cigars pervade one of Miami's most densely populated parks. Located at the corner of Calle Ocho and SW 15th Avenue, **Máximo Gómez Park** ⑲ (better known as **Domino Park**) are games tables covered by red-tiled roofs. Concerned about crime, Miami city officials have limited access to the park to those over the age of 55, and an identification card is required to get in, though exceptions are made for interested tourists.

A large mural at the park displays portraits of the leaders of every North and South American country who attended the 1994 Miami Summit of the Americas, offering an opportunity to have your picture taken with former president Bill Clinton.

A few blocks west of Gómez Park

is **La Casa de las Piñatas**, 1756 Calle Ocho, a store filled with cheerful *piñatas* (animal or human figures filled with toys and candy to hit with a stick until they burst), and other accessories for children's parties.

About 10 blocks farther west and left on SW 27th Avenue is **Botánica la Esperanza** at No. 901, a store with herbs, candles, dolls and small images of saints. *Botánicas* sell the ingredients and equipment required by the religious rites associated with Santería and Vodou *(see page 132)*. Customers and staff can regularly be heard discussing which herb to use for a particular problem, or which prayer to recite for a loved one.

Devotees buy Spanish-made wood-paste statues of Catholic saints such as St Judas Tadeo, the Virgin of Regla and the Virgin of Charity, Cuba's patron saint. These are to be set in small shrines, often in the worshippers' front yards. On Little Havana's Cuban Memorial Boulevard is a large Ceiba tree with its roots covered with candles. This, too, is of spiritual significance to those who practice Santería.

The many *botánicas*, scattered throughout Little Havana, Little Haiti and other Miami neighborhoods, are not intended as tourist sights. Outsiders are politely tolerated, but not particularly welcomed, and practitioners are sensitive about being misunderstood. Tact and discretion are useful companions.

Monuments and memories

Well worth a visit is the **Woodlawn Cemetery ㉠**, at the corner of Calle Ocho and SW 32nd Avenue. Anastasio Somoza, the Nicaraguan strongman unseated by his country's 1979 Sandinista revolution, rests here in a mausoleum marked only with his initials. Carlos Prio Socarras, the Cuban president elected in 1948 and deposed in a 1952 coup by Fulgencio Batista, lies beneath a tombstone that carries the colors of the Cuban flag. Also buried here is Gerardo Machado y Morales, Cuba's fifth president, a harsh dictator who fled the country after the 1933 revolt.

A more recent monument is that of Jorge Mas Canosa, founder of the Cuban-American National Founda-

Map on page 112

Statue of a deity in a Little Havana botánica.

BELOW: lighting up Little Havana.

tion and a burr under Fidel Castro's saddle for many years. He died in Miami in 1997. To the rear of the cemetery is another monument to veterans of the Bay of Pigs.

Little Havana is at its most accessible through the palate. The area is thronged with coffee shops and restaurants serving a range of Latin foods. Cuban cooking is homey – people's fare – and Calle Ocho offers a number of options. **Versailles** ㉑ *(see page 127)*, is one of the most popular eating establishments in Miami and the surrounding area.

The large mirrors and bright lights are unselfconsciously gaudy, and that is part of its charm. Versailles attracts a varied clientele, from large families and groups of businessmen to theatergoers dropping in for a late-night snack. It is also a stop for politicos courting the Cuban vote.

The menu is huge. Neophytes to Cuban cooking might try the restaurant's sampler of Cuban foods: roast pork, sweet plantains, ham croquettes and tamales. Also popular, and with a similar menu, is **La Carreta**, across the street, and one of the few places

that is open 24 hours. **Guayacan**, at No. 1933, is where local Nicaraguans sit down to homemade soups and delectable beef-tongue simmered in tomato sauce.

Cuban culture

The neighborhood is experiencing a cultural explosion with a surge of galleries, workshops and theaters. The **Latin American Art Museum** (2206 Calle Ocho) features works by Hispanic artists from all over the world, and is dedicated to the preservation of the cultures of Latin America and Spain.

Viernes Culturales (Cultural Fridays) take place the last Friday of every month. This is when Calle Ocho between SW 14th and 17th avenues fills with arts and crafts stalls, live music and dance. Walking tours of the neighborhood are conducted from 7–11pm.

On other days, try **Casa Panza** (1260 Calle Ocho; tel: 305-643-5343) which puts on live flamenco several nights a week. Audience members are encouraged to participate.

One of the most beautiful of the

Fidel Castro, the most hated man in Miami, spent his honeymoon in Miami Beach in 1948. According to Cuban archives, he ran out of money and had to pawn his watch, but Castro's bride liked the city so much they stayed several more nights.

BELOW: food *rapida*.

Little Havana theaters is the **Tower Theater** at 1508 Calle Ocho. Built as a movie palace in 1926 and remodeled five years later in the Art Deco style, its signature feature is a shiny steel spire. Now owned by the City of Miami, it has dance and theater performances as well as film festivals.

At **Teatro de Bellas Artes** (2173 Calle Ocho; tel: 305-325-0515) you might be treated to a Spanish tragedy or a contemporary anti-Castro comedy. The Hispanic Theater Guild is resident at **Teatro Ocho** (2101 Calle Ocho; tel: 305-541-4841).

The **Manuel Artime Theater** (900 SW 1st Street; tel: 305-575-5057) is home to the Miami Hispanic Ballet. The theater is named for the late Manuel Artime, who was one of the key figures in the Bay of Pigs invasion, and who had previously been instrumental in overthrowing Cuban leader Fulgencio Batista.

Sweetwater

Twenty years after Cuba's 1959 revolution, upheaval in Nicaragua began a new flow group of Latin American refugees to Miami, who found sympathy from Cuban exiles. By the time the Sandinistas were defeated in 1990, Miami's Nicaraguan community had grown to an estimated 150,000 residents. The exiles made most impact in East Little Havana and in the **Sweetwater** district on Miami's western edge, about 7 miles (11 km) west of Little Havana. Today, Sweetwater is more of a Cuban and Latin American mix as people from other Hispanic countries swell the population, but one Nicaraguan memory not only remains, but has thrived and grown.

Los Ranchos Restaurant (125 SW 107th Avenue; tel: 305-221-9367) opened in Sweetwater in 1981 with just 15 employees. It and four branches – in Coconut Grove, Coral Gables, Bayside Marketplace and The Falls shopping center – now employ 250 people.

Los Ranchos promotes its attraction as "Latin flavor with international ambience." So go along, savor the *churrasco* steak with *chimichurri* sauce, followed by the creamy house specialty, *tres leches*, and join in the *bueno* celebrations. ❏

Coffee shop chat: try it with café Cubano and a guava-filled pastry.

RESTAURANTS

Blue Sky Food By The Pound
3803 W Flagler St. Tel: 305-642-4388. Open: B, L, D daily. $
Locals love the hearty Cuban food, and feast on it here or take it out to enjoy as a picnic.

Casa Juancho
2436 8th St. Tel: 305-642-2452. Open: L & D daily. $$
Cuban-Americans throng to this Latin setting, voted many years running the best Spanish restaurant in Miami.

Guayacan Restaurant
1933 SW 8th St. Tel: 305-649-2015. Open: L & D daily. $$
Excellent Nicaraguan cuisine, well-served in a comfortable setting. Try the grilled meat with *chimichurri* – a parsley and oil sauce. The daily *sopa* specials are homemade and hearty.

Hy-Vong
3458 SW 8th St. Tel: 305-446-3674. Open: D Tues–Sun. $$
Vietnamese cuisine served in an unlikely setting. The owner can be brusque and the setting is seedy, but devotees line up for the highly spiced and French-inspired fare.

Islas Canarias
285 NW 27th Ave. Tel: 305-649-0440. Open: B, L, D daily. $$
Fast service and some of the best Cuban cooking in the neighborhood.

La Caretta
3632 SW 8th St. Tel: 305-444-7501. Open: 24 hours a day. $$
Outlets are all over the city, and this one has a huge replica water wheel. This rustic fast-food chainlet offers cheap Cuban fare, especially welcome after a night on the town.

Versailles
3555 SW 8th St. Tel: 305-444-0240. Open: B, L, D daily. $$
Feel the pulse of the Cuban community and enjoy tasty, traditional and hearty Cuban fare at its finest.

● ● ● ● ● ● ● ● ● ● ● ●
Prices for a three-course dinner per person with a glass of wine:
$ under $25, $$ $25–$40, $$$ $40–$60, $$$$ over $60

UPPER EAST SIDE AND NORTH MIAMI

The art explosion trained a spotlight on the Wynwood Art District and the Design District. Music and murals define Little Haiti, while other areas have outrageous architecture or cultural gems

The **Upper East Side** is the name of a loose collection of neighborhoods north of Downtown. Some are old and established; some are very new. The term is very much in vogue with property developers right now, to hype up two areas in what was previously a rundown part of town, now revived under the stylish banners of the Wynwood Art District and the Design District.

Art: Miami style

The colors here are electric – cobalt blue, or tropical, sunset oranges. At the edges are ochres and browns – New York cool. Art: Miami style. Some call it "Miami Noir"; others are giving it time to define itself. All froth and hype, or here to stay? The answer remains to be seen. The one sure thing is that the art scene in Miami is – right now – hot, hot, hot.

The transformation began a few years ago, as artists unable to afford rising rents near the beach, crossed Biscayne Bay to colonize warehouses and 1920s stores. Designers followed, seduced by period architecture and huge spaces that offered perfect showcases for their often large furniture. The creative influx has bathed these areas in a wash of cool.

At the same time, an artistic explosion rumbled in Miami. Art Basel, the prestigious Swiss trade fair came to the beach in 2002. Its glittering success drew the eyes of the art world to Miami. There was money here, inexpensive real estate, young artists from South America and year-round sunshine. Wynwood and the Design District became even more hip. Curators and dealers, fleeing from the sky-high prices in New York's SoHo, turned into modern-day snowbirds – albeit with more exotic feathers.

At no time is this transformation more apparent than during the five days of Art Basel. Although primar-

Map on page 130

LEFT: Carlos Betancourt in Wynwood.
BELOW: December's Art Basel sparks off events galore.

This car on the side of a wall at 38th Street is a former exhibit from the Police Museum. The museum has moved, and the car is now beige, but it's still a startling sight.

BELOW: dog day afternoon in the Design District.

ily staged in the Miami Beach Convention Center, parallel events, collectively known as "Alt. Basel," contribute to the flurry of artistic excitement and display.

Some are prestigious shows organized out of New York, some are late-night hot spots for the foot-weary and thirsty *afficionadi*. There are parties and events everywhere. Galleries (many open until 2am) not chosen by the official selection committee, often stage their own shows, in the style of the Salon d'Refuses that exhibited the artists rejected by the Paris Salon in 19th-century France.

Work in progress

The **Wynwood Art District** ❶ (www.wynwoodartdistrict.com for map) is an association of art institutions, museums, galleries, collections, studios, and alternative art spaces, approximately 60 in all. But Wynwood, spanning NW 19th to 37th streets, is a work in progress.

Warehouses are large and brightly painted, but it's a rough, sprawling area, needing more urban pioneers to make it coalesce. Visitors also need a car, and to take care after dark.

Two streets lined by galleries, make an easier visit. The first is **NW 23rd Street**. Don't miss **World Class Boxing** (No. 170) which used to be a sparring venue, and is now a leading multimedia site. Nearby is the **Javogue Design Collection** (No. 123). As soon as the buzz became a humming chorus, galleries moved in from Coconut Grove or Coral Gables, like the well-respected **Fredric Snitzer Gallery** (2247 NW 1st Place).

A few blocks north is **MoCA at Goldman Warehouse** (404 NW 26th Street), a temporary satellite branch – until 2009 – of the Museum of Contemporary Art *(see page 135)*; in wintertime, shuttle buses connect the two. A discreet white building with a green door about a

block northwest is the excellent **Margulies Collection ❷** (591 NW 27th Street; open winter Fri, Sat 11am–4pm; closed summer; free; tel: 305-576-1051). With soaring ceilings and an attractive balcony, it's a spacious venue for installations by Frank Stella and a fine collection of photography, with an emphasis on social realism.

Housed in a former warehouse used by the US Drug Enforcement Administration, the most established collection is the **Rubell Family Collection ❸** (95 NW 29th Street; open winter Wed–Sun 10am–6pm; closed summer; charge; tel: 305-573-6090). Don and Mera Rubell are from the New York art world – Don is the brother of the late Steve Rubell, of Studio 54 fame. The collection, majoring on the work of young artists, began four decades ago. Almost every important artist since the 1970s is represented, including Keith Haring, Jeff Koons, Damien Hirst, Paul McCarthy and Cindy Sherman. The Sculpture Garden is a balmy outdoor setting for large works.

The other street with galleries galore is **NW 36th Street**. The **Bikeko Gallery** (No. 215) is just a few steps away from **Abba Fine Art** (No. 233). The **Jakmel Gallery** (No. 147) showcases Haitian art. Low-key and funky, the gallery entices with good-humored, voodoo charm. The white 1950s curvy beauty with black porthole windows is the **Bernice Steinbaum Gallery** (36th Street and N Miami Avenue). Bernice earned her reputation showcasing women artists, and relocated to Miami after 23 years in New York.

Square mile of style

Called "one square mile of style," the **Design District ❹** (www.miami designdistrict.net for map) regularly draws movers and shakers from the beach to this side of the bay. The area embraces 16 square blocks, from NE 36th to NE 41st streets, between NE 2nd Avenue and North Miami Avenue. Encompassing the old Buena Vista neighborhood, built in the early 1920s by pineapple-planter and furniture-tycoon T.V. Moore, the compact area is perfect for a stroll.

Map on page 130

TIP

Most Wynwood galleries are closed on Sundays and Mondays, and the major collections are closed May through August. The Wynwood Art District Gallery Walk takes place on the second Saturday of each month, from 7 to 10pm.

BELOW: Antoni Miralda's shoe made from a real gondola on display in the Design District.

Voodoo Boutiques

The first thing you notice at the door is the smell – sweet, pungent and intoxicating. Listed in the Miami telephone book under religious goods, *botánicas* (shops that sell magical herbs and religious paraphernalia) provide working testament to the fact that African mysticism thrives in South Florida. (Further proof: in 2006, a woman was arrested at Fort Lauderdale airport after luggage screeners found a human head in her suitcase. The woman, just off a flight from Haiti, said it was to ward off malign spirits).

Usually tucked away in neighborhood shopping centers, *botánicas* cater to practitioners of the Afro-Caribbean religions of Santería and Vodou (voodoo). Shelves are stacked with a spiritual potpourri of aromatic roots, tranquility balm, serenity salve, virility pills, black cat repellent, dried alligator flesh, floor polish to ward off greed, rosary beads, statues of saints, black candles, bile of bullock, bones arranged as crosses, books of numerology, stuffed monkey heads and voodoo dolls, supplied with pins.

While *botánicas* are most popular in the neighborhoods of Little Haiti and Little Havana, they are found throughout the city and all have a combination Jesus Christ, Black Magic, and Alice in Wonderland persona.

Both Vodou and Santería have their roots in the religion of the Yoruba tribes of West Africa. The practices were carried to the Caribbean by slaves, and took on a Christian mantle when the slaves were forced to adopt Christianity. The religion was practiced with secrecy because of the colonizers' fears that it could unite the slaves and help fuel rebellion. In Haiti, it became Vodou. In Cuba and other islands, it became Santería. Both came to Miami with Caribbean immigrants.

While there are differences between the two, both are animistic and pantheistic and use drum-beats, chanting and the offering of animal sacrifice. Followers communicate with spirits who are found in nature; occasionally beat themselves with twigs to ward off evil spirits; and cast magic spells to influence fate and the future. Sociologists say that the practice among Miami's Caribbean immigrants is a remedy for the pressures they feel to assimilate to American life.

Botánicas, which never existed in the Caribbean – medicinal herbs were sold at marketplaces, not stores – are a relatively modern phenomenon in Miami. While the *botánicas* themselves are a peculiar yet peaceful addition to Miami, the eccentric and exotic ceremonies of Santería and Vodou have provoked some controversy.

In some neighborhoods, locals have complained about the disappearance of dogs and cats, and animal rights groups have protested against the killing of chickens and goats in sacrifices. Practitioners have also been accused of breaking into coffins in city cemeteries and stealing human remains for ritual use. In their defense, adherents have complained of prejudice and persecution, and petitioned the US Supreme Court for their practices to be awarded the status given to other legitimate religions.

It is difficult to determine how many devotees of Santería and Vodou there are in Miami, as most ceremonies take place at home, and in secret. But the number of *botánicas* indicates a figure in the tens of thousands. ❑

LEFT: ceramic "saint" in a Little Haiti *botánica*, showing the influence of Christian iconography.

This is the place find urban art toys, hand-forged iron-brass lighting, or holistic solutions for kitchen living spaces. Have a drink in a basement bar, or just indulge in a little high-end window shopping. T.V. Moore's store at 4040 2nd Avenue, now called the **Moore Space**, is an impressive structure with a lounge where visitors and artists can watch videos and socialize. Also worth seeking out is the modern installation *The Living Room*, a three-story outdoor cutaway, with purple-flowered wallpaper and a towering floorlamp. In a neat trick of perspective, spectators feel like Alice down the rabbit hole, dwarfed by the outsize furnishings.

The houses on tree-lined **42nd to 48th streets** date from the Buena Vista boom time. Among them are fine examples of Mission, Craftsman and Art Deco-style homes.

Little Haiti

Music draws you to **Little Haiti ❺**, an enclave of Caribbean culture on the site of Lemon City, an earlier neighborhood. Storefronts vibrate to the Haitian music, blaring from side-walk speakers. Multilingual signs advertise peculiarly Haitian products – the latest *compas* records, custom-tailored "French-style" fashions and culinary delights like *lambi* (conch) and *griot* (fried pork). And, unlike many neighborhoods, Little Haiti's streets are thronged with pedestrians.

Houses painted pink, blue, red, and yellow – the colors of the Caribbean countryside – are nothing like the Art Deco pastels of Miami Beach. The vivid hues of the sunlit tropics sing out of **folk-art murals** on storefronts, walls and billboards, especially along **NE 2nd Avenue** and **54th Street**.

These murals, painted by local artists, have subjects ranging from political demonstrations and floral collages to Haitian people. The colors are also seen in Little Haiti's **Caribbean Marketplace** (5925 NE 2nd Avenue), a modern replica of Haiti's famous iron market, designed by Charles Pawley. This signature structure is awaiting restoration.

Along NE 2nd Avenue from 45th to 84th streets, Haitian stores predominate. At the corner of NE 1st Avenue and 54th Street, stop for a

Map on page 130

Homes in Little Haiti are painted bright Caribbean colors.

BELOW:
herb and grocery vendors in Little Haiti.

All dressed up for church: there's wonderful music at the Sunday services at Notre Dame d'Haiti.

tastebud treat at **Lakay Tropical Ice Cream** store. Exotic flavors include *cachiman* (sweetsop), *corosol* (soursop), mango, tamarind, and more. The bakery sells good paté, too.

A few blocks north is **Libreri Mapou** (5919 NE 2nd Avenue; tel: 305-757-9922), a bookstore with a large selection of Creole and French publications, as well as Haitian paintings and crafts. Owner Jan Mapou, an enthusiastic promoter of Haitian culture, founded the **Mapou Cultural Center**, where readings and other cultural events take place.

Around the corner, at 120 NE 59th Street, is the **Toussaint Louverture Elementary School**, the only Miami-Dade County school named after a Haitian hero. Toussaint Louverture, a freed slave, led the uprising against the French, spurring the emancipation of slaves and the first modern free black republic. There's a statue of the hero, donated by the Haitian community. The school's walls reflect bold Caribbean colors.

Back on NE 2nd Avenue, at the junction with NE 60th Street, is Little Haiti's spiritual center, the **Church of Notre Dame d'Haiti** and the **Pierre Toussaint Haitian Catholic Center**, in a former Catholic girls' high school. The chapel's splendid stained-glass windows depict the family of the freed Haitian-born slave Pierre Toussaint, a tireless worker for charity in New York in the late 18th century. In 1996, he was declared Venerable by Pope John Paul II, in the first step toward sainthood. There's another mural depicting the journey of Haitians to South Florida.

Mass is held most days, but try to attend a Sunday service, when the chapel overflows with immaculately dressed worshippers. A Haitian band and choir often provide the music, a blend of French melodies and African rhythms, more mellow and mellifluous than most Afro-Caribbean music.

Notable neighborhoods

East of Little Haiti are several picturesque neighborhoods. Like pearls strung on a necklace, these residential areas on wide tree-lined avenues line the western rim of the bay in an area known as the **Biscayne Corridor**. Miami's very first historic district was

Morningside ⑥. Designated in 1984, the status preserved its fantastic Mediterranean-Revival and Art Deco homes between 55th and 60th streets. Farther north are the pretty enclaves of **Bayside**, **Belle Meade** and **Shorecrest**.

On June 6, 2006, Biscayne Boulevard between 50th and 77th streets was designated the **MiMo/Biscayne Boulevard Historic District**. This is seen as a significant victory for the campaigns to preserve Miami's 1950s and '60s MiMo architecture *(see page 104)*. In among the jubilation has been dissent, however; one disgruntled business owner declared the date – 6/6/6 – an ominous day to approve the controversial application.

North Miami

The **Museum of Contemporary Art** ⑦ (770 NE 125th Street; open Tues–Sun; Sun pm only; charge; tel: 305-893-6211) is situated in the City of North Miami. MoCA is known for provocative and innovative exhibitions, with a fresh approach to contemporary art. The buzz since MoCA opened has drawn a number of galleries into the streets around the museum, providing a mini-boom within the boom that is this part of town and spawning the nickname **NoMi**. MoCA hosts hot-ticket events for the "see and be seen" crowd. Parties everyone can enjoy are the free jazz concerts on the last Friday of each month. After live music under the stars, visitors can go inside to tour the museum, which suspends its admission charge and asks for a voluntary donation only.

Farther north is a hidden jewel – the **Ancient Spanish Monastery** ⑧ (16711 W Dixie Highway; open Mon–Fri; charge; tel: 305-945-1461). This 12th-century monastery was bought in Spain in 1925 by newspaper magnate William Randolph Hearst, who arranged to have it shipped to the US stone by numbered stone. Upon arrival, the shipment was quarantined because of foot and mouth disease in Spain. The crates were opened and the hay cushioning the stones was burned.

Unfortunately, the men responsible for repacking the crates failed to put the stones back in the correct

Map on page 130

The neighborhood of El Portal, just north of Little Haiti, is the site of a Tequesta village dating from AD 500. Pottery and arrowheads have been unearthed, but all you can see above ground is a burial mound at 500 NE 87th Street.

BELOW:
the streets of Little Haiti are seldom silent.

Map on page 130

Opa-Locka architecture.

BELOW: Museum of Contemporary Art.
RIGHT: Ancient Spanish Monastery.

order. Shortly after, Hearst encountered financial problems and postponed the monastery's' reassembly. When it was finally rebuilt in 1952, some stones did not fit, and several of these can be seen in the back lot.

Northwest suburbs

Northwest of downtown Miami are the cities of Opa-Locka and Hialeah, suburbs that were created during the real-estate boom of the 1920s, and which used exotic architectural themes as marketing schemes to attract potential buyers.

In 1921, Glenn Curtiss, an early aviation pioneer, teamed up with cattle rancher James Bright and began the development of Hialeah. The architecture of the new city was based on the Spanish churches of the California missions. Four years later, Curtiss embarked on plans for the city of **Opa-Locka** ❾. An outrageous Moorish-Revival theme was inspired by the *Arabian Nights* stories. Buildings had horseshoe arches, domes and minarets, and streets had names like Ali Baba and Sharazad.

The Opa-Locka Company Admin-istration Building, currently **Opa-Locka City Hall**, has been restored to its former splendor of embellished domes and crenellated parapets.

Opa-Locka train station is probably the finest example of the fantasy Moorish-Revival style. Built in 1927, it uses multicolored, glazed ceramic tiles in an array of patterns. Two domes faced in the direction of south-bound trains and heralded the arrival of visitors to this Arabian fantasy. The station was derelict for many years, so neglected, in fact, that trees grew inside. Its demise seemed imminent. But after a 10-year restoration – in the course of which time the team endured a hurricane, a fire and a tornado – the station is now home to a community museum.

Hialeah ❿ is just south of Opa-Locka. Its major attraction was always Hialeah Park, one of the most beautiful horse-racing venues in the country, built in 1925. But in 1999, the last race was won and the buildings have been empty ever since. Designs for the use of the site are in consideration, including residential and commercial possibilities. ❑

RESTAURANTS, CAFES & LOUNGES

Restaurants

Canela Café
5132 Biscayne Blvd (at 51st St). Tel: 305-756-3930. Open: Mon–Sat L & D. **$$**
Excellent *tapas* are served at night at this Latin café. The *paella* is the best in town, and the lunch menu includes Cuban sandwiches, *ropa vieja*, and grilled meats. Great sangria, too.

Dogma
7030 Biscayne Blvd (at 70th & 71st sts). Tel: 305-759-3433. Open: L & D daily. **$**
A real gourmet weiner stand, this busy outlet also offers good Greek salads, chicken sandwiches and wraps. The thick-cut fries, mint lemonade or the thick shakes always delight.

Michy's
6927 Biscayne Blvd (at 69th St). Tel: 305-759-2001. Open: Tues–Sun L & D. **$$$**
Book well in advance for this charming 50-seat bistro. Celebrity chef Michelle Bernstein, with husband David running the front of the house, ensures a charming evening and delicious meal.

Sheba Ethiopian Restaurant
4029 N Miami Ave. Tel: 305-573-1819. Open: Mon–Sat L & D; Sun D only. **$$$**
Miami's first Ethiopian restaurant, this sexy outpost draws the artsy crowd from the nearby Design District. Low wooden tables and brightly colored paintings make for a very appealing setting.

Soyka
5556 E 4th Ct (at Biscayne Blvd). Tel: 305-759-3117. Open: L & D daily, BR Sat and Sun. **$$**
Large and not too pricey portions keep loyal patrons coming back to this industrial-chic spot. Offerings like grilled salmon, big burgers and hummus and pita make it an appealing choice for family meals, too.

Sushi Siam
5582 NE 4th Ct (at 54th St). Tel: 305-751-7818. Open: L & D daily. **$$**
A taste of the East on the Upper East Side, this popular Thai restaurant hides in the shadow of neighboring Soyka. Pad Thai and other classics please the locals.

Cafes & Lounges

A
4582 NE 2nd Ave. Tel: 305-972-3358.
This is an artists' collective serving good food, including a range of vegetarian and vegan options. Open every night after 8pm for dinner. No liquor license, so bring your own alcohol.

Jakmel Art Gallery and Haitian Cultural Center
147 NW 36th St. Tel: 305-573-1631. Open varied hours.
Drumming, yoga and African dance classes share time with the all-night parties and performance art that take place here.

Karu & Y Restaurant and Ultra Lounge
59 NW 14th St. Tel: 305-403-7850.
This multi-million-dollar lounge, club, restaurant, and performance space is a sanctuary for art, cuisine and entertainment in lush surroundings.

The Pawn Shop
1222 NE 2nd Ave. Tel: 305-373-3511.
An especially happening scene erupts here on Saturday nights with '80s music. The all-round good time atmosphere continues until the wee small hours.

XXI Amendment
190 NE 46th St. Tel: 305-571-7200.
With a full liquor license and a bordello-like setting, this enticing space hosts live music and other cool performances. A *tapas* menu sates the palates of the hip young crowd.

PRICE CATEGORIES

Prices for a three-course dinner per person with a glass of house wine:
$ = under $25
$$ = $25–$40
$$$ = $40–$60
$$$$ = over $60

RIGHT: Upper East Side treats.

CORAL GABLES

**A dreamy haven from the Miami hustle, this
planned city of the 1920s has oak-lined streets
to explore and architectural delights to discover**

Entrepreneur and developer George Merrick called it the City Beautiful, and Coral Gables is certainly that. Its most distinctive features include towering Mediterranean and colonial-style homes with manicured lawns, and quiet, tree-lined streets, monumental gateways, pergolas of flowing vines and ornate fountains that look as if they have been transplanted from a square in Seville.

It is also the City Prosperous. Its 43,000 residents earn nearly twice as much as their neighbors throughout Miami-Dade County. The healthy economic climate has attracted the headquarters of a number of prestigious firms, adding to the atmosphere of wealth and privilege.

Quality of life

It is certainly the City Confusing. The streets have small, white, sometimes illegible signs, with mainly European names in no logical order. Visitors have to navigate a warren of avenues like Caligula, Savona and Luenga running one after the other, off Le Jeune Road.

Coral Gables is bordered in the north by the Tamiami Trail (SW 8th Street), and encompasses the next 5 miles (8 km) or so south, through the Granada and Biltmore public golf courses, the private Riviera Country Club and the University of Miami, to Sunset Drive. Southeast, it includes the area between Old Cutler Road and Biscayne Bay, then south for about 3 miles (5 km) to just beyond Fairchild Tropical Botanic Garden.

Strict zoning laws forbid the removal of any tree without the permission of the city, the keeping of more than four cats or dogs per household, and the parking of boats or trucks in residents' driveways (these must be kept out of sight in garages or behind homes).

Map
on page
140

LEFT: classical statues line the pool of the Biltmore Hotel.
BELOW: decorative coral-rock planters.

Coral Gables and Coconut Grove

N

1 mile

1 km

0

Rickenbacker Causeway

VIRGINIA KEY
BEACH

Key Biscayne →

Virginia
Key

Miami
Seaquarium

BRICKELL
HAMMOCK

Brickell Ave

I-95

Biscayne Bay

BAY
HEIGHTS

ALICE
WAINWRIGHT
PARK

Ermita de la Caridad 20

Vizcaya 22
Miami Museum
of Science
& Planetarium 21

SW 13th
Avenue

SW 7th Ave

SW 22nd Avenue

SW 22nd St

Coral Way

Metrorail

GROVE KEY

Grove Isle

KENNEDY
PARK

Dinner Key

Picnic I.

C
O
C
O
N
U
T

G
R
O
V
E

Bird Road

South Dixie Highway

Main Highway

Grand Avenue

SW 27th Ave

Coconut
Grove
Cemetery

Coconut Grove 10

DOUGLAS
PARK

SW 37th Avenue

Ponce de Leon Blvd

SW 37th Avenue

Poinciana Street

SUNRISE
HARBOR

ISLA
MARINA

ISLA
GRANDE

COCO
PLUM

ISLA
DORADO

Coral Gables Waterway Drive

Old Cutler Road

GABLES
ESTATES

Old Cutler Road

MATHESON
HAMMOCK PARK

Fairchild Tropical
Botanic Garden 10

Snapper Creek

9

SW 57th Avenue

Davis Road

North Kendal Drive

Ponce de Leon Road

SW 72nd Street

Sunset Drive

Red Road

University Drive

South Miami 10

South Dixie Highway

Maynada Street

Granada Blvd

Dutch South
African Village 8

French
Country Village

Cartagena

South Plaza

Chinese
Village 6

Italian
City
Village

Colonial
Village

RIVIERA
COUNTRY
CLUB

Student
Lake

University
of Miami

Lowe
Art Museum 7

Coral Gables Canal

Granada Boulevard

Bird Road

SW 40th Street

Red Road

Le Jeune Rd

BILTMORE
GOLF
COURSE

Biltmore
Hotel 5

Coral Gables
Congregational
Church

GRANADA
GOLF COURSE

Merrick House 3

Venetian
Pool 4

Granada Boulevard

French
Normandy
Village

Italian
Village 2

Coral Gables
City Hall

SW 42nd Ave

Le Jeune Ave Rd

SW 42nd Avenue

Merrick Park

Douglas
Road

Coral Gables
Village 6

Dutch South
African Village

Coral Gables

Hyatt Regency
Coral Gables 1

Miracle Mile

Miracle
Theater

Ponce de Leon Blvd

CORAL
GABLES

Coconut Grove

N

400 yds
400 m

0

0

Key Biscayne →

The Chart House

Miami
City Hall 19

Dinner Key 18
Marina

Scotty's
Landing 19

Pan American Drive

Coconut Grove
Exhibition Center

Grand Bay
Hotel

SW 27th Avenue

Chart House Drive

South Bayshore Drive

Darwin Street

Biscayne
Bay

BAYSIDE
PARK

PEACOCK
PARK

16

McFarlane Avenue

Chamber of
Commerce 12

The Barnacle
State Historic
Site 13

Via Abitare

Monroe Drive

Main Highway

Franklin Avenue

Royal Road

Plymouth
Congregational
Church 11

Charles Avenue

William Avenue

Margaret Street

Thomas Avenue

Franklin Avenue

Grand Avenue

Coconut Grove
Playhouse 12

Commodore Plaza

Coconut
Grove Realty

Fuller St

Old Bank
Bldg

CocoWalk 15

Mayfair
Hotel
& Spa

Florida
Street

Rice Street

Virginia Street

Oak Avenue

Day Avenue

Mary
Street

Florida Avenue

Mary Street

SW 27th Avenue

Public
Library 17

Grand Avenue

MUNROE
PARK

14

McDonald Street

Percival Avenue

Florida Avenue

Lamb Ct

Gifford Lane

Oak Avenue

Day Lane

Day Avenue

Matilda
Street

Lime
Ct

Virginia Street

Oak Avenue

Day Street

Florry Avenue

Florida Avenue

Grand Avenue

Elizabeth St

Biscayne Bay

Cornelia Drive

Tigertail Avenue

All this goes to make Coral Gables an immaculate and fascinating city. Restaurants have architecture as inviting as the food, high-end stores have red-tiled roofs and arched windows, and at the foot of its sloping gardens are sleek yachts moored on winding waterways. It's a city that, in the understated words of a former preservation administrator, "tries to maintain the quality of life."

This quality dates back to the 1920s, when property developer George Merrick first imagined turning the area's citrus groves into a residential community with a Mediterranean theme. By the mid-1920s, 600 homes had been built, roadways constructed, and thousands of trees, shrubs and flowers planted (*see page 142*).

Enter the City Beautiful

Coral Gables is a delight to wander around. One of the most striking features of Merrick's vision are the **elaborate limestone arches** that mark the entrance to the city from the Tamiami Trail. At Granada Boulevard is a copy of the city gate

to Granada in Spain, and Country Club Prado has an elegant entrance popular as a backdrop for bridal photographs. A good entry point is on Douglas Road where a towered building has a 40-ft (12-meter) arch, built in 1924 on the corner of Douglas Road and the Tamiami Trail, now part of a modern complex.

South from here is the Gables' shopping area, **Miracle Mile ❶** (also known as SW 22nd Street or Coral Way). Just a few blocks long – running from Douglas to Le Jeune roads – it's full of upscale cafés and well-appointed stores, especially shoeshops and bridal boutiques.

Miracle Mile is visitor-friendly. Many stores and restaurants offer a centralized valet parking system. Cars can be dropped off at any valet station on the local map and picked up at another, more convenient departure point. These maps are available from participating merchants and hotels. The cute, efficient **Coral Gables Trolley**, Florida's first hybrid-electric shuttle fleet, is also helpful for visitors and shoppers who want to travel around.

Map on page 140

Trolleys connect the Miracle Mile to local hotels; other trolleys go to the Village of Merrick Park mall.

BELOW: Miracle Mile is lovely, but it's really only half a mile long.

The Alhambra Water Tower, disguised as a lighthouse, was designed by George Merrick's uncle, Denman Fink.

BELOW: a home built to Merrick's masterplan.

An excellent first stop is under the red-tiled roof of the **Chamber of Commerce**, a block north of Miracle Mile, where brochures on local attractions and a good map of the area are available.

The predominant structure on the Mile is the **Colonnade Building** at the corner of Ponce de León Boulevard. Built in 1925, it has a huge baroque front door, a rotunda with marble floors and a central fountain. The home of the Florida National Bank, it is connected to the 13-story **Omni Colonnade Hotel** (180 Aragon Avenue; tel: 305-441-2600).

At the corner of Douglas and Alhambra is a modern development on Merrick's theme. Built in 1987 by Gables architect John Nichols, the **Hyatt Regency Hotel** (tel: 305-441-1234) takes a cue from the location. The 242-room hotel's Moorish architecture is inspired by the sensual Alhambra in Granada, Spain.

It's a miracle

Near the western end of the Mile at No. 280, is the **Miracle Theater** (tel: 305-444-9293), a 600-seat, 1940s Deco movie theater that was converted into a playhouse in 1995 and has a year-round resident company. Owner Mitchell Kaplan, co-founder of the Miami Book Fair International, sponsors lectures and book signings at Books & Books, a block north again, at 265 Aragon Avenue. There's also a Barnes & Noble on the Mile.

At the foot of the Mile, on the other side of Le Jeune Road, is **Coral Gables City Hall ❷**. Built in the late 1920s, the graceful semi-circular building has a columned facade and a Spanish Renaissance-style clock tower.

West along Coral Way is a tunnel formed by mature banyan and oak trees dripping with Spanish moss. A few blocks west, at 907 Coral Way, is the **Merrick House ❸** (open Wed and Sun afternoons; donation; tel: 305-460-5361), the boyhood home of George Merrick. The house was built between 1899 and 1906 of oolitic limestone – a rock plentiful in South Florida and often mistaken for coral – with a multi-gabled roof of coral-colored tiles. The house dis-

George Merrick

Born in 1886, George Merrick was the son of a minister who moved from Massachusetts to South Florida when he was 12. His father built a home with a gabled roof from what he thought was coral rock and called it Coral Gables. He planted groves of avocados and citrus, and his son would deliver the produce at 2am in a horse-drawn wagon. When his father died, George took over the property and built it into Florida's most prosperous fruit and vegetable business. Later, he bought the adjoining land and set about developing his vision of a residential community – a South Florida city with a Mediterranean feel. To do this he assembled a team that included architect Phineas Paist, landscaper Frank Button and artist Denman Fink, his uncle. The homes and buildings were intended to reflect the best of Spanish and Italian design, and he named the city Coral Gables after his childhood home. By 1926, the year-old city had 2,153 families, 11 schools and six hotels, but a subsequent hurricane and a property crash sent Merrick and his city into bankruptcy. At the celebration of Coral Gables' 15th anniversary, Merrick predicted the city would again see prosperity. He was right, but did not live long enough to see it happen.

plays Merrick family art treasures, furniture and personal effects, and has been restored to its 1920s look.

Farther west, turn right on Alhambra Circle to pass the **Alhambra Water Tower**, cleverly disguised as a lighthouse, with Moorish designs.

Swim like a mermaid

The flamboyance of Coral Gables' heyday is exemplified at the gorgeous **Venetian Pool ❹** (2701 De Soto Boulevard; hours vary seasonally; charge; tel: 305-460-5306). Acclaimed with some justification the "world's most beautiful" public swimming pool, this 820,000-gallon (3-million liter) pool was previously a 1920s coral-rock quarry. Converted into a pool by Phineas Paist and Denman Fink in 1923, it is listed in the National Register of Historic Places.

Fed every day with cool spring water, and featuring waterfalls and coral caves, the pool is surrounded by Venetian-style loggias, porticos and a cobblestone bridge. Beauty pageants were held in the pool's early years, and swimming champ-

turned-Hollywood star Esther Williams swam here. In 1989, the pool had a $2.3 million restoration.

Nearby, another fine example of Merrick's legacy is **Venetian Villas**, at 2800 Toledo Street. With Moorish arches, Spanish tile fountains and wrought-iron balconies, the villas opened in 1926 as a winter retreat for wealthy northerners. Later converted to a 22-apartment building, it then fell into disrepair. The Edelman Restoration Company gave the villas a facelift in 1989, and converted the property into six luxury condominiums.

Flanking the western edge of the city is Merrick's elegant resort, the **Biltmore Hotel ❺** (1200 Anastasia Avenue; tel: 305-445-1926). With a grand tower modeled on the Giralda in Seville, the spectacular opening in 1926 followed a successful $10 million construction.

In its heyday, the Biltmore Hotel attracted celebrities from Judy Garland to Al Capone. Industrial barons rode gondolas on its waters and hunted foxes in its grounds. The hotel fell into disrepair during the

Map on page 140

TIP

Pick up a map of the area at the Coral Gables Chamber of Commerce, located on the corner of Aragon and Galiano. The map has local attractions and a self-guided tour.

BELOW: the Venetian Pool, on the National Register of Historic Places, is open to the public.

Depression and stayed that way until 1943, when it became a World War II army hospital. It was not until 1987 that hotel guests returned to the 280 opulently remodeled rooms.

The Biltmore is a favored hideaway for visiting movie stars and royalty. It is also a highly prized fashion-shoot location. The hand-painted ceilings, Spanish tiles and marble floors are well worth seeing. Weekly tours start in the lobby, and the swimming pool is not to be missed – it's said to be the largest hotel pool in the country. Johnny Weissmuller, bronzed star of the *Tarzan* movies, set a world swimming record here in the 1930s.

The Biltmore spa features 12,000 sq. ft (1,100 sq. meters) of pampering. Located on the hotel's seventh floor, each treatment room offers a view of Coral Gables and beyond. The hotel also offers complementary horse-drawn carriage rides through the Gables to guests or restaurant diners on weekends, weather permitting. As an added attraction, local lore has it that there is a ghost among the hotel guests.

The University of Miami's football team, the Hurricanes, are local heroes, with a good reputation for spotting talent for the National Football League. Hurricane home games are played at the Orange Bowl Stadium.

BELOW: Coral Gables City Hall has 12 columns and a Spanish-style clock tower.

Directly across the street from the Biltmore is the **Coral Gables Congregational Church**. This pretty Spanish baroque-style church is regularly a setting for lectures, book readings and concerts.

Northwest of Ponce de León Boulevard, and taking up almost an entire city block, is the **Village of Merrick Park** ❻, on Avenue San Lorenzo. Stores are centered around decorative open gardens, with fountains, shade and cool benches. High-end labels for the ladies who lunch here include Gucci, Hugo Boss, Roberto Cavalli and La Perla.

Lowe Art Museum

To the south is the area's prestigious private university, the **University of Miami**, which has one of the best college football teams in the US. UM has long lost its image as Suntan-U, where students were supposedly more interested in lazing in the sun than in learning, and now has a fine academic record. The enrollment is close to 16,000 and a full-time faculty of 2,600 occupy the pretty 260-acre (105-hectare) campus. The School of Medicine opened in 1952, and the School of Marine and Atmospheric Science in 1969, but the attraction for visitors here is the university's art museum.

The **Lowe Art Museum** ❼ (open Tues–Sun; Thur and Sun pm only; charge; tel: 305-284-3535), on UM's campus at 1301 Stanford Drive, is one of Miami's best museums. Its permanent collection of 8,000 works includes Egyptian, Greek and Roman antiquities, Renaissance and baroque art, 19th- and 20th-century European and American pieces, ancient art from Latin America and an impressive Asian collection. Highlights include the Alfred I. Barton Collection of Native American art – one of the finest in the country – with Pueblo and Navajo weavings, and the Samuel H. Kress Collection, which

includes works of European masters like Tintoretto and Cranach the Elder.

Villages of the world

Around Coral Gables are small, village-like enclaves created by Merrick's architects to widen the influences from the Mediterranean Revival theme.

A drive around some of **Merrick's Villages** ❽ rewards with an exotic range of styles: there's the **Chinese Village** (on Riviera Drive at Menendez Avenue); the **Dutch South African Village** (Le Jeune Road at Maya Street) modeled on the farmhouses of 17th-century Dutch colonialists; the **French City Village** (Hardee Road at Cellini Street); the **French Country Village** (Hardee at Maggiore Street); the pretty **French Normandy Village** (Le Jeune at Viscaya Avenue); the **Italian Village** (Altara Avenue at Monserrate Street); and the **Colonial Village** (Santa Maria Street), with a wooden clapboard New England theme.

The petite and hidden 27-room **Hotel Place St Michel** (162 Alcazar Avenue; tel: 305-444-1666) was also built during Merrick's era, with high ceilings and rooms individually furnished with antiques. The atmosphere is attentive and low-key and the hotel's restaurant (open to the public) is charming and intimate.

Ponce de León is one of the starting points of Gables Gallery Night, a once-a-month tour (usually the first Friday of each month) that takes art-lovers to nearly 20 Coral Gables galleries. Free open-air trolley cars move from gallery to gallery allowing visitors freedom to come and go, to peruse the art, photography and antiques, and to sample a little complementary wine and cheese along the way.

South of Sunset Drive

The wealthy neighborhoods in the southeast are south on Le Jeune Road, across US 1, and over a waterway to **Cartagena Plaza**, where Le Jeune, Sunset, Cocoplum and Old Cutler roads converge by the giant sculpture of a shoe in the traffic circle. Southwest on Old Cutler Road, the Cocoplum mansions that line the waterways are in a world of their

Map on page 140

This classic facade is characteristic of houses in the French City Village. The homes have enclosed courtyards and kitchen gardens.

BELOW: the Biltmore Hotel opened in 1926.

own. Local authorities insist on the colors and roof styles of the multi-million-dollar homes conforming to strict zoning laws, all of which highlights the visual harmony. The roads around here have names like Mira Flores and Vistamar.

Parks and gardens

Coral Gables has two other luxury-home divisions, called Casuarina Concourse and Arvida Parkway. Both of these are on the way to **Matheson Hammock Park ⓿** (9610 Old Cutler Road; open daily; free), a 100-acre (40-hectare) park.

Developed in the 1930s on land donated by Commodore J. W. Matheson, Matheson Hammock Park is a popular weekend retreat for locals. It has a marina and a small beach. The man-made tidal pool, which was once a coconut grove, is separated from the bay by a walkway and provides a calm place for small children to play in the water.

There are plenty of amenities for outdoor recreation, like picnic facilities and walking trails through the mangrove swamp. Sailboat rentals

provide opportunities for day-time fun, and the Red Fish Grill is a lovely place for dining in the evening.

Next door to Matheson Hammock Park is lovely 83-acre (34-hectare) **Fairchild Tropical Botanic Garden ⓿** (10901 Old Cutler Road; open daily; charge; tel: 305-667-1651), the largest of its kind in the continental United States. The garden, which has been open to the public since 1938, was founded by Col. Robert H. Montgomery. The gardens were named for the botanist Dr David Fairchild, who provided many of the specimens.

In addition to lakes and winding paths are an outstanding collection of tropical flowering trees, and around 5,000 exotic ferns, plants, and orchids, including the fire tree from Australia, the talipot palm from Sri Lanka, and the ponytail tree from Mexico. Many species in the park are rare and endangered. Trams tour the garden regularly, but a tour with a guide provides a closer look at the labeled flora, as well as a sensual, sweetly-scented walk in the sunshine.

The City Beautiful it is indeed, right to the end. ❏

Locally produced, sun-drenched peppers are a regular feature on Miami's restaurant tables.

BELOW: graduation day at the University of Miami.

RESTAURANTS

Cacao
141 Giralda Ave (at Galiano & Ponce de León Blvd). Tel: 305-445-1001. Open: L & D Mon–Fri, D only Sat, closed Sun. **$$$$**
Exciting Nuevo Latino cuisine is served in a stunning setting to make this a popular gathering spot for foodies seeking the finer things in life. These do come at a price, though.

Fleming's Prime Steakhouse
2525 Ponce de León Blvd (at Andalsuia Ave). Tel: 305-569-7995. Open: D daily. **$$$**
It may be a chain but this value-priced chophouse gives the other nearby steak spots a good run for their green. The exceptional wine list features more than 100 wines by the glass to help fuel the race.

Francesco
325 Alcazar Ave. Tel: 305-446-1600. Open: Mon–Fri L & D, Sat D only, closed Sun. **$$$**
This tiny, little-known Peruvian restaurant specializes in superb *ceviche*. Those in the know come for the catch, fresh from the docks. Squid ink pasta and other divine and exotic dishes thrill the gourmands. A decent wine list helps, and dull decor doesn't detract.

Miss Saigon Bistro
148 Giralda Ave (at Ponce de León Blvd). Tel: 305-446-8006. Open: L Mon–Fri, D daily. **$$$**
Waiters in Vietnamese garb sing and sometimes even dance, and are not the only attractions at this Restaurant Row veteran. Dishes also include authentic or more Americanized dishes, all very fresh and tasty. Ask for it spicy and you will get it spicy.

Ortanique on The Mile
278 Miracle Mile (at Le Jeune Rd). Tel: 305-446-7710. Open: L Mon–Fri, D daily. **$$$$**
Caribbean cooking goes upscale at this permanently lively and crowded tropical oasis. Chef Cindy Hutson is a regular on the Food Network and festival circuit, and serves up specialties like jerk chicken, penne pasta, and lobster with mango to Coral Gables' beautiful people.

Palm d'Or at the Biltmore
1200 Anastasia Ave (at Granada Blvd). Tel: 305-445-1926. Open: D only Tues–Sat. **$$$$**
Small plates of exquisite New French cuisine are served in one of Miami's most romantic settings. Deft wine pairings and a truly professional staff add to the experience.

Pascal's on Ponce
2611 Ponce De León Blvd (at Almeria & Valencia Aves). Tel: 305-444-2024. Open: L Mon–Fri, D Mon–Sat, closed Sun. **$$$**
Magnifique French fare draws Francophiles to this pocket-size hideaway. Chef Pascal Oudin and his wife Ann-Louise make perfection part of the allure. Leave space for an exemplary soufflé to finish.

Randazzo's Little Italy
150 Giralda Ave (at Ponce de León Blvd). Tel: 305-448-7002. Open: L Mon–Fri, D Mon–Sat. **$$**
Randazzo's serves Italian food to transport you to Mott Street in New York City with big servings of primo spaghetti and monster meatballs.

Villagio Restaurant
358 San Lorenzo Ave (at Le Jeune Rd). Tel: 305-447-8144. Open: L & D daily. **$$$**
A regular muster point for the ladies who lunch, joined by others who appreciate a fine Italian meal. The prices won't pinch the budget for Jimmy Choos, and the cuisine and service in this upscale Village of Merrick Park *bella ristorante* please the pickiest of customers.

PRICE CATEGORIES

Prices for a three-course dinner per person with a glass of house wine:
$ = under $25
$$ = $25–$40
$$$ = $40–$60
$$$$ = over $60

RIGHT: chef Cindy Hutson of Ortanique.

COCONUT GROVE

Sparkling as much in the sun as under the stars, and once a writers and artists colony, Coconut Grove has fantastic festivals, savvy stores and a breezy night-time buzz

Coconut Grove is a free-wheeling, laid-back community with great style and Bahamian roots. At midnight, only the streets of South Beach buzz brighter than those of the Grove. Diners linger over coffee at outdoor cafés after evenings at the theater, and couples stroll on the red-bricked sidewalks, lined with trees and streetlamps. Jamming the streets and bars, cruising in cars, on rollerblades or skateboards, youthful residents and visitors make the scene and check each other out.

The Grove groove

One of the oldest Miami neighborhoods, for many years the Grove was home to writers and artists, a little like New York's Greenwich Village or London's Chelsea, but bathed in Florida sunshine and dancing to a Caribbean beat.

Artistic residents were often eccentric, like the leonine Eugene Massin, an award-winning sculptor and painter with a laugh that could shatter glass, or the nomadic Bill Hutton, a New York advertising man turned painter, who captured scenes of Grove life on pieces of wood, then hawked them on the street for money to buy food and jugs of wine. Later came free-loving hippies and Vietnam War protesters.

Coconut Grove now has chic stores, good restaurants and dozens of bars. It's a great place to be, but new Mediterranean-style townhouses have sprung up by the bougainvillea-draped pioneers' homes, and boutiques have replaced hippie head shops. The Grove groove has been gentrified.

The Bohemian spirit still shines brightly, though. Few months pass without a party. There are pajama parties in the park, bed races on the streets, and the hugely popular Goombay Festival (see page 152).

Map on page 140

LEFT: outdoor dining is part of life in the Grove.
BELOW: Bahamian looking party pretty.

The year kicks off with January's Taste of the Grove, where live jazz wafts through the scents of sauce and spices, as 30 chefs serve signature dishes. Waiters race through an obstacle course, carrying trays laden with food and drink.

In February, like the swallows returning to Capistrano, artists from all over the country flock to the three-day Coconut Grove Arts Festival. They meet the public, and display watercolors, oils, graphics, ceramics, photography and sculpture.

The Barnacle historic home hosts an old-fashioned Fourth of July party for guests dressed in period clothes. The house is decorated in bunting, and thronged with antique cars.

In December is the irreverent King Mango Strut, a spoof of the buttoned-down Orange Bowl Parade in downtown Miami. The King Mango parade pokes fun at just about everyone, including local politicians and national figures.

Arboreal canopy

Entering the Grove from Coral Gables along Main Highway, the road runs under a canopy of beautifully foliaged, long-rooted trees. On the way is one of Florida's most beautiful churches. Looking like a venerable Spanish monastery, with bell towers and a niche with a small saint sculpted in coral, **Plymouth Congregational Church** ⑪ (3400 Devon Road) only dates back to 1916. True to style, though, the iron-framed black wooden door is from a 17th-century Pyrenean monastery. The facade often lends a romantic backdrop to wedding photographs.

The **Memorial Gardens** are tranquil oasis behind the church, with borders of impatiens, palms and a huge poinciana tree. South American macaws and cockatoos of brilliant reds and greens are regular visitors.

Bahamian pioneers

Along Main Highway are remnants of Coconut Grove from when it was Miami's first black settlement. Residents of Charles Avenue and the neighboring streets to the west were mainly Bahamian pioneers, immigrant "conchs" drawn to work at the nearby Peacock Inn. Their experience with tropical building materials and plants was key to the development of Cocoanut Grove (as it was spelled then). Some of the small, shotgun-style wooden houses here date from the 1890s.

Grove streets like Charles, Mary and Frow are named after Bahamians. In the summer of 1896, when the vote was held on whether to incorporate the new city of Miami, 5 miles (8 km) to the north, 43 percent of the 368 men who voted were black, mostly of Bahamian ancestry.

At the junction of Charles and SW 37th avenues is the **Macedonia Baptist Church**, which served the first black congregation here. The AME Methodist Church, which housed the community's first school, stood nearby. Also here is the **Coconut Grove Cemetery**, first

Sip on a cool, cool coconut in one of the many Coconut Grove bars; the atmosphere is always buzzing.

BELOW: Plymouth Congregational Church.

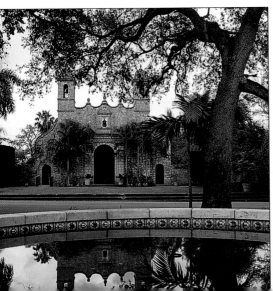

Map on page 140

used in 1906. Some tombstones are carved as torsos, and some as gumbo limbo trees – a symbol of regeneration. The style can be traced back to the Bahamas. Those people too impoverished to buy a grave marker broke off a tree branch to plant on the grave.

Back on the main road, **Cefalo's Wine Corner** (3540 Main Highway) marks the southern end of Coconut Grove village. This wine bar and cellar, owned and operated by former Miami Dolphin football player Jimmy Cefalo, is in a one-story cypress building built in 1922, with oak beams and tables made from ships' doors.

Just up the street is the **Coconut Grove Playhouse ⑫** (3500 Main Highway; tel: 305-442-4000). The blue building, with a Mediterranean-style roof and white curlicued pillars, opened as a cinema in 1926, the brainchild of industrialist George Engle. It became a live theater in 1956, establishing cultural credentials with the US premiere of Samuel Beckett's *Waiting for Godot*. The Playhouse attracted stage luminaries like the maverick Tallulah Bankhead, who once conducted a press interview seated on a toilet. The 1,100-seat theater was taken over by the state of Florida and stages Broadway-style plays and musicals.

Commodore Munroe

Shielded from the busy highway by a forest of trees, and with grounds leading to the bay is the **Barnacle State Historic Site ⑬** (3485 Main Highway; open Fri–Mon; charge; tel: 305-442-6866). Deep in Peacock Park, Commodore Ralph Munroe built the Barnacle in 1891 on a coral ridge, overlooking Biscayne Bay. It was just a bungalow until 1908, when Munroe raised the original bungalow to become the second floor, and built a new floor underneath. Munroe obviously had good technical skills: the Barnacle survived both the devastating hurricane of 1926 and Hurricane Andrew in 1992, with remarkably little damage. Inside the house are Munroe family's heirlooms, period appliances like an early refrigerator and other original furnishings.

Marjory Stoneman Douglas, leading campaigner for the preservation of the Everglades, lived in Coconut Grove from 1926 until her death in 1998. Her cottage is at 3744 Stewart Avenue, south of the village center.

BELOW: strolling the Grove's Bahamian streets.

BELOW: Coconut Grove's nightlife is second only to the scene in South Beach.

Ralph Munroe was a significant force in the development of the character and prosperity of Coconut Grove. When he bought the Barnacle property, he left the hardwood hammock in its natural state. He was also a builder of sailboats, and the last in existence, the ketch *Micco*, was displayed here until Hurricane Andrew smashed the 101-year-old boat to splinters. *Egret*, a replica of one of his boats, is anchored offshore.

Main Highway's first major intersection, and entry into Coconut Grove proper, is named for Monroe. **Commodore Plaza** is a short street of shops and eateries. On the corner is **Coconut Grove Realty**, its design all circles and swirls.

Party, party

Commodore, just a block long, ends at Grand Avenue, one of the main streets of the Grove. This block is busy all year round, but it is especially lively in May. One spring evening each year, the plaza is closed off on both ends for the Coconut Grove Block Party. The square is filled with stages, entertainers, and sidewalk vendors. Many Commodore restaurants provide tasty samples, as does an English pub, the Firkin Friar.

West along **Grand Avenue**  leads into the "Black Grove" – a vibrant but poor neighborhood compared to the visible wealth in the village. Grand Avenue, too, has its own party – and what a grand party it is.

The Goombay Festival is held the first weekend in June. It is one of the largest black heritage festivals in the US, and a time when the Grove celebrates its Bahamian roots. Costumed junkanoo groups dance to Caribbean rhythms playing rake 'n' scrape instruments. There are three sound stages, and more than 400 brightly dressed vendors sell arts and crafts, as well as lots of delicious, spicy Bahamian food.

In addition to Commodore Plaza, another short road of stores called **Fuller Street** links Grand Avenue with Main Highway. The Old Bank Building, at the corner on Main, is still a busy bank frequented by locals, managing to escape the fate of many by turning into a wine bar. Also on Fuller is a collection of good-looking boutiques and sports-ware outlets known collectively as the **Florentino Shops**.

Heading northeast along Main Highway leads to the nerve center of the Grove – the intersection of McFarlane, Main and Grand. This is dominated by **CocoWalk** ⑮, a huge, Mediterranean-style open-air mall with towering palms and three levels of terraces and balconies.

CocoWalk houses a number of restaurants, dozens of stores and a 24-screen movie theater. The shops are mostly of the chain-store variety (Banana Republic, Gap), but they do stay open until midnight on Friday and Saturday nights (until 10pm during the week). Day or night, there is always something happening at CocoWalk – artists sketching caricature portraits, or sensual flamenco dancers working up a sweat for themselves or their audience. Live, free concerts are held here almost every evening.

Coconut Grove has followed the trend started in South Beach, converting many hotel rooms into shared condos, rented like hotel suites to short-stay guests, but accessible for a fixed number of nights each year to the condo owner. This makes economic sense for hoteliers, but is less advantageous for the tourist industry as a whole, where the livelihood is dependent on visitors spending dollars generously on attractions, in stores or at restaurants.

Urban delight

One establishment that manages to do both is the **Mayfair Hotel & Spa** (3000 Florida Avenue; tel: 305-441-0000), which mixes traditional amenities with modern style.

The atmosphere is tranquil and luxurious, but with an added attraction of Eastern ease. The lobby is set within a sunny, soaring central atrium, with stairs at different levels and plants mixed with soft fountains – the ambience is like being in an outdoor garden when you are, in fact, inside the hotel. The sound of running water in the fountains is soothing to urban ears.

Each guestroom has a two-person Japanese soaking tub and a private balcony. The spa offers a variety of

Map on page 140

This art-themed eatery opened in CocoWalk in 1991. Now there are Tu Tu Tangos across the States, with several in California.

BELOW: CocoWalk is the hub of activity both day and night.

TIP

A fun way to explore Biscayne Bay off the Coconut Grove coast is to rent a sailboat or a kayak. Shake-A-Leg Miami (tel: 305-858-5550) has both craft and crew, and good access for the disabled. They operate from 2600 S Bayshore. Go to www.shakealeg miami.org for details.

BELOW: the Barnacle, built in 1891, is one of Miami's oldest homes.

treatments, including two-person massages (four hands). The rooftop Jacuzzi gives views of the village and the bay, and completes the image of a hidden idyll in the city.

Towards Biscayne Bay

Heading down McFarlane Avenue, at the southern end of S Bayshore Drive, is **Peacock Park 16**. It was here that the Peacock Inn, South Florida's first hotel, was built in 1882 by Charles and Isabella Peacock. At that time, it was the only hotel along the 230-mile (370-km) stretch between Lake Worth in the north and Key West in the south.

The park – which sweeps down to the bay – has a baseball field and the woodsy Chamber of Commerce building, where there is a walk-in **Tourist Information Office** (open Mon–Fri 9am–5pm; tel: 305-444-7270). Small and staffed by friendly, well-informed locals, the information office is a good place to stop by for maps, brochures and local information about the Grove.

Across from Peacock Park, near where S Bayshore Drive meets

McFarlane Avenue, is the **Coconut Grove Public Library 17** (closed Fri, Sun), a coral-rock building with a sloping tiled roof and veranda that would not look out of place as a luxury jungle safari lodge. The land was donated by Commodore Munroe – his first wife is buried in the grounds – and the library was started in 1895 by a reading group called the Pine Needles Club. After the original building opened in 1901, the group used to send books by boat to the new Miami settlement that was growing just along the coast. The library overlooks Biscayne Bay and provides Internet access.

Next door to the library is the clubhouse of the **Woman's Club of Coconut Grove**, another example of coral-rock construction. Built in 1921, the building is on the National Register of Historic Places.

Take S Bayshore Drive as it heads toward downtown Miami, and pass by the **Coconut Grove Exhibition Center**, which hosts a number of exhibitions and conferences every year. Beyond the exhibiton center, bougainvillea-draped balconies sig-

THE BARNACLE
STATE HISTORIC SITE
DEPARTMENT OF NATURAL RESOURCES
DIVISION OF RECREATION AND PARKS

nal the **Grand Bay Hotel** (Wyndam's Grand Bay, 2669 S Bayshore Drive; tel: 305-858-9600). Shaped like a Mayan temple, the entrance is dominated by a bright red steel funnel-shaped sculpture tied with what looks like a convoluted bow. This untitled sculpture is a work of the artist Alexander Liberman.

Flying clippers

To the east is a view across a forest of masts, bobbing in Biscayne Bay. These belong to the yachts tied up at the **Dinner Key Marina** ⓲, one of the city's largest moorings. Also here, at the end of Pan American Drive, is **Miami City Hall** ⓳. This attractive Art Deco structure was built by Pan American Airways to serve as a terminus for their flying boats. When it was first opened in 1934, the terminus was popularly heralded as "the most beautiful air transport base in the world."

From 1930 to 1945, in the heyday of romantic air travel, Pan Am took passengers in luxury seaplanes known as "clippers" from Biscayne Bay to faraway destinations like China and Brazil. Some of the earliest flights were undertaken without radios, and carrier pigeons were brought along – to be released to summon help if the plane ditched into the sea. A display case inside the building contains models of the various clippers.

The area has a number of good spots to dine with a view of the bay for a backdrop. Take your pick. Next to City Hall is the casual outdoor setting of **Scotty's Landing** *(see page 157)* or the classier dining option of the **Chart House** (tel: 305-856-9741). Back on Bayshore Drive, at No. 2550, is **Monty's Stone Crab Seafood** (tel: 305-858-1431), where staff are accustomed to serving fish and seafood specialties to as many as 700 people at a time.

Heading north, Bayshore Drive becomes Miami Avenue, but the laid-back ambiance of the Grove reaches out to **Kennedy Park**. This is where fit Groveites come to jog or cycle in the early morning, pausing only to turn toward the bay and watch the sun rise up from behind Key Biscayne. Between Kennedy and Peacock parks

Map on page 140

Dinner Key Marina makes a calm change from the Grove's sociable streets.

BELOW: marching with a message at the King Mango Strut.

Map
on page
140

Astronomy shows are held inside the soaring dome of Coconut Grove's planetarium.

BELOW: Deco details on Miami City Hall.

are three sailing clubs: **Coral Reef Yacht Club** (established in 1955); the **Coconut Grove Sailing Club** (1946) and the granddaddy of them all, the **Biscayne Bay Yacht Club**, founded in 1887, once again by busy pioneer Commodore Ralph Munroe. The club moved to its present site as recently as 1932. Applicants to join the Biscayne club must be recommended by three of its 250 members, and, once accepted, wait for a vacancy to occur. This only happens on the demise of a present member.

Farther north, the first right after Mercy Hospital leads to a serene spot on the edge of the bay with an unusual conical church. Built in 1966, and sacred to the Cuban population, **Ermita de la Caridad 20** is a shrine to Cuba's patron saint, the Virgin of Charity. A mural inside depicts the history of Catholicism in Cuba and shows the Virgin and her shrine on the island. The altar is oriented toward Cuba, instead of the more customary eastward direction, reminding parishioners of their "lost" homeland across the waves.

Farther along the coast is one of Miami's most beautiful attractions – **Vizcaya 21** (3251 S Miami Avenue; open daily; charge; tel: 305-250-9133). This grand, Italian Renaissance-style mansion is set among nature trails and manicured gardens *(see pages 158–59).*

Planetarium

The **Miami Museum of Science & Planetarium 22** (3280 S Miami Avenue; open daily; charge; tel: 305-646-4200) is across the street. The museum explores the mysteries of science with more than 150 exhibits, demonstrations of scientific phenomena, and natural history specimens. Hands-on exhibits allow children to touch items in order to learn more about physics, light and sound, electricity, and health.

The outdoor wildlife center rehabilitates injured birds of prey and reptiles, and houses live hawks, snakes, insects, and other creatures. The planetarium gives laser and astronomy shows, as well as lectures. On certain evenings (weather permitting), there are inspiring views of the heavens through huge telescopes. ❑

RESTAURANTS

Berrie's
2884 SW 27th Ave (at 28th Ter). Tel: 305-448-2111. Open: B, L & D daily. **$$**
A popular hangout with the knowledgeable locals, this little juice bar has transformed into a full-fledged restaurant with worthy salads, sandwiches, wraps and handmade pastas as well as fresh blackened mahi mahi. The setting, with wooden tables, brick flooring and market umbrellas, is charming and the daily Happy Hour is the best in town.

Bizcaya Grill at The Ritz Carlton Coconut Grove
3300 SW 27th Ave. Tel: 305-644-4675. Open: B, L & D daily. **$$$$**
This Ritz Carlton Mediterranean stunner is perfect for an elegant meal in the otherwise very casual Grove. Set against a cascading waterfall with accents of wood and marble, the food and service are top-notch to match.

Café TuTu Tango
3015 Grand Ave (at Main Highway). Tel: 305-529-2222. Open: L & D daily. **$$**
A swinging singles scene fueled by imaginative drinks and small eclectic, international dishes, this is a perennial favorite in CocoWalk. All this is coupled with a killer sangria and an abundance of art, tango performance, belly dancing and tarot reading.

Green Street Café
3110 Commodore Plaza (at Main Highway). Tel: 305-567-0662. Open: B, L & D daily, BR weekends. **$$**
A child- and dog-friendly café with great views of colorful characters gliding by one of Coconut Grove's busiest corners. The French-Med fare includes a good snapper in white wine sauce, vegetable lasagne, lamb burger with goat cheese on brioche, as well as divine desserts.

Jaguar Grill
3067 Grand Ave (at Virginia St). Tel: 305-444-0216. Open: L & D daily, BR Sun. **$$**
Just steps from Coco-Walk, the local outdoor mall, this gorgeous ocher and saffron Latin American eatery has the best *ceviches* and grilled meats in the area. The lively bar scene and fruity sangria provide still further attractions.

Las Culebrinas
2890 SW 27th Ave. Tel: 305-448-4090. Open: L & D daily. **$$**
A bigger version of the old Little Havana favorite, this Cuban landmark serves classics like *ropa vieja*, *picadillo* and *arroz con pollo* in a festive environment.

Le Bouchon du Grove
3430 Main Highway (at Grand Ave). Tel: 305-448-6060. Open: B, L & D daily, BR weekends. **$$$**
The friendly and flirtatious owner offers a taste of Paris in this perpetually packed French bistro, and the terrific staff serve *moules frites*, duck confit and escargot with panache. The tables, practically on top of each other, only add to the atmosphere.

The Original Daily Bread
2400 SW 27th St (at 24th and 27th Aves). Tel: 305-856-5893. Open: B, L & D Mon–Sat, L & D Sun. **$**
A real find, this veteran Middle Eastern market and cafeteria-style eatery serves Miami's best hummus and *baklava*. There are seats inside among the racks of dried beans and bins of olives, as well as outdoor tables, although no view to speak of.

Scotty's Landing
3381 Pan American Dr (at S Bayshore Dr). Tel: 305-854-2626. Open: L & D daily. **$$**
A salty shack with million dollar views, this old-time Miami hangout on the marina offers grilled dolphin sandwiches, cole slaw and tasty burgers.

PRICE CATEGORIES

Prices for a three-course dinner per person with a glass of house wine:
$ = under $25
$$ = $25–$40
$$$ = $40–$60
$$$$ = over $60

RIGHT: savoring a moment in the sunshine.

Vizcaya: Palazzo Luxury by the Bay

This bayfront villa set in formal gardens gives an evocative glimpse into bygone days and moonlit nights

Inspired by country houses in the opulent Italian region of Veneto, tycoon James Deering built his bayside winter retreat in 1916. Constructed on 180 acres (73 hectares) of spectacular shoreline, pineland and hammock, the house was designed to resemble an Italian Renaissance villa, but also has baroque, rococo and neoclassical features. The estate's name is from the Basque word for "elevated place," also the name of a Basque province on the Bay of Biscay, which itself gave the name to Miami's Biscayne Bay.

Deering, his architect Burrall Hoffman Jr and painter Paul Chafin traveled for inspiration to Italy to study architectural details. Along with imported doors, ceilings and fireplaces, native Florida materials such as limestone were employed to maintain a local ambience.

The house has 70 rooms and needed a staff of 30 during the four months the Deerings stayed. Today, half of the rooms are open to public view. Every detail is exquisite, from the black-and-white marble tub to the gold-leaf cornices, especially the swimming pool, extending from the sun-lit exterior to a grotto beneath the house, its ceiling decorated with shells and carved stone.

Above: At one end of the sea wall, a bridge leads to the delightful Tea House, inspired by French architecture.

Left: Deering named each guest room after its design style. The Cathay Bedroom is decorated with chinoiserie, popular in the 18th century.

Left: The 17th-century statuary populating the gardens includes busts and mythological figures like Neptune, Minerva, and Apollo.

ABOVE: The villa's south side faces the Italian Renaissance-style formal gardens. Unlike flower gardens, these feature stone, water and greenery.

RIGHT: The floors in Vizcaya are laid out in geometric patterns of richly colored marble, a style based on Italian palazzi.

BELOW: Decorated in the lively spirit of Italian Rococo, the Music Room has an 18th-century harpsichord and a Louis XVI harp.

VIZCAYA BY MOONLIGHT

"Miami by Moonlight" has long been a romantic angle for poets and songwriters. Now visitors can enjoy "Vizcaya by Moonlight" on an evening spent wandering among the sweetly scented gardens, guided by a knowledgeable docent.

The tours are only once a month, on the night of the full moon, and only in the more temperate season, January through April, weather permitting. The visit begins inside the palazzo of Vizcaya itself, with a short talk on the gardens and statuary, including tips on the sights that unfold in the moonlit grounds, and what views to look out for along the way.

Programs begin at about 7.30pm, and last approximately 90 minutes. The tour takes in Vizcaya's subtropical forest, proceeds toward the main house along a lit walkway lined with fountains and foliage, and includes views of Biscayne Bay and the gorgeous orchids in the David A. Klein Orchidarium. Vizcaya's café and gift shop remain open on these evenings.

Vizcaya is open every day except Christmas from 9.30am to 4.30pm. For information on tours, go to www.vizcayamuseum.org or tel: 305-250-9133.

BELOW: The three arches of the East Facade, between the fortress-like corner towers, lead out to the sea-wall promenade by the bay, and to a stone barge.

KEY BISCAYNE

Get set to jet ski, windsurf or just listen to
the drawl of the sea. Some of the best
beaches and oceanfront parks are in
sight of Miami, just across the bay

Just minutes from the hustle of
Miami are golden sands, great
watersports, secluded coves,
and even a picturesque lighthouse.
High-rise resorts and expensive condominiums appear to be taking hold
of Key Biscayne, but seclusion and
solitude are still easy to find in this
5-mile (8-km) by 1-mile (1.5-km)
sliver of sun-soaked land.

The modern Key Biscayne community began when the remarkable
Rickenbacker Causeway opened
in 1947, with a then-steep 25¢ toll.
Built by, and named after, a World
War I flying ace, it loped over Biscayne Bay, a waterway shared with
the rest of Miami. With the bridge
came "mainlanders," out to exploit,
according to local Key Biscayners.

In the early 1950s, the Mackle
Brothers developers built affordable
housing to lure World War II veterans with GI loans. Working-class
neighborhoods emerged on the des-
olate island. Then, as in other parts
of Miami, construction fever caught
on in Key Biscayne, and zoning
went awry. Apartments turned into
huge blocks of condominiums. As
President Richard Nixon brought the
winter White House to the island in
the 1970s, homeowners watched the
rest of the world discover Key Biscayne. Amid gentrification, a Mackle
home, bought for $15,000 in 1955

and sold for $200,000 in 1985, would
now fetch millions. The boom has
been partly fueled by South Americans with deep pockets, who value
the area's security and seclusion.

Virginia Key

Between Key Biscayne and Miami is
Virginia Key, over the Rickenbacker
Causeway across Biscayne Bay from
Brickell Avenue and South West 26th
Road, about 2 miles (3 km) south of
downtown Miami. Before the main
span, about 200 ft (60 meters) east of

Map
on page
162

LEFT: cycling over
the Rickenbacker
Causeway.
BELOW: Key
Biscayne is wonderful
for watersports.

the tollgate, is **Hobie Beach**, popular for catamarans. Ribbons of cement, pebbles and sand edge the bay, with parking and picnicking spots nearby.

Water sports

Windsurfer Beach (first past the tollbooth) captivates the windsurfing *aficionados*. Averaging 18 knots in March through April, winds from the east and southeast move sailboards along at an easy pace. Flat, shallow, waveless water makes for ideal beginners' surf, while the late summer high winds thrill the daredevil pros. Equipment rentals and lessons are negotiable on the spot.

Sailboard fans gather at Windsurfer Beach and then head out into the steady winds of Biscayne Bay.

Stretching parallel, north of the causeway, is **Jet Ski Beach**, where motorized skiers roar free – jet skis are banned from many other areas around Miami because of their danger to swimmers, manatees, other marine life, and the peace and quiet generally. Stands along this stretch offer windsurfing classes and board

BELOW: a fishy scene at Jimbo's Shrimp.

rentals as well as jet skis, bicycles and scooters for rent. You can even sample an ultra-lite flight over the bay.

On the far side of the bridge, the Rickenbacker Causeway alights on **Virginia Key ❶**, a popular hideaway for celebrities seeking privacy. Pretty **Virginia Key Beach** is a 2-mile (3-km) stretch of sand, with water deep enough to truly indulge swimmers; just be aware that the undertow can be strong in these waters.

For a break from the sun, follow the dirt roads to the northeast of the island, which offers magnificent views over the bay to Miami. **Jimbo's Shrimp**, an old-style Florida fish smokehouse and bar, hangs on against encroaching development. The agreeably ramshackle shack has a shaky future but a loyal following: Mariah Carey shot her first album cover here. Sample the legendary home-smoked salmon with a cold, cheap beer while you still can.

Virginia Key's most popular

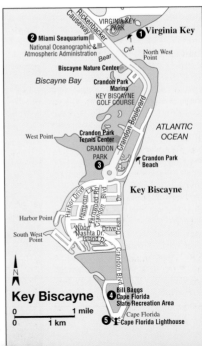

Map on page 162

attraction for kids is the 35-acre (14-hectare) **Miami Seaquarium** ❷ (4400 Rickenbacker Causeway; open daily; charge; tel: 305-361-5705), where sea lions and dolphins can be met, petted and fed, and sharks can be seen feeding, too. A descendant of the world's most televised dolphin, Flipper, and a 5-ton killer whale named Lolita perform daily. Endangered birds and reptiles nest in the Lost Islands, a wildlife sanctuary for threatened species. Energetic rescue, rehabilitation and breeding efforts have carried on here since 1955.

Reefs and beaches

Beyond Virginia Key, the causeway crosses narrow **Bear Cut** to **Key Biscayne** itself. East along its sandy northern shore, Key Biscayne has its own petrified forest – a black mangrove reef of fossilized wood and roots, the only such site known in the world. Wearing sneakers you can hike in the waters to explore this unique environment, which stretches along the shore for about 1,300 ft (400 meters), and juts seaward 350 ft (100 meters). The **Marjory Stoneman Douglas Biscayne Nature Center** (4000 Crandon Boulevard; tel: 305-361-6767), sometimes offers guided walks along this shore.

On the northern part of Key Biscayne is **Crandon Park** ❸. Donated by the Matheson family, its 1,400 acres (570 hectares) of royal palms and mangroves echoes the park's heyday as a coconut plantation. Slogs through the seagrass and coastal hammocks in the northeast wilderness take visitors back even farther.

At the northern end of the park is the **Crandon Park Marina**. Here, captains of charter boats dock to clean and sell their catch. Half- and full-day excursions follow sailfish and dolphin. Anchor at **Sundays on the Bay** (tel: 305-361-6777) for a spot of brunch or night-time reggae. Alternatively, watch the sunset over

Miami's skyline from the **Rusty Pelican** (tel: 305-361-3818). Sure, Rusty's is a tourist trap and the seafood could be better, but a drink served on the terrace overlooking the city is an only-in-Miami experence.

On the Atlantic side of the Key is **Crandon Park Beach**, a 3-mile (5-km) swathe of sand, consistently rated among the US's top 10 beaches. The beach and nearby parkland amenities include soccer and softball fields, an 18-hole public golf course and 75 barbecue grills.

Favored as the best "party beach" in Miami, Crandon can become pretty boisterous when the four parking lots are jammed by fun-seeking visitors in the midsummer months. A carousel dating from 1949 has been renovated and gives rides on the weekend. The exotic birds and iguanas in the nearby **Quiet Gardens** are a reminder of the long-lost days of Crandon Park Zoo.

Top-ranked tennis players compete in the NASDAQ-100 Open for 12 days in March at **Crandon Park Tennis Center**. As many as 200,000 swivel-necked spectators turn out

This is one of the few structures still fending off the wind and waves in Stiltsville; see them soon before they fall into the bay.

BELOW: dinnertime at Miami Seaquarium.

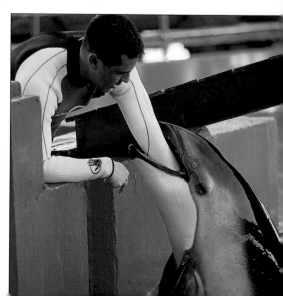

BELOW: secluded cove on Key Biscayne.

for the contest, worth millions in prizes. It's a stellar affair, with sports personalities, fashion shows, champagne tastings and celebrity chefs. The tennis courts are open to the public during the rest of the year.

Save for occasional summer onslaughts and the tennis Open, the island has a soft, quiet tempo, with few traffic lights or traffic jams. In "the village" beyond Crandon Park, tourist season means a few seconds' wait for a left turn, or a couple of minutes' search for parking by the grocery. Visitors are treated the same as locals, with no routes designated scenic, few tourist brochures and no crucial road signs.

Most stores are clustered along **Crandon Boulevard**, which bisects the island north to south. With the Atlantic as a backdrop, the island's two hotels: the **Ritz-Carlton** and the **Silver Sands**, have private beachfronts away from the public parks. All year round, residents cycle, walk or jog along the beach, causeway or in the parks. For no-sweat cycling on almost completely flat terrain, enquire about rentals at **Mangrove**

Cycles in the Square Shopping Center (260 Crandon Boulevard; open Tues–Sun; tel: 305-361-5555).

Cape Florida

For the real Key Biscayne experience, take a walk into **Bill Baggs Cape Florida State Recreation Area ❹**, (open daily; charge; tel: 305-361-5811). In the 494-acre (200-hectare) preserve, the dense canopy of Australian pine and sea-grape trees, was the main attraction, but Hurricane Andrew changed all that. At the southernmost tip of the Key, with nothing to break the winds, **Cape Florida** took a massive hit in the 1992 storm and was one of the most devastated areas in Miami.

Park rangers began industrious re-greening efforts in the mid-1990s, planting millions of tiny native seedlings, and with help from nature, the park is making a botanical recovery. Even now, though, Cape Florida attracts nature and sun lovers in both the winter and summer months.

The outdoor scene is well-known to local hedonists: swim, sunbathe, picnic, fish, cycle, jog, hike or, as

Baggs, the *Miami News* editor whose crusade preserved the park, said himself, "listen to the drawl of the sea."

The white sand beach is not postcard-pristine, and is dotted with seaweed and stinging man-o'-wars, but for its location, it's excellent. Treats include tropical fruit drinks and Key Lime Pie at the island's most eclectic concession stand. Anglers cast for bonefish, grouper, jack, snapper and snook on the seawall.

Lighthouse and Stiltsville

The 109 steps up the 95-ft (29-meter) **Cape Florida Lighthouse** ❺ lead to the top of the oldest structure in South Florida. Perched on a sand dune, the handsome 1825 lighthouse has been fully restored. Tours are at 10am and 1pm, Thursday through Monday; arrive early as places are limited to ten people.

The lighthouse kept ships afloat through storms, uncharted waters, sandbars and submerged reefs. In 1836, during the second Seminole War, the lighthouse was attacked by Seminoles, angry at the land being appropriated by settlers. The light-

keeper clung to the lighthouse platform until he was rescued by a Navy schooner. Damaged by Confederates in the Civil War – to prevent Union sailors using it as a navigational aid – the lantern was extinguished in 1878, and not lit again until 1978. The surf is classic, too. It was here that John Wayne waded into the water to escape the PT boat in the 1945 movie *They Were Expendable.*

Just offshore, near the Key's southern tip, where the Atlantic Ocean meets Biscayne Bay, is **Stiltsville**, a huddle of bungalows on stilts in the ocean. Built as weekend getaways, only a few of the structures remain, standing in the water like concrete-and-wood flamingos. Dr George, of the Historical Museum of Southern Florida, conducts trips to Stilsville, where dolphins are likely to follow your boat (tel: 305-375-1621 for reservations).

Charter boats pass on their way to deep-sea fishing in the Gulf Stream, their wakes rocking bonefishers, who are standing on flat-bottomed boats. Then the quiet returns, broken only by curious cormorants. ❏

Map on page 162

Cape Florida Lighthouse dates back to 1825. Tours can be taken to the top.

WELCOME TO...

Burr's

STRAWBERRY FARM

FRESH DAILY

We Eye Catchers Signs
852-3333

FRESH!
Strawberry
ICE CREAM
CONES

FRESH!
Strawberry
MILK
SHAKES

HOT
DOGS!

We Eye Catchers Signs
852-3333

HEADING SOUTH

Fruit and spice and all things nice, including old-fashioned kids' attractions and a celebrated racetrack, lie just south of Miami. There's also a ruined mansion built for unrequited love

outh Miami-Dade County, encompassing the pretty community of **Homestead** and a disappearing agricultural area from the 1900s known as the **Redland**, is 25 miles (40 km) from downtown Miami but years away in time. South Miami-Dade is rural, small town, Southern, more a place for a barbecue than a *boulangerie*.

In 1992, Hurricane Andrew charged right through this district, the hardest-hit section of the Miami area. Businesses and homes were flattened, and many years of regeneration brought some modernization, or at least yuppification. Hurricanes Katrina and Wilma hit the farms and the Everglades again in 2005, but with less lasting damage *(see pages 172–73)*. Some scientists said that South Miami-Dade – particularly the farmlands and the Everglades – got a much-needed pruning by Mother Nature, and would be in better shape because of the storms.

Old Florida

Hurricanes notwithstanding, Homestead and its surrounding area are still "old Florida." This is a place with the smell of the earth, with pick-up trucks, turnip greens, two-lane streets lined with tunnels of majestic Royal Palms, and a hardware store on the main street. Drive through farmland

in the Redland in winter and you'll smell the lime trees in blossom. There is an annual rodeo, and cowboy boots are worn not as a fashion accessory but as everyday dress. But change, like the lime blossom, is in the air. Once as corny as Kansas, South Miami-Dade is becoming a yuppie frontier. The Volvos and Saabs are heading south.

The area is now the gateway to the Keys, the Everglades and the water wonderland of Biscayne National Park. Homes from the 1920s are

Map on page 168

LEFT: buy the best berry shakes here.
BELOW: Miami Metrozoo residents.

BELOW: plane speaking at the Wings Over Miami Museum.

being done up; new homes to young families with money who want to escape the urban sprawl for a more relaxed, rural lifestyle.

Cultural detours

A possible detour before you head south is the Tamiami campus of Florida International University (FIU), which lies between Southwest 8th Street, Coral Way and SW 107th and 117th avenues. The **Patricia and Phillip Frost Art Museum ❶** (open daily; Sat and Sun pm only; free; tel: 305-348-2890) has an extensive collection of contemporary sculpture on display throughout the grounds of its 26-acre (11-hectare) **Art Park**. The collection emphasizes Latin American and 20th-century American art and includes pieces by Alexander Calder and Willem de Kooning.

Another cultural attraction on the way south is the **Deering Estate ❷** (16701 SW 72nd Avenue; open

daily; charge; tel: 305-235-1668). Here you can experience the elegance of a lost era in the renovated historic home of industrialist Charles Deering, brother of James Deering, who built Vizcaya in Coconut Grove. In 1913 Charles bought the 420-acre (170-hectare) estate to build a winter residence for his family, and to store his yacht, furnishings, fine paintings and tapestries. It had previously been the site of Richmond Cottage, the first hotel between Coconut Grove and Key West, which opened in 1900.

Deering had his winter home built in the Mediterranean-Revival style, to remind him of the castles he owned in Spain. Visitors can tour the house and take nature trails that meander among rare native plants in the hardwood hammock.

Inland from the Deering Estate is the **Wings Over Miami Museum ❸** (open daily; charge; tel: 305-233-5197), an homage to airplanes of days past. The museum is adjacent to the

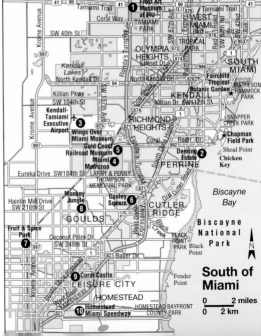

Kendall-Tamiami Executive Airport, and features a changing collection of vintage planes, many under loving restoration by pilots of the present and past. Military memorabilia from World War II and later are also on display.

Talk to the animals

South Miami-Dade, known for its farms and flora, is also a place for fauna. **Miami Metrozoo ❹** (12400 SW 152nd Street; open daily; charge; tel: 305-251-0400) is one of the best zoos in the country, a cageless sprawl over 290 acres (115 hectares) that has wisely specialized instead of trying to be a Noah's Ark of every animal.

Opened in 1981, the zoo is dedicated to tropical life; there are no polar bears here. The zoo has more than 225 species living in "natural" island sites surrounded by moats. The animals come from as far afield as the African and Asian plains and jungles, Asian forests, Eurasian steppes and Australia. There are first-rate exhibits: a koala park, Komodo dragons, a rare and endangered white Bengal tiger, two other tigers, a petting zoo, plus an ecology theater. Metrozoo had quite a set back from Hurricane Andrew. More than 5,000 trees were lost, and the huge free-flight aviary, Wings of Asia, built to withstand winds of up to 120 mph (193 kmph), was reduced to rubble. Fortunately, the zoo is now recovering nicely.

Adjacent to Metrozoo is the **Gold Coast Railroad Museum ❺** (SW 152nd Street; open daily; charge; tel: 305-253-0063), featuring 50 pieces of railroad equipment from different eras. The 1942 *Ferdinand Magellan* was the presidential car for Franklin D. Roosevelt, Harry S. Truman, Dwight D. Eisenhower, and Ronald Reagan. Walk through the narrow confines of a working dining car, see steam and diesel engines and peer out of a 1948 stainless-steel, domed passenger car used by the *California Zephyr*. On certain weekends the museum fires up a train, and it chuffs up and down a small track.

Almost directly south of Metrozoo is **Cauley Square ❻**, a former railroad town that still faces the old

Map on page 168

Some of the best kids' attractions around the Miami area are here.

BELOW: white-handed gibbons at Miami Metrozoo.

tracks and Highway US 1 at 224th Street. It is 10 acres (4 hectares) of nostalgia, featuring stores selling crafts and antiques, all of which are linked by paths. There is a charming tea room for lunch. This is not Disneyland, not a mall, but the way things used to be, insists the owner.

Blushing berries

The nearby flatland is ideal for bike rides and a 20-mile (32-km) loop can be wound through the Redland. Or pop the top down for a drive in a convertible, poking around country lanes looking out for homes and farmsteads, many of which are officially designated by the county's historic preservation division; a quarter of the county's older buildings are here. And berries abound.

From Christmas to April, South Miami-Dade fills with rows of vivid strawberry plants stretching to the horizon. For decades, people have been waiting in line at the stand at **Burr's Berry Farm**, SW 127 Avenue, for the best berry shakes around. A family-run affair, the three Burr brothers came to South Florida

Pick-your-own fruit and veg places are getting rare, so ask locally for directions.

BELOW: Coral Castle is one man's testament to unrequited love.

in 1876. Another older property is **Knaus Berry Farm**, at 15980 SW 248th Street. Run by a religious order called the Duckers (an offshoot of German Baptists), Knaus has fresh berries, too (pick your own in the back to the shop), but the thing that makes the trip worthwhile are the melt-in-your-mouth pies and cakes. Be sure to try the yummy cinnamon buns.

Due west of Knaus is **Fruit and Spice Park** ❼ (187th Avenue and SW 248th Street; open daily; charge; tel: 305-247-5727), a 35-acre (14-hectare) tropical botanical garden. Here you can travel the world through 500 varieties of fruits, herbs, spices, and nuts from Asia, Africa, South America, and the Mediterranean. Depending on the season, the grounds are lush with trees and shrubs in bloom or in fruit. Sampling fallen fruit is allowed, but picking or harvesting is forbidden. A gourmet store sells dried fruits, jellies, jams, and cookbooks.

Even more exotic blooms can be enjoyed at **R.F. Orchids** (28100 SW 182nd Avenue; open Tues–Sun 9am–

5pm; tel: 305-245-4570), where thousands of the exquisite flowers grow among ponds and gazebos.

About 3 miles (5 km) west of Cauley Square is **Monkey Jungle** ❽ (14805 SW 216th Street; open daily; charge; tel: 305-235-1611), a roadside attraction dating from 1935 with walking tours of shaded grounds full of primates. At Monkey Jungle the residents roam free in the trees while you watch from fenced enclosures. A tropical rainforest is filled with monkeys and rare parrots.

Coral Castle

Outside Homestead, at 28655 S Dixie Highway, is an extraordinary attraction. **Coral Castle** ❾ (open daily; charge; tel: 305-248-6345) is a ruined coral-rock mansion hand carved by a Latvian immigrant in the 1920s and '30s, presumably to his fiancee, a girl of 16 who jilted him on the eve of their wedding.

Awash with crescents, a moon fountain, a sundial, and objects like the "Feast of Love" table – a 5,000-lb (2,268-kg) platform in the shape of a heart – Coral Castle is a remarkable feat of engineering and a melancholy testament to unrequited love.

The town of **Homestead** is coming back strong after hurricanes Andrew, Katrina and Wilma. Pretty houses have been restored, and the town, already known for good home cooking, now has Mexican restaurants that have grown up to serve the numbers of Mexican farm workers.

Near Palm Drive, one conspicuously successful post-hurricane project has been the **Homestead Miami Speedway** ❿, site of the Toyota Indy 300, the NASCAR Nextel finals, and the Ford Championship Weekend. Thought by many fans to be the most beautiful speedway facility in the land, the Homestead property includes four lakes and a new Turn One Tower.

Promoter Ralph Sanchez made the 2.21-mile (3.5-km) track and the 600- acre (243-hectare) site a major regeneration effort after Hurricane Andrew. In 2005, Hurricane Wilma brought a little damage, too, but race and test run schedules remain uninterrupted, running from May through December each year. ❏

Map on page 168

TIP

The best on-site tour to this area is Rob's Redland Riot, billed as a "fruity, tropical tour down south." The tour visits Cauley Square, historic Homestead, the 1904 Redland Hotel, and fruit stands galore: www.redlandriot.com

BELOW: Homestead Miami Speedway has over 1,000 palm trees.

Hurricanes

Just before dawn on August 24, 1992, a storm of 160-mph (260-kph) winds and a 12-ft (4-meter) tidal wave slammed the southern part of Florida.

Andrew was a Category 5 hurricane and, at the time, the most destructive natural disaster to hit the US. Over 60,000 homes were destroyed and 150,000 people were left homeless. Forty lives were lost in a 30-mile (48-km) wide path of damage, estimated at $25 billion.

Rural areas about 20 miles (32 km) south of Miami – Homestead, Kendall, Florida City – were hardest hit, and parts of Coconut Grove and Coral Gables were badly damaged. Cape Florida, at the tip of Key Biscayne, suffered a direct hit. One homeowner woke to find a shark floating in his swimming pool; others found fish in their television sets.

Thousands of civilian volunteers from around the country, along with the American Red Cross, poured in to help. The President deployed 20,000 US troops to the area to deter looting, clean up debris, and build temporary tent cities. But, as happened later with Hurricane Katrina, locals complained of officials caught in bureaucratic confusion with no

one in charge, taking too long in mobilizing assistance. Tens of thousands of people waited days in the summer heat without food, water, medical care, or shelter.

One positive outcome was that Dade County, with a problem of racial conflict, became a more cohesive community. Residents – white, black, Cuban, and Haitian – worked together. "As one we will rebuild" was the spirit. Fortunately for the vital tourist industry, the damage wrought by Andrew to most busy tourist areas was slight. Had the hurricane's eye hit just a few miles to the north, Miami could have been wiped out.

Records broken

Poised between the Caribbean and the Gulf of Mexico, hurricanes are simply a feature of the South Florida climate, a sales tax on the bill for all that sunshine. In fact, each spring Florida gives a sales tax amnesty on storm-precaution goods like flashlights, storm shutters, and portable generators.

The formation of hurricanes over the oceans has been a seasonal event as far back as climatologists can detect, and the intensity of a hurricane appears to be governed mainly by the temperature of the water below it.

Hurricanes are the Atlantic version of one of nature's fiercest forces. They form in the tropical zone when two or more storms gather in high humidity over warm seas, and winds from different directions cause the storms to spin. Beneath the storm, warm air and water vapor rises, causing an area of low pressure; meanwhile, cold air is drawn down from above the storm. A funnel of cool, low-pressure air is created, surrounded by whirling storms gathering in intensity.

While the storm remains over warm water, the hurricane becomes stronger, the warmer the seas; the more violent the storm. Storms of the same type, broadly speaking, that occur in the Pacific are called cyclones, and storms in the Indian Ocean and China seas are called typhoons.

Seasonal hurricane activity has risen since 2004, and Florida has endured an unprecedented number of impacts. Hurricanes Frances and Jeanne (2004) made landfall only three weeks apart (Jeanne was, at the time, the costliest hurricane to date.) Hurricane

Wilma (2005) cut off the electrical power to 98 percent of South Florida. Miami's Vizcaya, Seaquarium, and Downtown skyscrapers were damaged, but most of the city was relatively unscathed. Everglades National Park suffered extensive damage to trees, and its Flamingo Lodge closed for good.

Since 1851, when records began, the most active hurricane season was 2005, with 2004 coming second. Twenty-eight named tropical storms occurred in 2005, and of those, 15 rose in intensity to become hurricanes, beating the previous record of 12.

The first season ever to produce four storms of categories 3–5 – Emily, Rita, Katrina, and Wilma – was 2005, and these were some of the strongest storms on record. Wilma was the strongest, with a pressure of 882 millibars. The year 2005 was also the longest hurricane season, the earliest to begin and the latest to end, as Hurricane Epsilon lasted into mid-January, 2006.

Names retired

The names of exceptionally deadly and/or destructive hurricanes are "retired," meaning that for reasons of sensitivity, as well as for scientific practicality, those names will not be used for future storms. Five names: Dennis, Katrina, Rita, Stan and Wilma were all retired, marking another record for 2005.

Whether the increased activity is due to global warming is still hotly debated, although the scientific community seems mostly convinced that it is. Beyond dispute are the facts that the 10 years from 1995 to 2005 have seen the highest sea temperatures on record; the largest number of hurricanes; and the fiercest hurricane activity. The sea temperature is predicted to remain high until 2025, and so intense hurricane seasons are forecast to be a regular feature.

Valuable lessons have been learned since Hurricane Andrew, however, and South Florida has shown itself not only well-prepared, but energetic in recovering. ❏

LEFT: Hurricane Wilma (2005) created problems in Miami, but was not as deadly as Andrew.
RIGHT: Hurricane Andrew (1992) killed 40 people, caused $25 billion in damage, and wrecked boats against the sea wall at Dinner Key, Coconut Grove.

Hurricane Watch

A Hurricane Watch is signaled when the National Hurricane Center determines that a hurricane may hit within 36–48 hours. Precautions should be taken against a direct hit: for example checking your vehicle's gas tank is full, gathering together emergency supplies and so forth. Tune to a local radio or TV station for storm updates.

Hurricane Warning

This is issued when the storm reaches winds of at least 74 mph (119 kph) and high water and storm surges are expected in a specific area within 24 hours. Warnings will identify coastal areas where these conditions may occur. Be ready to evacuate your home or hotel. Finish preparing what you will take to a shelter, or anything you will need if you stay in place.

Hurricane Categories

Hurricanes are categorized from one to five according to the Saffir Simpson Scale, which measures the wind speed per hour:
Category 1: 74–95 mph (119–153 kph)
Category 2: 96–110 mph (154–177 kph)
Category 3: 111–130 mph (178–209 kph)
Category 4: 131–155 mph (210–249 kph)
Category 5: over 155 mph (149 kph)   ❏

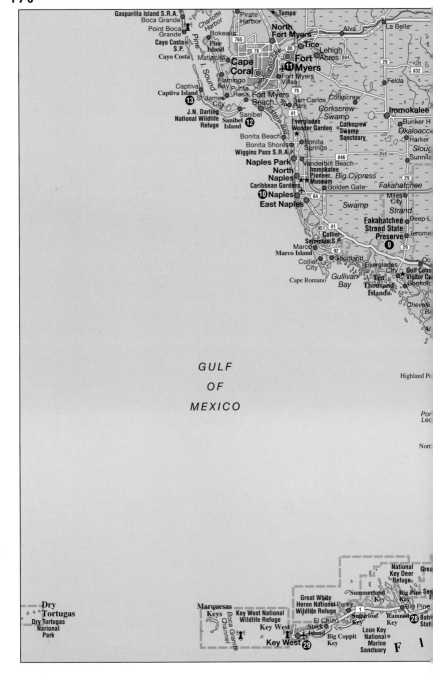

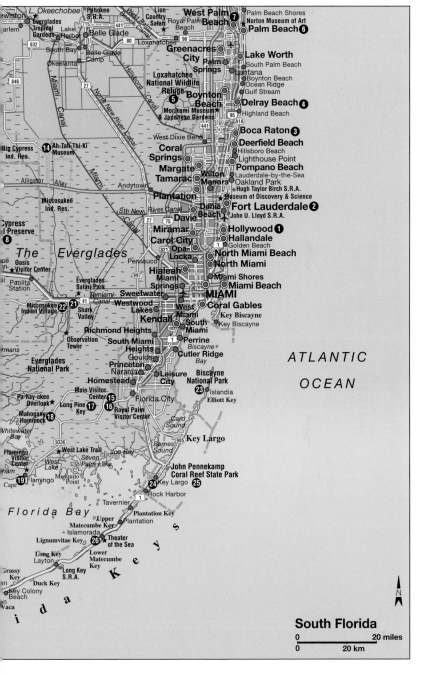

South Florida

0   20 miles

0   20 km

THE GOLD COAST

A shimmering strand of beachfront resorts, from the sailors' delights around Fort Lauderdale to the millionaires' playground of Palm Beach, beckon with hot sun, warm seas and golden sand

Driving north up the coast from Miami, Alternate 1 Atlantic, or as it is known locally, Highway A1A, is the best way to travel. Following the coast as closely as possible, the road is occasionally scenic, and occasionally overwhelmed by the condos and hotels that blot out the ocean. It can often be crowded, but it's rarely dull. The reward for enduring the traffic lights and detours is memorable rides sweeping through seaside resorts that beg for longer stops.

Here and there, mom and pop motels hang on, and garden apartments with names like Betsy-Marv or Blue Sea Kitchenettes sit behind white board fences. Interspersed are strips of fast-food restaurants and tee-shirt stores.

Florida's Turnpike, Interstate 95, is a much faster way to drive to Boca Raton or Palm Beach, but, unless your schedule absolutely demands it, take the slow road and allow Florida to unfold some of its state's less hectic coastal charms. Morning and evening, joggers pack the A1A roadsides. On weekend mornings, skin-suited cyclists whirr colorfully close to the curbs. Docks and marinas shelter boats along baysides. As the road extends north, counties and towns more generously preserve the beachfront for parks. Finally, 70 miles

(110 km) north of Miami, you will arrive in Palm Beach, where the legacy of Henry Flagler, South Florida's railroad tycoon and tourism pioneer *(see page 187)*, endures in gorgeous testaments to a bygone age.

Broward County

The first notable town after Miami is **Hallandale**. Halland was a Swede from New York enlisted by Henry Flagler in the late 1890s to farm tomatoes west of the railroad. However, times changed. By the 1930s

Map on pages 176–77

PRECEDING PAGES: sailing South Florida. **LEFT:** a quiet moment on Via Mizner, Worth Avenue in Palm Beach. **BELOW:** a picture of wintertime and wealth on the Gold Coast.

TIP

In Fort Lauderdale, you can walk, jog, take a water taxi, a rickshaw, or a Segue Human Transporter. There's also a hop-on, hop-off trolley service linking Downtown with the beach. It's free on weekends.

Hallandale had become a notorious gambling town controlled by the Lansky brothers. Hallandale today forms a vast "U" along the beach; at the bottom the four boulevard lanes of A1A travel between high-rise walls of condominiums. The pretty **Diplomat Country Club and Spa** has been the city's landmark leisure facility since 1957.

Hooray for Hollywood

Next up is **Hollywood ❶**. Joseph W. Young, an Alaskan goldminer and sometime newspaper publisher, rode the crest of the land boom until he crashed into the triple wall of the 1926 hurricane, the land bust and the Great Depression. The scale of his style, if not the grace, endures at the **Hollywood Beach Hotel** (now a Ramada Inn) and with a painted-up complex of shops and restaurants called **Oceanwalk**. Take a look at the photo blow-ups that recall the hotel's heyday – it was a Mediterranean classic: solid, grand and dripping in grotto moss. Elaborate colonnades lifted ceilings heavenward for America's boom-time elite.

These days Hollywood Boulevard, dividing around wide circles on its way from town, dumps and collects its traffic along ramps that swerve daredevil-close to the front of the hotel, its elegance, sadly, forever blighted.

At the rear of the hotel and facing the beach, is the **Hollywood Broadwalk**, a pedestrian promenade lined with French-style restaurants, cafés, and souvenir shops. Thousands of French Canadians flocked to Hollywood for winter vacations, and transformed it into a bilingual community. Skaters, bikers, and joggers weave around retirees and tourists, who appear to be in no hurry.

In recent years, Hollywood's reputation has risen. Artists and yuppies-on-a-budget have been driven out by high Miami prices, and relocated up the coast to Hollywood. Both the **Art and Culture Center** on Harrison Street, and the active **Performing Art Center** on Monroe Street, are well-regarded for their innovative events. In 2007, the 10-acre (4-hectare) **ArtsPark** opens, which includes a state-of-the-art

BELOW: symphony by the seaside, with fan.

amphitheater, a smaller studio theater, gallery space, and artists' workspaces. One of the area's newer attractions is the **Seminole Hard Rock Hotel & Casino**, a massive resort proclaiming, "hot shops, cool restaurants and wild nights." Good rock acts perform here.

North, beyond the Dania Beach Boulevard cut-off, the road extends to **John U. Lloyd State Recreation Area**, which has a fine beach. Footbridges cross a creek into pine forests that border the beach. In winter, old-timers in webbed beach chairs sunbathe and gossip behind their massive campers, living the retirement dream. At the far end of the park road, cruise liners dock across the channel at Port Everglades, one of the world's largest cruise ports and part of neighboring Fort Lauderdale.

Dania Beach Boulevard carries A1A briefly inland to US Highway 1 between two sections of huge **West Lake Park**; its 1,300 acres (525 hectares) make this the largest urban park in South Florida. Its entrance is to the south, on Sheridan Street. The town of **Dania Beach**, to the west, was settled by Danes and is known for the pretty antiques shops lining US 1 through town.

If angling is your pastime, head west to the **International Game Fish Association World Fishing Museum** (open daily; charge; tel: 954-922-4212), just off I-95 south of Griffin Road. Try your hand at virtual fishing and visit the fishing Hall of Fame to see those big ones that didn't get away. Next door is Bass Outdoor World, one of the biggest sporting goods stores around.

Fort Lauderdale

The skyscraper landscape of **Fort Lauderdale ❷** pops up like the land of Oz from where US 1 lifts to accommodate the vast spaghetti of the I-595 airport interchange. Beyond the junction, A1A bears right toward Port Everglades and the beach, but US 1 carries you on to downtown Fort Lauderdale.

The city, especially the ocean-front area known as **The Strip**, was long associated with youthful exuberance. The 1960 beach-party movie and song *Where the Boys Are*

Map on pages 176–77

Las Olas Boulevard connects downtown Fort Lauderdale to the beach.

BELOW: aerial view of the Las Olas section of Fort Lauderdale.

Stranahan House, which overlooks the attractive New River, is Fort Lauderdale's oldest building.

romanticized this stretch of beach for college students on Spring Break. Throughout the 1970s, The Strip became one huge drunken beach party, just like the movie. By 1990, though, the location for the students' antics had shifted north to Daytona Beach, and by 2006 they were back in Miami.

New River

Fort Lauderdale is all grown-up now, and known for its outdoor dining and cultural attractions. The neighborhood along the north bank of the **New River**, which 1920s filmmaker Rex Beach used to call "the most beautiful stream in the world," has good places for eating and entertainment.

Downtown to the west are the **Old Fort Lauderdale Village and Museum** (219 SW 2nd Avenue; open daily; charge; tel: 954-463-4431) and the immense **Museum of Discovery and Science** (401 SW 2nd Street; open daily; Sun pm only; charge; tel: 954-467-6637). The latter is the largest science museum in South Florida, and an ideal attrac-

tion for children, with hands-on educational exhibits like video games and a bubble-making machine, an indoor citrus grove, and an IMAX theater. A few blocks east is the **Fort Lauderdale Museum of Art** (1 E Las Olas Boulevard; open Tues–Sun; charge; tel: 954-525-5500). The museum has the US's most extensive collection of CoBrA paintings, sculptures and prints. Named for the artists working in **Co**penhagen, **Br**ussels and **A**msterdam between 1948 and 1955, the style paralleled the American abstract expressionist movement.

East along the **Riverwalk** is **Stranahan House** (335 SE 6th Avenue; open Wed–Sun; closed public holidays; charge; tel: 954-524-4736). Restored to its 1913 appearance, this is where, 20 years earlier, Frank Stranahan settled the trading post that became Fort Lauderdale. His house is now a museum.

A vehicle tunnel separates Stranahan House from the **Riverside Hotel** and the stores along busy, attractive **Las Olas Boulevard**, where visitors are treated to boutiques, galleries,

and restaurants along a gas-lighted avenue of luxuriant landscaping. The hotel has been a town favorite since 1936, with tropical gardens extending to the river. Riverwalk itself is a stretch of mini parks and walkways by the New River.

Cruises to nowhere

Head east to the other end of Las Olas to rejoin the beachside, palm-lined A1A. The route takes in the striking canalfront subdivisions that line Fort Lauderdale's many miles of **inland waterways**. Water taxis shuttle visitors from place to place along a 7-mile (11-km) inland route.

Fort Lauderdale claims to berth more pleasure craft than any other Florida city. Many tie up at Bahia Mar Yacht Center off Seabreeze Boulevard. The real things sail from **Port Everglades**, in the south of the city. Once a landlocked lake, the port opened to the Atlantic with a channel blasted in 1928.

"Cruises to nowhere" last for a day or an evening's entertainment; you can also take a cruise ship out into the Atlantic and take advantage of the unrestricted waters in order to gamble. The more intimate, old-fashioned paddleboat *Jungle Queen* (tel: 954-462-5596) navigates the New River from Bahia Mar on 3-hour afternoon trips or longer dinner cruises. Guides confide nuggets of intelligence about the millionaires who live in the fancy riverside homes.

North of Bahia Mar, beyond Las Olas, is **Beach Place**, an entertainment and dining complex in the heart of the old Strip. Farther north, and behind seagrape trees just before Birch Park, is **Bonnet House** (open for guided tours Tues–Sun; closed public holidays; charge; tel: 954-563-5393), possibly the most curious sight in the city.

The creation of the late artists Evelyn and Frederick Bartlett is a mansion of artistic whimsy, with unusual antiques and bizarre knick-knacks. The huge beachfront estate was given to Frederick by Hugh Taylor Birch, his father-in-law by an earlier marriage. In 1942, Birch gave the state the 180 acres (73 hectares) of the land that bears his name, **Birch Park**.

Map on pages 176–77

The BBQ and Shrimp Dinner Cruise on the Jungle Queen *has been popular for six decades. It lasts 4 hours and includes a vast meal and a vaudeville show. Tel: 954-462-5596 for reservations.*

LEFT: Bonnet House, home of artists.
BELOW:
near Palm Beach.

On the drive north from Fort Lauderdale, beach resorts melt from one to the next until at last you hit **Pompano Beach**, at one time a busy agricultural center, and where a Farmers' Market is now held on Saturday mornings.

Farther north, the lighthouse at **Hillsboro Inlet** is on private property, but its site is forever rooted in the tale of the barefoot mailman. From 1885 until just before Henry Flagler built his railroad, when there was no land route to the settlements, letters were carried by contract mailmen walking the beaches. They crossed inlets by boat, and left the boats tied to trees.

When one day his boat drifted to the wrong side of an inlet, carrier Ed Hamilton attempted to swim the channel and was never seen again. He lost his life to duty at Hillsboro. At least one book, a resort, and many yarns have kept the legend of the barefoot mailman alive.

Beyond the inlet is **Hillsboro Beach**, a mere sand spit that has been built upon. The road curves between expensive oceanfront estates buffered by heavy plantings, and the bayside rimmed by private docks; a large swath of beachside has submitted to the zealous claws of commercialism. Spirits lift, however, as A1A swings across Boca Raton Inlet into Palm Beach County and Boca Raton.

Boca Raton

Boca Raton ❸ was the creation of the eccentric architect Addison Mizner (1872–1933), the darling of Palm Beach society in the 1920s and the aesthetic arbiter after Henry Flagler. His graceful Mediterranean mansions still stand along the ocean road. About the time that George Merrick was creating Coral Gables in Miami Beach and Joseph Young was building Hollywood, Mizner dreamed of Boca Raton.

Indulged by the open wallets of his devotees, Mizner formed the substance of a fantasy resort, which he called, "the greatest in the world." He imagined a fleet of gondolas romantically roving a man-made canal through town, but the waterway was never completed. The filled-in ditch instead became the **Camino Real**,

More of the elegant architecture of Addison Mizner (1872–1933) can be admired by driving around the Old Floresta district, which is west of Boca Raton Town Hall.

BELOW: Boca Raton Museum of Art.

where tall palms grace the route to the **Boca Raton Resort and Club**, one of Mizner's greatest achievements. The resort incorporates the original, pink **Cloister Inn**, whose loggias, archways, tiles and fountains convey the opulence of the 1920s.

After the boom burst, Boca limped along until after World War II but has since emerged as one of the best-managed communities along the Gold Coast. The town seashore is a varied series of excellent parks and open beachfront, and in one respect Boca still manages to eclipse its posh neighbor, Palm Beach: it fields a better polo team.

The **Boca Raton Museum of Art** (open Tues–Sun; charge; tel: 561-392-2500) in attractive **Mizner Park** is also well supported. In addition to exhibits of modern masters and American art is an extensive display of outdoor sculpture.

Like Boca, **Delray Beach ❹** is largely open to the sea, and gives a pleasant, inexpensive alternative to the plush resort cities to the north and south. On the seafront, a marker sites the **Orange Grove House of Refuge**, one of a number of primitive shelters that were spaced along the wilderness beaches between 1876 and 1896 from Cape Canaveral to Cape Florida. The shelters were put here for the protection of those who had the misfortune to be shipwrecked and fetch up in these remote parts.

On a winter visit, drive west a short way along Atlantic Avenue and stop at the **Colony Hotel and Cabana Club** (tel: 561-276-4123). The Moorish stucco facade, lobby and rooms, on the main street of Delray, date from 1926. After a renovation, the hotel is now a chic, trendy and environmentally friendly retreat for a young, well-to-do crowd, who enjoy the private beach and the oceanfront beach club with its heated saltwater pool. Note: the Colony is a no-smoking hotel.

Three miles (5 km) farther west along Atlantic Avenue and south on Carter Road is the stylish **Morikami Museum and Japanese Gardens** (open Tues–Sun; closed public holidays; charge; tel: 561-495-0233), a 150-acre (60-hectare) park and museum of Japanese culture that marks the site of a thriving Japanese agricultural community from the early 1900s.

Just 10 miles (16 km) inland from here is the **Loxahatchee National Wildlife Refuge ❺** (open daily; charge; tel: 561-734-8303), which includes the most northerly part of the Everglades. The wildlife is well worth seeing, ranging from alligators to a great variety of birds. An informative visitor center is the starting point for two fine nature trails.

Seaside towns

Back at the coast, and back on A1A, head north to **Gulf Stream**, a town so private it barely lets on that it's a town. No name appears on the ornate, Mizner-designed Gulf Stream Club. The Gulf Stream School is private, as is St Andrew's Golf Club,

Map on pages 176–77

Silhouette by sunset.

BELOW:
the Boca Raton Resort has its own private oceanfront.

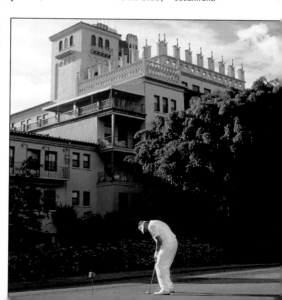

but a beautiful concourse winds under a casuarina canopy that anyone who comes can enjoy.

In **Manalapan** the scene is South Seas languid. Thatch roofs line the beach under swaying palms. Rows of drive-out mirrors are arranged for drivers emerging from hidden mansions to avoid traffic, otherwise obscured by the great walls and privacy hedges. Coppery sea grape leaves color-coordinate with barrel-tile roofs. No buildings obtrude along the waterway. Look instead for yachts tied up to private docks, next to Rolls-Royces and Jaguars. Cyclists with surfboards under their arms pedal by.

High-rises reappear in **Lantana** but are better spaced apart on reaching **South Palm Beach**. Across **Lake Worth** and on the Intra Coastal Waterway is the **GulfStream Hotel**, a 1920s survivor and now an old-fashioned inn.

Palm Beach is farther north on the A1A. Suddenly, the garish shopping centers and neon hotel signs vanish, and clean, uncluttered streets of class take over. The structures behind the high walls of concrete and ficus aren't museums, just second homes to Palm Beach residents. Signs warn that no stopping is allowed – Palm Beach encourages people it doesn't know to keep moving, or to stay in town without straying very far.

Palm-fringed island

Henry Flagler fell in love with the palm-fringed island in 1892 and bought out the landholders who preceded him. His first Breakers Hotel burned down. So did the second. By the time the third one went up in 1926 – it is no less opulent today – Palm Beach was the winter watering hole for American society.

The rich were here to play. They dressed up and partied in the name of charity. Their benefit balls for every worthy cause ennobled their wealth. The Palm Beach way of life became a crowning sanction for American ambition. For many, it still is today.

So, to appreciate Palm Beach in full swing – unless you prefer to gaze on empty mansions in the throes of restoration and garden manicures – you should visit during "the season,"

In exclusive Palm Beach, it's against the law to own a kangaroo or any other exotic animal, to hang a clothes line, or to park almost anywhere.

BELOW: the Breakers resort has a staff of 1,800 who speak a total of 56 languages.

that indeterminate period somewhere between Thanksgiving and Easter. The annual migration of wealth ignites a round of galas, charity balls, and, in election years, political cocktail parties.

Palm Beach

Approaching **Palm Beach** ❻ from the south, Highway A1A leads to South Ocean Boulevard, which runs past the fabulous 117-room estate of the late cereal heiress, Marjorie Merriweather Post, at No. 1100. It's called **Mar-a-Lago** and is now owned by tycoon Donald Trump, whose purchase included 17 acres (7 hectares) of land and a golf course. Trump added a new ballroom, which is hired out for lavish events. At 702 South Ocean Boulevard is a home formerly owned by John Lennon. Next door is a house that belonged to Woolworth Donahue, heir to the dime-store fortune.

The first stop in Palm Beach is **Worth Avenue**, Addison Mizner's substantial contribution to local charm and retail. If Flagler gave Palm Beach stature, Mizner gave it

grace – his Mediterranean-style mansions and shops, with all their rich ornamentation and colorful shrubbery, were legendary attractions in their time, and are still delightful to admire in the sunshine.

Worth Avenue was begun in the 1920s and has been one of the world's premier shopping streets since 1945, often compared to London's Bond Street and Paris' Faubourg St Honoré. Buildings are mostly two or three stories.

Shops are set among villa-like facades, extended by colorful canopies and graced by Palladian windows. Bougainvillaea entwines wrought-iron gates that top ceramic staircases. Little *vias* (alleys) lead off to patios with fountains.

The Breakers, Flagler's famous hotel and the town's pre-eminent landmark, is farther north, at 1 South County Road. This Beaux Arts eminence dominates the oceanfront like a leviathan at sea.

From its fountains and towers to its frescoed ceilings, the Breakers is the very articulation of order in a world of chaos, exactly how Flagler

Map on pages 176–77

The Rambler, *Henry Flagler's railroad car, dates from 1886.*

BELOW:
Worth Avenue in Palm Beach.

Henry Flagler (1830–1913)

South Florida's standing as a vacation mecca for millions owes much to Henry Flagler, railroad- and hotel-builder extraordinaire. Born in Hopewell, New York, Flagler struggled in his early ventures but finally made his fortune in the oil business, as a partner of John D. Rockefeller. Honeymooning in Florida in 1883, he saw the state's vast tourist potential and turned his attention to hotel construction, beginning in St Augustine. To attract visitors in numbers Florida needed transportation, and Flagler began constructing the East Coast Railway to link his resorts along the coast. In 1894 he brought the railroad to Palm Beach, where his hotel, the Royal Poinciana, was the world's largest wooden structure and a playground of the rich and famous.

A year later, Julia Tuttle convinced him to continue the tracks to Miami, and when the government announced the construction of the Panama Canal in 1905, the possibilities for trade persuaded him to push all the way to Key West. The prodigious feat of engineering, linking island to island in a 100-mile (160-km) arc across the sea, reached Key West in 1912, in time for Flagler's 82nd birthday.

Map
on pages
176–77

Golden-haired boy on the Gold Coast.

BELOW:
glass ceiling by Dale Chihuly at the Norton Museum of Art.

saw himself in the dog-eat-dog world of 19th-century capitalism.

Flagler's personal style is also exemplified at Whitehall, on Whitehall Way. This was the $3-million palace he built in 1901 for his third wife, Mary Lily. Called the "Taj Mahal of America," the house has marble interiors and fabrics of gold, as well as private collections of porcelain, paintings, silver, glass, dolls, lace, and costumes. Flagler's private railroad car, *The Rambler*, has been restored alongside. Today, the house serves as the **Flagler Museum** (open Tues–Sun; Sun pm only; charge; tel: 561-655-2833), where docent led-tours are available.

Back toward Worth Avenue is the **Society of the Four Arts** (open daily; Sun pm only; closed public holidays; free; tel: 561-655-7227), on Four Arts Plaza. This complex includes exhibition galleries (open Dec–Apr only), a formal garden, and the stunning Four Arts Library building designed by Mizner's contemporary Maurice Fatio.

Whitehall, The Breakers, and Worth Avenue are the crown jewels of Palm Beach, but in this town, every street is beautifully landscaped. The best view is by bicycle, which can be rented locally; there's also a 3½-mile (6-km) lakefront trail where cars are not allowed.

Just beyond 1075 North Ocean Boulevard is the former estate of the Kennedys, known in the 1960s as the "Winter White House" when John F. Kennedy wintered here. It was at this mansion that Kennedy's nephew, William Kennedy Smith, was staying in 1992 when he was charged with the rape of a young woman he met in a Palm Beach bar. After a sensationalized televised trial, Smith was found not guilty.

The other Palm Beach

Across Lake Worth, the city of **West Palm Beach** ❼ was conceived as an asterisk by Flagler. The town was reserved for servants, gardeners, and others who toiled to keep Palm Beach sparkling, while their employers played polo and made money. It's an unpretentious town, but one reason to visit is the **Norton Museum of Art** (open Tues–Sun; Sun pm only, closed May–Dec and public hols; charge; tel: 561-832-5196). Works by French Impressionists and also Post-Impressionists from Cézanne to Picasso are displayed, as well as fine 20th-century American works – including pieces by Georgia O'Keeffe, Winslow Homer and Andy Warhol – and a wonderful ceiling of glass by Dale Chihuly.

Fifteen miles (24 km) west of downtown West Palm Beach is **Lion Country Safari** (open daily; charge; tel: 561-793-1084), the area's top family attraction, where you can drive along miles of jungle trails past hundreds of roaming animals. The well-fed lions seem to be rather lazy, but it's thrilling to watch one lead a parade of cars, or see a giraffe peering in through the windshield. Keep the windows closed, though. ❑

RESTAURANTS

Fort Lauderdale

Himmarshee Bar & Grill
210 SW 2nd St (Brickell Ave). Tel: 954-524-1818. Open: L Mon–Fri, D daily. **$$$**
Run by two graduates of Mark's Las Olas School of Cooking (see below). Try plantain *empanadas* stuffed with curried lamb, or duck confit over golden raisin polenta.

Indigo Restaurant
At the Riverside Hotel, 620 E Las Olas Blvd. Tel: 954-467-0671. Open: B, L & D. **$$**
Imaginative seafood and salads dominate the menu, complete with accents from Malaysia, Indonesia and Singapore. Sidewalk seating and friendly service.

Johnny V
625 E Las Olas Blvd. Tel: 954-761-7920. Open: L & D daily. **$$$**
Chef Johnny Vinczencz, the Caribbean cowboy, pleases precious diners with a shortstack of portobello mushrooms, great salads and other modern interpretations of classics.

Mark's Las Olas
1032 E Las Olas Blvd. Tel: 954-463-1000. Open: D daily. **$$$$**
This superior seafood haven has a chic bar scene and plenty of innovative dishes. Chef Mark Militello reels 'em in with sesame dolphin or quail and crab cakes with mango slaw.

Sunfish Grill
2771 E Atlantic Blvd. Tel: 954-788-2434. Open: D Tues–Sat. **$$$**
Tony Sindaco may have what is affectionately known as "a joint," but this is still the best place in town for fresh fish. Put aside the frat house decor and dig in. Great wines and experienced service, too.

Palm Beach

32 East
32 E Atlantic Ave (at Swinton Ave). Tel: 561-276-7868. Open: D daily. **$$$**
Good-looking diners come for chef Nick Morfogen's New American cooking, and the lively bar scene. The sexy wood-accented dining room has low lighting and a young, energetic staff. Book early as the place gets packed and loud, but it does offer some of the best food in the zip code.

Café Boulud Palm Beach
The Brazilian Court, 301 Australian Ave. Tel: 561-655-6060. Open: B, L & D daily. **$$$$**
Chef Daniel Boulud opened his first eatery outside New York in this lush hotel with seating inside, and in a stunning courtyard with a fountain as a calming background. The food is divinely French, and the service is excellent.

Echo
230A Sunrise Ave (at N County Rd). Tel: 561-802-4222. Open: D daily Oct–May; Wed–Sun June–Sept. **$$$$**
A sleek and sophisticated setting for sushi and other Asian-inspired fare. Spicy coconut shrimp and curried fish precede outrageous desserts. The great bar scene make it a real Happy Hour hit.

Taboo
221 Worth Ave. Tel: 561-835-3500. Open: L & D daily. **$$**
California cuisine served in a kitschy retro setting, complete with cozy fireplace. The food majors on pizzas, pastas, and big salads.

Toojay's Palm Beach
313 Royal Ponciana Way. Tel: 561-659-7232. Open: B, L & D daily. **$**
A real New York-style deli in blue-blooded Palm Beach. Specials include pastrami on rye, matzo ball soup, and mile-high chocolate cake.

PRICE CATEGORIES

Prices for a three-course dinner per person with a glass of house wine:
$ = under $25
$$ = $25–$40
$$$ = $40–$60
$$$$ = over $60

RIGHT: Café Boulud at the Brazilian Court, Palm Beach.

TOWARD THE GULF COAST

Moody swamplands, captivating islands
and Native American sites are just some of the
attractions on this route from the east to the west
coasts of Florida. You can reward yourself
with a beautiful beach at the end

Miami

I n 1928, the wilds of Florida's
southern tip were made accessible by the construction of a road
known as the **Tamiami Trail**. Officially designated as US Highway
41, the highway begins as Calle
Ocho in Miami's Little Havana and
heads west toward that vast river of
grass, the Everglades, and other
attractions *(see page 197)*.

Skirting the northern boundary of
Everglades National Park, the road
crosses Big Cypress Swamp before
reaching Florida's west coast at the
town of Naples, about 2 hours' drive
from Miami. As well as the fascinating natural habitats along the way,
the journey is easily worthwhile for
the west coast's irresistible beaches,
lapped by the calm, warm waters of
the Gulf of Mexico and graced by
gorgeous sunsets.

Big Cypress Swamp

A ridge riddled with hammocks and
evocative cypress trees separates the
Everglades proper from impressive
Big Cypress Swamp, which is actually closer to the traditional image of
a swamp than its more famous
neighbor. It consists of marshes,
sandy islands of slash pine and large
stands of dwarf cypress sprouting
from knee-deep water and mud.
Giant bald cypress trees that once
distinguished the area were nearly

wiped out by loggers for use in the
manufacture of boat hulls and
coffins. The few that remain are
thought to be 700 years old.

The swamp is a 2,400-sq-mile
(6,200-sq-km) basin, of which about
40 percent is within the **Big Cypress
National Preserve ❽** (open daily;
free; tel: 941-695-4111). The main
access point for the preserve is the
Oasis Visitor Center, on the Tamiami Trail, about 60 miles (100 km)
west of downtown Miami. There is
scope for swamp-hiking here, but

Map
on pages
176–77

LEFT: watersports on
the west coast are
worth traveling for.
BELOW: dancer on the
Seminole Indian
Reservation.

The Tamiami Trail crosses the Everglades and is the most scenic route to the west coast.

permission is needed from park rangers. Most people are happy to drive along the **Loop Road** – a 23-mile (37-km) dirt road running south of US 41 between the Tamiami and Monroe ranger stations. On weekdays, few cars use this road, because, in its very worst sections, it is so pot-holed that anything over 20 mph (32 kph) requires a Jeep.

The road narrows to one lane and enters a beautiful swamp of clear, fresh water. A natural amphitheater of wildlife hovers, with orchids and exotic red flowers shooting from cypress-rooted bromeliads to fire the imagination.

Florida panther

Hiking in the swamp, you may see paw marks of one of the few remaining Florida panthers *(see page 202)*. Watch also for the endangered Everglades swallow-tail kite. This area was once home to about 2 million wading birds, but plume hunters reduced their numbers to only a few hundred thousand by the late 19th century. Laws protected the fowl and helped boost their numbers, but

BELOW:
the natural beauty
of Naples beach.

flocks have diminished again. The decline was steep among wood storks – a population of 50,000 in the 1930s has dwindled to about 10,000. One of the best places to see them is at Corkscrew Swamp Sanctuary *(see page 194)*.

Farther west on the Tamiami Trail, and then south on SR 29, leads to **Everglades City**, the last outpost on the edge of a wildlife kingdom, the watery gateway to a labyrinth of very photogenic mangroves called the **Ten Thousand Islands**. Guided boat trips originate at the Gulf Coast Ranger Station here. Some months, sunset cruises go into upper **Chokoloskee Bay** for the spectacle of as many as 20,000 birds returning to roost.

West again, and the Tamiami Trail leads to the **Fakahatchee Strand State Preserve ❾** (open daily; free; tel: 239-695-4593), the world's only known forest of royal palm and cypress combined. A short trail at Big Cypress Bend leads to a whole array of flora, including magnificent orchids. The preserve has one of the largest concentrations of native orchids in the United States, with about 44 identified species, including the catopsis, which grows only here. Some cypress trees along the trail are more than 500 years old.

As the Tamiami Trail reaches the west coast, SR 951 branches south to **Marco Island**, once a gorgeous seascape, and fought over by environmentalists and developers. The latter won, though with concessions; some say the new developments are among the state's better-planned communities. Developers erected artificial bald eagles' nests in the shadow of the condos, hoping the birds will stay – evidence, they say, of a balance between the needs of modern man and nature.

The villages of **Marco**, at the north end of the island, and pretty **Goodland**, on the southern tip,

retain cottages and memories of an older Florida. Archeologists have found carvings, tools, masks, and weapons of the Calusa people, who lived here as long ago as 500 BC.

Naples

To the north, **Naples ⑩** is the most southerly town of any size on Florida's Gulf Coast, still good-looking in the midst of a population explosion that has dissected the land into subdivisions of mobile homes, waterfront suburbs and condo complexes. The self-proclaimed "Golf Capital of the World" (it has the most golf courses in Florida), this sedate and somewhat snooty town does not appeal to everyone. At the end of the scrubbed avenues are excellent beaches, and an attractive pier for fishing.

Interesting stores are off US 41 at the **Old Marine Market Place**, a collection of tin fishing shacks transformed into a trendy enclave of art galleries and boutiques.

One of the area's oldest attractions still offers a chance to interact with the wildlife. **Caribbean Gardens** (open daily; charge), formerly Jungle Larry's Caribbean Gardens, has a path winding for a mile (1.5 km) past lions, kangaroos, monkeys, African wild dogs, Asian deer, and more in a 52-acre (21-hectare) jungle of exotic plants. The attraction was first planned in 1919. A variety of nature programs and tours are offered, including an alligator feeding.

Next door is one of the area's newer attractions, the **Immokalee Pioneer Museum** (Roberts Ranch, 1590 Goodlette Road; open by appointment only; free; tel: 239-658-2466). The 15-acre (6-hectare) site recreates the story of cattle ranching, one of the region's oldest industries, and portrays day-to-day life on an early 20th-century pioneer homestead.

At **King Richard's Medieval Family Fun Park** (6780 North Airport Road) kids – and adults – can enjoy the "medieval" fun of go-carts, bumper boats, and a batting cage. The park has the area's only permanent roller coaster, plus a water-park area called Merlin's Moat and a dozen more rides.

Map on pages 176–77

A few miles east of Everglades City is the village of Ochopee, famous as the site of the smallest post office in the United States. It measures just 8 ft (2.4 meters) by 7 ft (2.1 meters).

BELOW:
Naples has the greatest concentration of golf courses in Florida.

A popular event on Radio Road west of Naples Airport has captured national attention. Here, the waist-deep **Mile-O-Mud Track** hosts the World Championship Swamp Buggy Races every year. The race course is flooded with water for two weeks before the races to ensure that it's in the worst possible shape to race on.

Naples forms the western edge of Big Cypress Swamp. Northeast of town, on SR 846, is the worthwhile **Corkscrew Swamp Sanctuary** (open daily; charge; tel: 239-348-9151), a haven for the rare wood stork. Here you can stand on the swamp boardwalk, look up at the canopy of nests in the trees overhead and hear the giant birds squawking as they glide through the air in search of food for their young. For any hope of seeing the wood storks, though, you need to visit in wintertime.

Fort Myers

From Naples, take US 41 or I-75 to **Fort Myers ⓫**, which, with neighboring **Cape Coral**, was the fastest growing metropolis in the US during the 1970s. The population growth continues. The inventor Thomas Edison (1847–1931) beat the rush when he built a home here in 1886, at the age of 39.

The **Edison Winter Home and Museum** (open daily; Sun pm only; charge; tel: 239-334-7419) sprawls across both sides of McGregor Boulevard (SR 867), beautified by the royal palm trees planted by Edison himself. The home and guest house, among the first prefabricated buildings in the US, were constructed in Maine and brought to Fort Myers by schooner. Tropical gardens engulf the homes.

It was here that Thomas Edison contemplated the future and entertained famous friends like his next-door neighbors Henry Ford and Harvey Firestone. He offered to light up his new city with electrical installations, but the townspeople refused for fear that the lights would keep their cattle awake at night.

Over the road, the museum displays photographs, personal items such as a gold watch, a collection of automobiles, and a treasure house of inventions, including 170 phonographs with huge, handpainted speakers and – of course – dozens of light bulbs.

Sanibel and Captiva islands

Fort Myers is the gateway to two islands where you can commune with nature just an arm's length from lots of modern amenities. In the 1960s and '70s, uncontrolled development threatened to turn pretty **Sanibel Island ⓬** and equally attractive **Captiva Island ⓭** into uninteresting places with high-rises.

In 1974 Sanibel seceded from Lee County, set up its own city government and immediately put an almost complete halt to further growth. Now, although there are still plenty of hotels and restaurants, a few shopping centers, and, of course, popular beaches, Sanibel

Guided tours of the Thomas Edison estate take in the adjacent home of car manufacturer Henry Ford. Historical and botanical tours are available (tel: 239-334-7419).

BELOW: Edison Winter Home in Fort Myers.

also has protected wildlife areas.

The tranquil **J.N. "Ding" Darling National Wildlife Refuge** (open daily; charge) includes a 5-mile (8-km) drive, the highlight of which is the rare sight of roseate spoonbills, wheeling and turning in flight formations as tightly organized as air force display teams. Anhinga "snake" birds, herons, and vultures are among the hundreds of birds that make the refuge home. Fortunately, these preserves are of secondary importance to the many tourists who descend on Sanibel so they tend to be relatively quiet. Captiva receives even fewer visitors than Sanibel.

Tropic Star Cruises (tel: 239-283-0015) offers boat trips to **Cayo Costa Island State Park**, north of Captiva. This is one of Florida's most unspoiled barrier islands, with a wonderful diversity of bird life and 9 miles (14 km) of dune-backed beaches. For the full experience, stay overnight in one of the cabins on the island, but be prepared for quite basic facilities (i.e. no hot water or electricity), and you'll need to take your own supplies for food and comfort.

Heading back

An alternative route back to Miami is along "Alligator Alley" (I-75), which crosses from Naples toward Fort Lauderdale and then turns south to Miami. For an interesting detour, leave the Interstate at exit 14 and head north on County Road 833 for 17 miles (27 km).

Here, in the Big Cypress **Seminole Indian Reservation**, is the interesting **Ah-Tah-Thi-Ki Museum** ⓴ (open Tues–Sun; charge; tel: 941-902-1113), dedicated to the culture and history of the Seminole Indians.

The Seminoles arrived in Florida in the 18th century, forced south by land-hungry Europeans. The stiff resistance they mounted to attempts to further evict them from the state resulted in what became known as the Seminole Wars.

The museum has exhibits about the Seminoles' survival in the inhospitable Everglades, and cultural artifacts like moccasins, turtle-shell rattles, and weapons from the Seminole Wars. Also on site are a working Seminole village and Everglades nature trails.   ❑

Map on pages 176–77

Seminole totem pole on display at the Ah-Tah-Thi-Ki Museum.

BELOW: a "shunter" doing the Sanibel stoop while looking for shells.

Shelling on Sanibel Island

The reputation of Sanibel is built on the shells that are tossed on to its beaches. Only Jeffreys Bay in South Africa and the Sulu Islands in the Philippines offer better opportunities for shell collecting. Here on Florida's west coast there is no offshore reef to break the shells; the warm, shallow waters encourage mollusc and crustacean growth; and the gently sloping sea floor south of the island allows the shells to roll ashore on the waves. The island also lies east to west, rather than the more usual north to south, helping more shells to roll in. Early morning, and after storms and heavy tides, are the best times for shunters (short for shell hunters). Look just under the sand where the waves are breaking.

Shunt for highly prized shells like the rare royal Florida miter, golden olive, and spiny oyster. More commonplace finds are the queen and horse conchs, murex, limpet, left-handed whelk, paper nautilus, cowrie, jewel boxes, jingles, tulips, and lion's paw. A shelling checklist, on sale on the islands, will enable you to identify your discoveries. Remember that live shelling is illegal – so please collect only uninhabited shells.

Just two hours' drive from Miami is the untamed heart of Florida – a swamp rich in wildlife and as raw in nature as the entire peninsula used to be

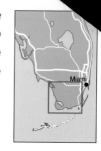

Miami

Protected as a National Park since 1947, much of the beauty and value of these fabulous wetlands is in the tropical wildlife and mangrove forests. While the Grand Canyon, Yellowstone, and Yosemite offer vistas of majestic geology and topography, the Glades are themselves a low-key, living marvel. Mangroves and seas of sawgrass stretch in all directions, punctuated by islands of hardwood trees (known as hammocks) and stands of cypress – all of it alive with species from alligators and manatees to pelicans, anhingas, and even an occasional bald eagle.

Living laboratory

Hiking and biking trails, tram rides, boat tours, and seaplane trips give tremendous opportunities to see and get around the swamps, and local naturalists as well as knowledgeable rangers provide guided tours. This teeming carpet of earthy and watery environments, tropical and temperate plant and animal life is a living, breathing laboratory, where nature cooks up new recipes for her annual cycles of life and death.

Everglades National Park makes up only a fraction of a slow-flowing river, whose source lies in the Kissimmee River, northwest of Miami. The Glades flow for about 200 miles (320 km), bulging up to 70 miles (110 km) in width and at a mean depth of only 6 inches (15 cm). The water oozes down a gradual incline in Florida's surface, dropping just 15 ft (5 meters) over hundreds of miles, before flowing into Florida Bay. A drop of water takes over a year to make the journey.

Around 350 varieties of birds, 500 kinds of fish, 55 species of reptile, and 40 mammal species call the Everglades home. The park even has 45 indigenous species of plants that are found nowhere else.

Map
on pages
176–77

LEFT: the Everglades encompasses most of Florida's southern tip.
BELOW: easy access into the Everglades.

The mud... light pours over... green and brown expanse of sawgrass, and of water, shining and slow-moving below, the grass and water that is the meaning... of the Everglades... It is a river of grass.

— M. STONEMAN DOUGLAS

BELOW: Stoneman Douglas in the national park she helped found.

...ch ecosystem evolved over ...n years of sea action, lime-...uild-up and fertile tropical ...n, but has reached the brink of ...tion in less than a century. Man ...ed on its hammocks about 2,000 ...s ago with the arrival of Native ...ericans, but the Calusas mostly ...ved in harmony with the Everglades. It wasn't until the late 19th century that man started draining swamps, and serious concerns were to follow as a result *(see page 203)*.

Governor Napoleon Bonaparte Broward put government efforts into opening up the region, and, by 1909, the Miami Canal connected Lake Okeechobee to Miami in a sophisticated network of waterways through the Everglades.

In 1926 and 1928, two major hurricanes dumped waters from Lake Okeechobee on thousands of South Florida settlers, and the Army Corps of Engineers ringed the lake, the core of the Everglades, with the defensive Hoover Dike.

The first major road across the swamp took five years to build and finally opened on April 25, 1928. The highway linked Tampa and Miami, hence the name, the Tamiami Trail (also known as US 41).

A fragile environment

The trail was a great feat of engineering, but blocked the movement of water and wildlife so vital to the life of the Glades. Efforts by the Audubon Society, the Florida Federation of Women's Clubs and the Tropical Everglades National Park Commission brought the area's designation as a National Park by President Harry S. Truman in 1947.

Marjory Stoneman Douglas awoke public awareness of the fragility of the ecosystem with her book *The Everglades: River of Grass*, published the same year. Unlicensed draining and continued contamination by fertilizers and pollution have stunted animal reproduction and dramatically altered the vegetation; visitors today see a tenth of the bird life that was visible in 1947.

Since the 1980s, man has brought an even more insidious imbalance to the Glades. Exotic pets, released by their owners when they grow large

Marjory Stoneman Douglas

For more than 70 years, Marjory Stoneman Douglas (1890–1998), the first lady of Florida's environmentalists, fought against the destruction of the Everglades. She was opinionated, passionate and poetic. Without her, the great natural wonder of the Everglades would probably be little more than a memory.

A newspaper columnist and short-story writer, Douglas moved to Miami from New England in 1915. After a brief marriage, she lived alone in a one-bedroom cottage from 1926 until her death. She served on the original 1927 committee that pushed to declare the Everglades a national park. Her 1947 book *The Everglades: River of Grass* brought to public attention the importance of what was hitherto considered a useless swamp. Years later, she founded the Friends of the Everglades to fight plans for an international airport. She received numerous awards and honorary degrees, including the first "Floridian of the Year" citation in 1983.

Through the many battles to save her river of grass, Douglas was never sentimental about her cause. She died at the venerable age of 108, but her legacy will live forever.

or inconvenient – from African monitor lizards to vervet monkeys, and at least 16 species of non-native tropical fish – have been recorded. Many just add a tasty side-dish to the swamp menu, but some, like the recently released Burmese python, are equipped to make successful lives for themselves.

The pythons grow as long as 20ft (6 meters), and have been known to devour alligators. They are currently being caught by park rangers at a rate of up to 15 a month. The presence of a new top predator is affecting the balance of nature in the mangroves – yet another threat in the increasingly fragile Everglades.

River of grass

To reach the park from Miami, head south on either US Highway 1 or Florida's Turnpike and pick up SR 9336 at Florida City. This road takes you to the main park entrance, where you can get a crash course in Everglades ecology from the displays at the **Main Visitor Center** **⓯** (open daily; charge for park; tel: 305-242-7700). SR 9336 is the main

road through the park. It is about 38 miles (60 km) from the entrance to its southwest dead end at Flamingo. Don't miss the opportunity to leave the car and detour along at least a few of the fabulous trails and boardwalks along the way.

Right by the **Royal Palm Visitor Center** **⓰**, just 2 miles (3 km) from the park entrance, is the easy **Gumbo Limbo Trail**, which explores a typical hardwood hammock. The gumbo limbo tree is a common sight along the path. This is a cool, rainforest-type environment of ferns, air plants, and orchids. Careful examination of the tree limbs may reveal the *Liguus* snail, found only here and in Cuba, Haiti, and the Dominican Republic, but be warned that the mosquitoes are devilish here, even in winter.

There's also the **Anhinga Trail** boardwalk into a willow head at the tip of Taylor Slough. (A slough, pronounced "slew," is a natural drainage ditch.) In winter this is one of the best places for wildlife, since there is more water here than in many other parts of the park.

Long Pine Key **⓱** has nature

Map on pages 176–77

The best time to visit is in winter, when the wildlife is most active.

LEFT: alligator wrestling for fun.
BELOW: take mosquito repellent.

trails winding through slash pines, a tree unique to southern Florida; this lovely spot is also the site of one of the park's campgrounds, and there are picnic areas too. A few miles farther down the main road is soaring **Pa-hay-okee Overlook**, an observation tower in a hardwood hammock edged with cypress stands and a freshwater slough.

There are about 100 species of grass in the Everglades and most can be observed from the boardwalk here, although it takes study to distinguish between coinwort, marsh fleabane, love-vine, creeping Charlie, and ludwigia. Sawgrass, ironically, is not a true grass, but a sedge. With luck, there might be a sighting of a snail kite, once common in the Everglades. This endangered bird feeds only on apple snails, which live on the sawgrass.

Beyond, the road turns south toward **Mahogany Hammock** ⓲, where a trail winds under some of the largest mahogany trees in the United States. Rare paurotis palms, stretching 12–30 ft (4–9 meters) high, flank Paurotis Pond and its

The Miccosukee Resort is a few miles east of Miccosukee Indian Village. It has a hotel, big-name shows, and a casino.

BELOW:
Miccosukee storyteller at the Indian Village.

plethora of wildlife. Between Mahogany Hammock and Flamingo the road connects with canoe trails, in addition to the **West Lake Trail** footpath, which wiggles through sawgrass and cat-tails. Pink shrimp feed and breed among the mangroves in havens like this before migrating to the Gulf of Mexico.

The end of the road

Once a remote fishing village accessible only by boat, **Flamingo** ⓳ is now at the end of SR 9336, and mainly caters to tourists; there are motor campsites and tent plots here for extended stays. Until Hurricane Wilma in 2005, there was also the motel-like Flamingo Lodge, but due to a lack of funding, there are no plans to reopen it.

Check for activities at the ranger station. If you have your own boat or hiking gear, be sure to file plans with the rangers before slipping off into the backcountry; even well-informed locals have lost their bearings and gone astray in the maze of mangroves, rivers, and bays. Otherwise, you can rent whatever equipment you need. If you're planning to stay a while, you can even move into a fully-equipped houseboat and cruise the waterways in comfort.

Flamingo is the southern terminus of the **Wilderness Waterway**, a week-long 99-mile (159-km) canoe trip that begins near Everglades City *(see page 192)* and winds south through alluring niches like Chokoloskee Island, Big Lostman's Bay, and Shark River.

Shorter cruises and walks are also available. Easy, hiking trails include the **Snake Bight**, through tropical hardwoods to a boardwalk over Florida Bay; **Rowdy Bend**, under Spanish moss and brilliant red bromeliads; and **Christian Point**, which winds past giant wild pine bromeliads attached to the trees. For a real taste of the swamp, though,

take a "slough slog" – a watery walk through the Everglades guided by a park ranger. Tour boats also sail the white-sand shores of **Cape Sable** ❷⓪, the southernmost point in mainland Florida, and around the keys in **Florida Bay**. A boating or canoeing trip to Flamingo should include at least one night here.

Bird-watching is spectacular near Flamingo and in the bay. Flocks of gulls waft on the air currents. In winter, white pelicans with 9-ft (2.7-meter) wingspans migrate from the west. Ospreys build nests atop channel markers, and bald eagles are sometimes spotted. Manatees and American crocodiles (as distinct from alligators) inhabit the waters, but are endangered and rarely seen. Bottlenose dolphins, though, like to frolic in the bow wake of boats.

Alternative route

Another route to the Everglades from Miami is to head west on Calle Ocho for the Tamiami Trail *(see page 191)*, and stopping along the way at **Shark Valley** ❷①. In summer, most of the freshwater slough is underwater, and

in winter the park operates a tram ride through the sawgrass prairie, teeming with wildlife, up to a 60-ft (18-meter) **Observation Tower**. Alligators make a range of sounds in willows at the foot of the tower; a hiss is a warning to stay out of their way. The tram route can be hiked or biked, too. The **Otter Cave Hammock Nature Trail** has a pamphlet to guide you. Tread softly and you may see otters munching on live frogs' legs beside the road.

Near the valley is the **Miccosukee Indian Village** ❷❷ (open daily; charge; tel: 305-223-8380). Most of the Miccosukee Indian tribe live near here and along the Tamiami Trail. The village has cultural displays and demonstrations of traditional crafts, like basket making, beadwork, and palmetto palm dolls.

There are also airboat rides and alligator wrestling displays (not everyone's cup of tea). At the restaurant, when available, you can try alligator tails or frogs' legs. Beyond the village, the Tamiami Trail continues to Big Cypress Swamp and eventually out to the Gulf Coast. ❏

Map on pages 176–77

TIP

Be extra vigilant when hiking through the Everglades. The newest threat to this fragile environment is pythons, domestic pets that have been released by their owners and are now upsetting the ecological balance by attacking alligators (not people).

BELOW: solitude and sunset in a secluded swamp.

THE ECOLOGY OF THE EVERGLADES

This balance of tropical and temperate, of fauna and flora, is found nowhere else in the US. It is in danger of being lost

The Everglades' ecosystem depends on the subtropical cycle of dry (winter) and wet (summer) seasons. The inhabitants are adapted to the climate, often moving from one part to another with the changes in the water level – the lifeblood pulse of this mysterious wilderness.

EVERGLADES HABITATS

● **hardwood hammocks**: tree islands of mahogany and cabbage palm above the high-water level. A refuge for mammals in the wet season.

● **bayheads**: smaller, shallower islands of mainly bay trees, on rich organic soil.

● **willows**: wispy vegetation in deep water near hammocks – usually in a doughnut shape, with a gator hole at the center.

● **sawgrass prairie**: grows over much of the Glades on a thin soil formed by decaying vegetation on the limestone base.

● **freshwater sloughs**: fresh water channels that help plants and animals survive through the harsh dry season.

● **cypress swamps**: where water is deepest and the soil very thin, cypress are among the few trees able to thrive.

● **coastal prairie**: a habitat for salt-tolerant plants like cacti.

DANGER

DO NOT FEED OR MOLEST

GATORS CANNOT BE TAMED AND FEEDING THEM CAN RESULT IN THEIR MISTAKING A HAND FOR A HANDOUT! FLORIDA LAW PROHIBITS THE FEEDING OR MOLESTING OF ALLIGATORS!!

ABOVE: Alligators are a vital part of the ecology of the Everglades. During the wet season, they use their feet and snout to dig holes that store water in the dry months. These offer oases for animals, including turtles and birds.

BELOW: Also known as airplants, epiphytes are non-parasitic plants that grow on trees but take water and nutrients as they run down the bark. Here, cypress trees are host to tufts of stiff-leaved wild pine.

ABOVE: A sub-species of the cougar that has adapted to the subtropical climate of Florida, the big, shy Florida Panther lives in the most remote areas of the Everglades, particularly in Big Cypress Swamp. Only 50–70 of the endangered felines survive.

SAVING THE EVERGLADES

Almost 50 percent of the Everglades has been lost due to human intervention in the 20th century. Roads, canals, and dikes (such as Hoover Dike, *above*) impede the water's natural flow and the seasonal changes in water levels. Much land has been drained for farming, and expanding urban areas on the coast have drained water for washing machines and swimming pools.

The campaign to save the Everglades is dependent on the cooperation between farmers, environmentalists, water managers, and bureaucrats. It is a rocky, on-going process, and often involves legal issues. Restoring the quality of the water is a major priority; another is a reduction in the levels of phosphorus, used in fertilizers. Fertilizer upsets the balance of the Everglades' ecology by promoting growth in plants like cattails, which choke vast areas of marshland.

The campaigning work begun by Marjory Stoneman Douglas (*see page 198*) continues, but help is still needed. Find out more information by going to the Friends of the Everglades website: www.everglades.org.

ABOVE: A great expanse of sawgrass, punctuated by tree islands known as "hammocks," is the classic Everglades scene. This is how the park came to be called "the River of Grass." Sawgrass is a member of the sedge family (and one of the world's oldest plant species), which is tough enough to endure months of burning sun.

RIGHT: Apple snails are the sole diet of the endangered snail kite – a dependency typical of the Everglades. The snails' eggs also feed other birds in the region.

LEFT: One of the Everglades' most distinctive birds, the anhinga are often seen drying their feathers at the water's edge, with wings splayed. The anhinga swims with only its head above the water (a habit that has earned it the nickname "snake bird") and dives for fish, using its sharp beak to skewer its prey.

THE FLORIDA KEYS

The drive down the Overseas Highway is delightful, with water shimmering on both sides. This string of islands beckons with boating, fishing and snorkeling, with Key West waiting to entertain at the tip

Driving south on Overseas Highway, it is the scent that hits you first. Through the open window wafts a sharp melange of odors – salt, seaweed, fish residue, and marsh – a pungent reminder that the city is far behind, and that something unique is waiting around the corner.

There are two ways to drive to the Keys from Miami. The slower but more scenic route is to follow US 1 south beyond Homestead, then take a left at the fork in the road just past Florida City. On either side of Card Sound toll bridge, clumps of red and black mangroves poke up out of the sea like solid islands.

Stunning natural reefs

The bridge ends on North Key Largo. A right on SR 905 leads through bright hammocks of Jamaica dogwood, loblolly, feathery lysiloma, and mahogany trees until the road runs directly back into US 1. A left turn on 905 eventually takes you to the northern tip of the key.

Boat-lovers can explore **Biscayne National Park ㉓** (open daily; free; tel: 305-230-7275), 96 percent of which is underwater – in the form of stunning natural reefs, mostly located about 10 miles (16 km) offshore. The main starting point for trips is the headquarters at **Convoy Point**, back on the mainland, east of Homestead.

As well as guided trips of the park, snorkelling, scuba diving, and fishing expeditions can also be arranged.

The toll bridge and scenic detour can be avoided by simply continuing on US 1. This becomes the scenic **Overseas Highway**, which hops from island to island all the way to Key West, 160 miles (257 km) from Miami. Locations in the Keys are often given as a mile marker (or MM). This refers to the signs alongside US 1, which give the distance from Key West.

Map on pages 176–77

LEFT: the big one that didn't get away.
BELOW: a local getting upclose and personal with a gecko.

These mile markers (MM) along Highway 1 give the distance from Key West.

BELOW: an angler's ultimate catch.

The road through the Keys is mostly lined with tacky storefronts, billboards, and gas stations; like the Everglades, the Keys do not dazzle for the casual tourist behind the windshield. Park the car. Get on a bicycle or boat. Revel in the immense canopy of sky and the mounds of whipped cloud. Put on a snorkel and fins. Rent a rod and reel. You'll soon succumb.

Key Largo

Edward G. Robinson, the gangster in the 1948 movie *Key Largo*, is terrified of the brewing hurricane. Bogart tells him, "You don't like it, do you Rocco, the storm? Show it your gun, why don't you? If it doesn't stop, shoot it." In **Key Largo** ㉔, all that remains of that black-and-white era is the **Caribbean Club Bar** near MM 104. Some of the movie may have been shot inside. The bar's coquina veneer, stills from the movie, and still-rowdy reputation offer a step into the past.

Key Largo's other main attraction is North America's only living coral reef. The dive shops that clutter US 1 offer crash courses, and crank out certified scuba-divers in just a few days. They also have equipment and daily dive trips. **John Pennekamp Coral Reef State Park** ㉕ (open daily; charge; tel: 305-451-1202; entrance mid-key at MM 102.5), has better, more reliable concessions offering snorkeling and glass-bottom boat rides, in addition to full-blown scuba trips.

There are nine specific dive spots in the park. By far the favorite is **Key Largo Dry Rocks**, site of the famous *Christ of the Deep* statue. The 9-ft (2.7-meter) bronze sculpture, usually covered with algae, is a replica of the *Christ of the Abyss* statue off the coast of Genoa, Italy, and was donated by an Italian industrialist and sport fisherman.

The first underwater park in the United States, John Pennekamp encompasses 78 sq. miles (200 sq. km) of coral reef, and harbors more than 40 types of coral and 450 or more fish species. Snorkelers rub snouts with triggerfish, swim with schools of tang, and see the conch, queen of the Keys, in its natural habitat.

Collecting coral is strictly prohibited, and it should not be touched or

Fishing in the Florida Keys

Throughout the island chain, marinas bob with fishing boats of all shapes and sizes. On the Atlantic side, the warm waters of the Gulf Stream are rich with prize catches like marlin and wahoo. These big game fish can take hours to land but make great trophies. Closer in, tropical species like snapper and grouper are hooked in the coastal and reef waters. North of the Keys, the protected shallows of Florida Bay, known locally as the "backcountry," offer more tranquil angling. Here, knowledgeable guides pole flat-bottomed skiffs between the islands in search of inshore fish such as snook or pompano. In these waters, guile and stealth win the day.

At the marinas throughout Islamorada, Marathon, and Key West, trips can be arranged for all budgets and abilities. Boats can be chartered for solo trips and parties, local guides will offer their knowledge of the schools and the waters, and trips can be taken more economically on one of the large fishing party boats. A private boat and guide can cost $200–$500 a day. Good advice on local guides and fishing trips can be had from the many bait and tackle shops that line the Overseas Highway. The stores also sell fishing licenses.

stood upon – the slightest touch can kill it. Boats must anchor well away from live coral. The reef was seriously damaged in the 1930s and 1940s, when coral was broken with dynamite and crowbars to stock souvenir shops. Marine scientists and conservationists pushed the legislation that led to the creation of John Pennekamp Park in 1960. It was named for a *Miami Herald* reporter whose stories brought public attention to the offshore reefs.

Key Largo is also the site of the world's first underwater resort, the remarkable **Jules' Undersea Lodge** (tel: 305-451-2353), at MM 103, where guests swim to, and sleep in, an underwater hotel. If you don't have time to stay overnight, you can scuba to the lodge for a visit to take in a movie or some music.

To eat seafood sandwiches and Key Lime Pie with the locals, turn left by the Burger King, and follow the signs to the **Pilot House Tiki Bar and Grill**. The tiny key limes for this tangy dessert once grew in South Florida and all around the Keys, but now have to be imported.

Matecumbe Keys

Highway 1 continues spectacularly through Rock Harbor, Tavernier, Plantation Key, and Windley Key. The sensation of being on a small tuft of land surrounded by vast seas deepens on the bridge over Whale Harbor to **Upper Matecumbe Key**. Polished fishing vessels either side of the harbor flag the sport fishing trade, such a staple of the local economy. **Islamorada** ㉖ considers itself the world's capital of sport-fishing.

If you have the cash, and a hankering to battle a bonefish or haul home a sailfish, this is a place to spend a few days. The luxurious **Cheeca Lodge** (tel: 305-664-4651) at MM 82 is the hub of the trade. For a more local hang-out grab a beer waterside at **Holiday Isle's Tiki Bar** near MM 84.5.

To pet fish rather than catch them, visit Islamorada's landmark **Theater of the Sea** (open daily; charge; tel: 305-664-2431), which has been here since 1946. Located at MM 84.5, it features daily doings in a natural coral grotto, with sea lion and dolphin shows, glass-bottom boat rides

Map on pages 176–77

The unpopulated islands off the Keys are refuges for the shy Great White Heron.

BELOW: diving by Key Largo's *Christ of the Deep*.

around nearby lagoons, and even a shark pit. You might also want to enquire about the Dolphin Adventure package, which includes a swim with the dolphins, but this does have to be booked in advance.

Islamorada town proper has a **Spanish Mission House**, with an art gallery and a striking Art Deco-style monument to the Labor Day hurricane of 1935, in which more than 400 people died.

More bridges lead to **Lower Matecumbe Key**, an embarkation point for trips to Indian and Lignumvitae Keys, which are accessible by boat from the marina at MM 77.5 (tel: 305-664-9814). The weird and wondrous tropical foliage of **Indian Key** hides traces of the early Calusa Indian habitations and the remains of a settlement that occupied the island from 1831 to 1840.

Lignumvitae Key is a treasure trove of fauna and flora, with a wide variety of unusual trees and fascinating bird species. Call the marina between Thursday and Monday to reserve a place on the ranger-led tour of the islands.

Seven Mile Bridge

From the Matecumbes, US 1 winds across little keys and breathtaking waterscapes to Key Vaca and the town of **Marathon**. With a population of about 12,000, Marathon is the main settlement of the Middle Keys.

Near MM 47 is the **Seven Mile Bridge ㉗** – an engineering marvel. The span, actually just 110 ft (33 meters) short of 7 miles (11 km), is laser-straight save for a bend at Pigeon Key. Completed in 1912, it was the crowning achievement of Henry Flagler's East Coast Railway.

The 1935 hurricane destroyed the railroad but not the bridge, which was then converted to carry the Overseas Highway. The old bridge, a hair-raisingly narrow structure, was eventually replaced by a shorter, modern bridge in 1982. On Pigeon Key, which can still be reached via the old bridge, you can see some of the buildings used by Flagler's bridge construction crews.

Continue to **Bahia Honda State Park ㉘** (open daily; charge; tel: 305-872-2353), at MM 37, where another rickety old bridge parallels

In 1947, there were fewer than 50 key deer; now there are at least 600.

BELOW: a bird's eye view of Key Largo.

the newer one, providing a glimpse into the past. This lovely park has a beach that is generally agreed to be the best in the Keys and was once voted the finest in the entire US. Beautiful white sand is fringed by a dense forest, where trails wind among rare trees such as the yellow satinwood. The beach itself has campsites and water sports equipment available for rent.

Between Bahia Honda and Key West are a group of slightly larger islands that make up the Lower Keys. A highlight here is the **National Key Deer Refuge** (open Mon–Fri; free; tel: 305-872-2239), which spans a number of islands but has its headquarters on **Big Pine Key** (take Key Deer Boulevard, just beyond MM 31, heading for Big Pine Key Shopping Plaza).

The star attraction is a colony of diminutive key deer, a subspecies of the Virginia white-tail. The animals grow to about 30 inches (75 cm) tall and 38 inches (95 cm) in length. Hunters and developers had reduced the population to fewer than 50 by 1947, but conservation efforts by the refuge have since boosted numbers to several hundred. Before leaving Big Pine, keen snorkelers and divers should consider the 5-mile (8-km) boat trip south to the truly sensational stretch of reef at the showcase **Looe Key National Marine Sanctuary**. Almost all of the dive centers in the area will offer excursions to the sanctuary, as well as equipment to rent.

Key West

Some 25 miles (40 km) beyond Big Pine Key, you first reach Stock Island, and then the last bridge on the Overseas Highway. Crossing the bridge is a short hop into another, very different, world. This melange of Margaritaville and Hemingway is quite literally the end of the road. This is **Key West 29**.

On arrival, first impressions may be those of any resort city anywhere: Holiday Inn, Days Inn, Burger King, and company. However, the character of the town inevitably surfaces, slowly at first, then more quickly.

Tacky neon storefronts begin to alternate with dignified old homes buried under fragrant pink blooms

Maps:
Area 176
City 210

Spanish explorers said that they found Key West buried in human bones, a tale that may have led to its name of Cayo Hueso – "Island of Bones." The name was later anglicized into Key West.

BELOW: protected sands at Bahia Honda State Park.

of frangipani. The ambiance is not quite Bahamian, not quite Cuban, not quite nautical. It is instead, part parochial American coastal port, part paradise for exiles and misfits. And all very Key West.

Old Town Key West

In the **Old Town**, bars, restaurants, shops and homes – some restored, some still crumbling – merge in a collage of discordant color that somehow suits this city. The people who blend into this bizarre landscape are as incongruous as the colors. Among them are born-and-bred locals (known as conchs, pronounced "konks"), long-haired survivors of the hippie era, impeccably groomed gay couples, leather-faced fishermen, jet-setters in color-coordinated tennis ensembles – and, of course, a large helping of tourists.

The tourists come and go, engulfing and deserting the town like waves as huge cruise ships dock and depart. If you arrive during one of these brief stops take shelter in a bar or the aquarium until the hordes leave, otherwise it's almost impossible to enjoy the distinctive flavors that Key West has to offer.

The inimitable character of Key West evolved from its location, a geographical haven for transients at an end of the earth. Once the haunt of pirates, the island gained legitimacy in the early 19th century when the US Navy stepped in to police these waters. Soon the town was booming, largely from the business of "wrecking" – the licensed stripping of cargo from shipwrecks. In the early 20th century, Flagler's East Coast Railway added another dimension to the economy: tourism. And apart from a slump in the 1930s, this constant influx of visitors has kept Key West prosperous.

To appreciate Key West, it's a good idea to stay for at least a couple of nights. Popular sights are mainly in

Wreckers in the 1800s would race across the water if a sinking boat was spotted off the Keys: the first ship to arrive at the wreck was legally entitled to strip it – after rescuing any survivors.

BELOW: calm and casual in Key West.

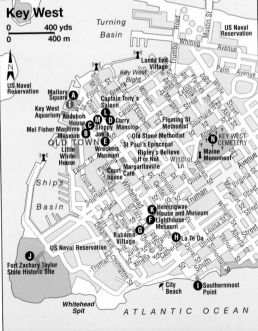

the western half of the city, with **Mallory Square** the usual starting point. This is the spot around which the city grew, and lately the spot around which its renaissance has revolved. Stock up on brochures and tips at the helpful information center. The popular souvenir market is a place to offload surplus cash.

On Mallory Square itself is the **Key West Aquarium** (open daily: charge; tel: 305-296-2051) and the **Key West Shipwreck Historeum** (open daily: charge; tel: 305-292-8990), a reproduction of the warehouse used for salvage operations.

The **Mel Fisher Maritime Museum** ⓑ (200 Greene Street; open daily; charge; tel: 305-294-2633) nearby displays treasures from the Spanish ships *Nuestra Señora de Atocha* and *Santa Margarita*, which sank in the waters off Key West during a fierce hurricane in 1622. Only a fraction of the hoard of gold, silver, and jewels is on view, but other exhibits tell the dramatic story of the treasure hunt and salvage operation.

Fortunately for visitors, Key Westers have indulged a passion for restoring their homes, and transformed the island into a stylish architectural museum. **Whitehead Street**, just beside the Mel Fisher Museum, displays some colorful examples. At No. 205 is **Audubon House** ⓒ (open daily; charge; tel: 305-294-2116), which was named for naturalist-artist John James Audubon (1785–1851), who spent a few weeks here while studying Florida's countless species of birds.

Bahamian style

Some of the best examples of local architecture are one block south, on **Caroline Street**. The Captain George Carey House at No. 410 is typical of the Bahamian style, as is the building at No. 310. The George A.T. Roberts House at No. 313, with its spacious veranda and "gingerbread" trim – the fancy wooden grillwork that is so typical of Key West – exemplifies "conch" architecture.

One of the city's best-known buildings is **Curry Mansion** ⓓ (511 Caroline Street; open daily; charge; tel: 305-294-5349), which admits visitors and is also a guest

Audubon House, built in 1830, has period furnishings, some of which were hauled off sinking ships.

BELOW: the rooftops of Old Town Key West.

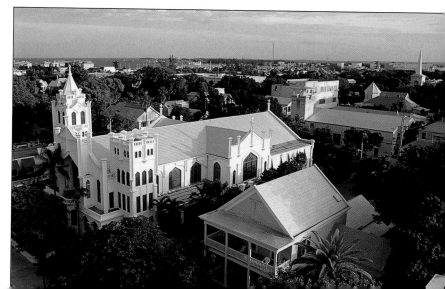

house. The house was begun in 1855 by William Curry, a wreck captain from the Bahamas who became the city's first millionaire. Much of the wood-paneling and electrical fittings are original. The furnishings, some of which are Victorian, were collected by the current owner.

Duval Street

Old Town's main drag is **Duval Street**. The word "drag" is used deliberately, for Key West has long been a popular spot on the map for gay and lesbian sun-seekers, many of whom come out in costume once the cocktail hour has arrived. Rowdy and riotous nightlife is guaranteed here: Happy Hours start early and bars close late, usually at around 2am.

South on Duval, the **Wreckers' Museum**  (open daily; charge; tel: 305-294-9502) at No. 322, attracts its fair share of visitors. Built in 1829 by Francis B. Watlington, a sea captain who made his money from wrecking, the house has been restored and refurbished with antiques; there are also displays of model ships, and documents and artifacts linked to the

At Key West's Southernmost Point, Cuba is only 90 miles away.

BELOW: Mallory Square market.
RIGHT: 19th-century lighthouse.

wrecking business. If you continue south, you'll reach the **Lighthouse Museum**  (open daily; charge; tel: 305-294-0012), pointing its head above the trees at 938 Whitehead Street. Although built back in 1847, the lighthouse is still functioning. Even better, visitors are permitted to climb up for the view.

The streets west of here make up **Bahama Village** , where the city's Caribbean atmosphere is at its strongest, with modest but often charming wooden houses. The Blue Heaven restaurant (*see page 215*) at 729 Thomas Street serves very good conch food and is popular with a young crowd.

La Te Da ⓗ (1125 Duval Street; tel: 305-296-6706) is a popular gay restaurant and bar that hosts drag shows a couple of nights a week. Lovers of gingerbread architecture should make a point to visit the two-story house next door. The building's details – bottles, hearts, and spades – reputedly served as a surreptitious sign to sailors and other fun-seekers that they would be able to find wine, women, and lots of gambling inside.

A beacon at the southern end of Duval marks the **Southernmost Point ❶**. While its title of the most southern point in the USA has passed to a point on the Big Island of Hawaii, this famous landmark is still 755 miles (1,215 km) south of Los Angeles and only 90 miles (145 km) north of Cuba. You can take a refreshing dip in the sea from the beach just a stone's throw from here.

Looming over the southwest tip of the island are the remains of **Fort Zachary Taylor State Historic Site ❿** (open daily; charge; tel: 305-292-6713), part of the 19th-century fortification of the United States' southern boundary. You can wander around the grounds and visit the military museum, but the main attraction is **Key West's best public beach**. A fair distance east along the shore are two **Martello Towers**, which were part of the same defensive network.

If you have a day to spare and aren't on too tight a budget, consider the 70-mile (110-km) trip into the Gulf of Mexico to **Fort Jefferson**. Construction of the fort, which covers Garden Key in the **Dry Tortugas National Park**, was started in 1846 but never completed. America's largest coastal fort, it was occupied by Federal troops during the Civil War and later became a prison. There are camping facilities on the island and the excellent snorkeling here offers the chance to see loggerhead and hawksbill turtles.

Day trips from Key West are via high-speed catamaran. The 9-hour excursion allows 5 hours at the fort. Choose between the *Yankee Freedom* (good for those who suffer seasickness), and the higher powered *Sunny Days*. Telephone 877-243-2378 for reservations.

Hemingway was here

For many, Key West is synonymous with Ernest Hemingway (1898–1961). You can visit his home, now called the **Ernest Hemingway House and Museum ❾** (open daily; charge; tel: 305-295-1575), on the corner of Whitehead and Olivia streets. He bought the delightful Spanish colonial building in 1931 and lived here until 1940, before

Map on page 210

A highlight of July's Hemingway Days festival is the Papa Hemingway look-alike contest held at Sloppy Joe's.

BELOW: Ernest Hemingway spent many evenings here.

Map
on page
210

The sunsets on the Florida Keys are particularly spectacular.

BELOW:
celebrating sunset on Mallory Square is a Key West tradition.

moving to Cuba. In the study of the pool house out back, he worked on *For Whom the Bell Tolls* and *A Farewell to Arms*.

After a hard day at the typewriter or fishing rod, Hemingway relaxed with a drink or a fist fight at Sloppy Joe's, now called **Captain Tony's Saloon** , at 428 Greene Street. The interior, wallpapered with business cards and clippings, is a transport back to those days.

The current **Sloppy Joe's** is at the corner of Greene and Duval. Hemingway also took his ease here, when it was called the Midget Bar. Old photos on the walls and memorabilia recall the writer's visits.

The city is also known for the ballads of singer Jimmy Buffett and his Coral Reefer Band. After years of visiting Key West, he now has a permanent home here and opened the first **Margaritaville Café** (there are now several around the United States) at 500 Duval Street. Buffett has also been energetic in efforts to save Florida's manatees.

Before leaving the Keys, it's perhaps fitting to visit the final resting place of many locals, the **Key West Cemetery** (tours available, tel: 305-292-6718). An intense maze of above-ground vaults (because of the high water table and hard foundation of the land), many of the tombs are marked simply by nicknames – Bunny, Shorty, The Tailor, Mamie. Some have or had signature expressions: "Call Me for Dinner," I Told You I Was Sick," and "The Buck Stops Here."

One offers the sentiment of a grieving widow: "At Least I Know Where He's Sleeping Tonight." Hot and glaring white in the sun, the cemetery attracts egrets, hawks, and gulls to the top of the tombstones and angel statues.

Sunset spectacle

To soak in a quintessentially Key West occasion, join the daily gathering for sunset at Mallory Square. The miniature Mardi Gras of jugglers, fire-eaters, acrobats, para-sailors, bongo players, cookie peddlers, peg-legged pirates, and a flotilla of boats compete with the natural spectacle to mark the event every evening.   ❏

RESTAURANTS

The Keys

Atlantic's Edge at the Cheeca Lodge
Mile Marker 82. Tel: 305-664-4651. Open: D nightly. **$$$**
Killer views and fine New American seafood are the distinctions of this hotel dining room.

Calypso Seafood Grille
Ocean Bay Marina, 1 Seagate Blvd, Key Largo. Tel: 305-451-0600. Open: L & D Wed–Mon. **$$**
Off the tourist map, this dockside seafood favorite pulls a strong local following for the friendly service, and the inexpensive, excellent, if slightly idiosyncratic dishes. Calypso caters to a lively bar scene.

Kaiyo
81701 Old Hwy, Mile Marker 82, Islamorada. Tel: 305-664-5556. Open: L Mon, Wed & Fri, D Mon–Sat. **$$**
Chef Dawn Sieber has many a fine way with seafood, and she serves sushi as well as tempura fried sea-bass and other cooked delights. The South Beach-style setting is a big local draw.

Key Largo Crack'd Conch
Mile Marker 105. Tel: 305-451-0732. Open: L & D Thur–Mon. **$$**
A dive by anyone's standards, this old time dockside spot still serves up great greasy fritters and salads, fried fish and super beers.

Lorelei's
Mile Marker 82. Tel: 305-664-4656. Open: B, L & D daily. **$$$**
Known for drinking and dancing more than for food, Lorelei's seaside setting is an excellent stop for sunset views and seafood, although prices can seem high.

Mrs Mac's Kitchen
Mile Marker 99.4, Key Largo. Tel: 305-451-3722. Open: B, L & D Mon–Sat. **$$**
This 1950's dive is popular with locals and bargain lovers for the chunky chili, fresh dolphin sandwiches, and burgers. For the authentic experience, perch up at the counter.

Pierre's and the Green Flash Lounge
Mile Marker 81.6, Bayside. Tel: 305-664-3225. Open: D daily. **$$$**
By far the classiest dining in the Keys, this New World stunner is a winner for food, service, and one of the best views around. The high price is justified. The beach café offers a more casual oceanfront setting.

Key West

Alice's Key West
1114 Duval St (at Amelia St). Tel: 305-292-5733. Open: B, BR, L & D daily. **$$$**
Alice Weingarten has been on the Key West culinary scene from the start, and she is as fun and outrageous as her food. Look out for Alice making dinnertime rounds in her puffy toques hat.

Blue Heaven
729 Thomas St (at Petronia St). Tel: 305-296-8666. Open: B, L & D daily. **$$**
Chickens and roosters, cat and kids crawl around picnic tables, set with some of the best food around. Be sure to try the snapper in mango sauce and yummy blueberry pancakes.

Café Marquesa
600 Fleming St (at Simonton St). Tel: 305-292-1244. Open: D daily. **$$$$**
The Marquesa Hotel's elegant pocket-size restaurant serves innovative Keys cuisine, complemented by an exceptional wine list.

Louie's Backyard
700 Waddell Ave. Tel: 305-294-1061. Open: L & D daily, BR Sun. **$$$$**
Fine American and Caribbean cooking is served in a romantic seaside setting with old Key West ambience. Booking is advised for this popular spot.

PRICE CATEGORIES

Prices for a three-course dinner per person with a glass of house wine:
$ = under $25
$$ = $25–$40
$$$ = $40–$60
$$$$ = over $60

RIGHT: drag queens enjoying a drink, Key West.

TRANSPORTATION

GETTING THERE AND GETTING AROUND

GETTING THERE

By Air

Most major US airlines and many international carriers serve Florida. Fare prices are competitive, so shop around before buying a ticket. A variety of discount fares and "package deals," which can significantly cut round-trip rates, are also available. Many scheduled services are supplemented by charter flights.

Miami International Airport (MIA) is one of the busiest and best people-watching airports in the US, with more than 800 flights daily. It serves as the main artery to the Caribbean and Latin America, and offers numerous flights to New York and the nearby Bahamas throughout the day. Just 8 miles (13 km) from Downtown, the airport is a city within itself, with over 32,000 employees. It has banks, restaurants, televisions, lockers, a hotel and an airfield sundeck for that last-chance tan.

The best way to get into town from the airport is **by taxi** or **SuperShuttle van** (which costs about half as much as a taxi). Taxis operate on a "zone" system, with a fixed rate to different parts of town frequented by tourists. These are posted on the back windows of each taxi, so it's easy to confirm the exact fare to South Beach, Coconut Grove, Biscayne Bay or wherever you are staying. An official attendant at Miami Airport will flag down a taxi for you, and make sure you know where you are going.

The SuperShuttle can take up to 11 passengers at a time and operates 24 hours a day, seven days a week. Taxis and the SuperShuttle can be picked up on the airport's lower level. There are also fairly unreliable bus and train services and, of course, all the usual car rental companies.

Some international airlines use **Fort Lauderdale Airport**, about 30 miles (48 km) north of Miami. Buses, trains and taxis are available to Miami. Various car rental companies are represented at the airport. The information numbers for Miami and Fort Lauderdale airports are (305) 876-7000 and (954) 359-1200 respectively.

For a small sum you can make your flight carbon neutral at www.climatecare.org or www. carbonneutral.com.

By Sea

The Port of Miami is one of the largest cruise ports in the world and welcomes well over 2 million passengers each year, which represents 75 percent of all cruise passengers worldwide. It is just a five-minute ride from Downtown with trolley service available.

For general information, telephone (305) 371-7678.

AIRLINE NUMBERS

For information on flights to and from Miami, call the following telephone numbers:
Air Canada, tel: (888) 247-2262.
Air France, tel: (800) 237-2747.
American, tel: (800) 433-7300.
Bahamas Air, tel: (305) 593-1910.
British Airways, tel: (800) 247-9297.
Continental, tel: (800) 525-0280.

Delta, tel: (800) 221-1212.
Lufthansa, tel: (800) 645-3880.
Northwest/KLM, tel: (800) 225-2525.
Southwest Airlines, tel: (800) 435-9792.
United Airlines, tel: (800) 241-6522.
US Airways/American West, tel: (800) 428-4322.
Virgin Atlantic, tel: (800) 862-8621.

Cruise Lines

Carnival Cruise Lines
Tel: (305) 599-2600.
Discovery Cruise Line
Tel: (305) 597-0336.
Norwegian Cruise Line
Tel: (305) 436-4000.
**Royal Caribbean International &
Celebrity Cruises**
Tel: (305) 539-6000.
Seabourne Cruise Line
Tel: (305) 463-3000.
SeaEscape
Tel: (800) 327-2005.
Windjammer Barefoot Cruises
tel: (305) 672-6453.

Marinas

For anyone who sails into the city independently, there are over 50 marinas with 350 sq. miles (900 sq. km) of protected waters that offer dock facilities for almost any size craft. The most centrally located marinas in Miami are:
**Biscayne Bay Marriott Hotel
& Marina**
1633 N Bayshore Drive
Miami
Tel: (305) 377-3625.
Crandon Park Marina
4000 Crandon Park Boulevard
Key Biscayne
Tel: (305) 361-1281.
Dinner Key Marina
3400 Pan American Drive
Coconut Grove
Tel: (305) 579-6980.
Haulover Park Marina
10800 Collins Avenue
Miami Beach
Tel: (305) 947-3525.
Mathesson Hammock Marina
9610 Old Cutler Road
Coral Gables
Tel: (305) 665-5475.
Maule Lake Marina
17201 Biscayne Boulevard
North Miami Beach
Tel: (305) 945-0808.
Miami Beach Marina
300 Alton Road
Miami Beach
Tel: (305) 673-6000.
Miamarina at Bayside
401 Biscayne Boulevard
Miami
Tel: (305) 579-6955.

Rickenbacker Marina
3301 Rickenbacker Causeway
Key Biscayne
Tel: (305) 361-1900.

By Rail

Amtrak is the passenger line that services Miami from most points across the country. Sleeping berths and restaurant cars are available on most trains. Extended travel passes are available. A trip from New York City takes 26 hours and costs about the same as an airline ticket. For information, tel: (800) 872-7245.

Tri-Rail links Miami-Dade County with the two northern counties of Broward and Palm Beach, with services available from the Metrorail station at 79th Street. Trains operate on a varied schedule. For information, tel: (800) 874-7245.

By Car

The major Florida highways leading to Miami are I-95 along the east, I-75 along the west, and the Florida Turnpike, which connects the central part of the state to the south. On all of them the roads are excellent with clean rest stops along the way (but don't stay in them overnight). US 1 runs all the way down the east coast of the United States to Key West. It isn't a fast through-route, as it's often lined with fast-food outlets and interrupted by traffic lights, but it is a good reference point throughout the Miami area.

GETTING AROUND

Orientation

Except for South Beach and parts of Coconut Grove, Miami is not a walking city; a car is needed to explore most neighborhoods. Good maps are available at most bookstores, news-stands and gas stations. Hitchhiking is illegal.

SOUTH BEACH LOCAL

The South Beach Local is an air-conditioned, pastel-colored shuttle bus serving South Beach only. The buses run every 10 or 15 minutes from 7.45am–1am Mon–Sat, and from noon on Sun, and go to and from on a route that takes in Lincoln Road, Washington Avenue and 5th Street. The shuttles have disabled access, and the fare is just 25¢.

Public Transportation

Buses

The **Metrobus** system that operates throughout Miami-Dade County services 200,000 riders a day on 65 routes. Hours of operation depend on the route, but are generally from 5.30am–11pm. For information, tel: (305) 770-3131. For maps of the system, tel: (305) 654-6586.

Trains

Metromover and Metrorail
An elevated electric train that locals call the "People Mover," the **Metromover** has an inner loop, which circles a 26-block area of downtown Miami, and an outer loop, which covers the same area but also branches off to serve Brickell Avenue in the south and the Omni Mall in the north. Its fun ride offers dramatic views of the city's bustling center. The system operates 5.30am–midnight on both the inner and outer loops.

Metromover's big sister is **Metrorail**, which serves stations on a 21-mile (34-km) arc that connects southwest and northwest Miami with the heart of the downtown area.

The service links up with Metromover at two stations, Government Center and Brickell. Exact change in quarters is required. Transfers to Metromover are free. Hours of operation are 5.30am–midnight, with special hours to accommodate festivals and special events.

Water Taxis

Little boats known as water taxis take passengers on two main routes. The first runs from Bayside Marketplace to 5th Street Marina in South Beach. The second serves various points on the Downtown waterfront, Watson and Fisher islands, the Port of Miami and a couple of stops up the Miami River. Both run daily from 10am to 11pm. For information, tel: (954) 467-6677.

Taxis

Taxis in Miami can be expensive. You usually have to call in advance for a pick up or your hotel can do this for you. Don't try to hail one in the street; it won't stop.
Flamingo Taxi, tel: (305) 885-1002.
Society Cab, tel: (305) 757-5523.
Tropical Taxicab, tel: (305) 945-1025.
Yellow Cab, tel: (305) 444-4444.

Limousines

Limousine service is available by the hour or day.
Admiral Limousine and Transportation Services, tel: (305) 271-0722.
BKTT Limo, tel: (305) 858-5466.
Brickell Limousines, tel: (305) 541-1311.
Limousines of South Florida, tel: (305) 940-5252.

Ocean Drive Limousines, tel: (305) 374-7182.
Red Carpet Transportation, tel: (305) 444-4635.

Driving

Rental cars in Florida are pretty inexpensive. A car can be picked up at the airport or you can have it delivered to your hotel the following day. Models range from modest economy cars to limousines and luxury convertibles.

Conditions

Most rental agencies require that you are at least 21 years old (sometimes 25), have a valid driver's license and a major credit card. Some will take a cash deposit in lieu of a credit card, but this might be as high as $500.

Travelers from some foreign countries may need to produce an international driver's license from their own country.

Arrangements

Visitors wishing to rent a car after arriving in Miami will find offices of all the main US firms at the airport and in town. Smaller local rental firms outside the airport are often less expensive than the national companies, but be sure to check the insurance coverage provisions before signing anything. If you are traveling from overseas, it is normally cheaper to arrange car rental in advance. Check for package deals that include a car,

since rental rates can be reduced by about 50 percent if you buy a "fly-drive" deal. However, be wary of offers of "free" car rental, which do not include extras like tax and insurance.

Insurance

Be sure to check that your car rental agreement includes Loss Damage Waiver (LDW), also known as Collision Damage Waiver (CDW). Without it, you will be liable for any damage done to your vehicle in the event of an accident, regardless of whether or not you are to blame.

Driving Tips

Try to avoid the main highways, Interstate 95, 826, 836 and US 1, during rush hours. Pay special attention to parking signs. Many parts of South Beach have parking limited to residents only. Be warned: cars may be towed. Yellow curbs usually indicate a "No Parking Zone." Many areas use meters or ticket machines. Remember you can turn right on a red light, unless a sign indicates otherwise, but you have to come to a complete stop first.

Bicycle and Scooter Rental

For information on bicycle or scooter rentals contact:
Broken Spokes
10451 NW 7th Avenue
Miami
Tel: (305) 758-3045.
Mangrove Bicycle Rentals
260 Crandon Park Boulevard
Key Biscayne
Tel: (305) 361-5555.
Miami Beach Bike Center
601 5th Street
Miami Beach
Tel: (305) 674-0180.

Inline Skate Rentals

Fritz's Skate Shop
730 Lincoln Road
Miami Beach
Tel: (305) 532-1954.

CAR RENTAL AGENCIES

Alamo
Tel: US (800) 327-9633
International +1 (954) 522-0000
www.alamo.com
Avis
Tel: US (800) 831-2847
International +1 (918) 664-4600
www.avis.com
Budget
Tel: US (800) 527-0700
International +1 (305) 871-3053
www.budget.com

Dollar
Tel: US (800) 800-4000
International +1 (813) 887-5507
www.dollar.com
Hertz
Tel: US (800) 654-3131
International +1 (405) 749-4424
www.hertz.com
National
Tel: US (800) 227-7368
International +1 (612) 830-2345
www.nationalcar.com

A CCOMMODATIONS

SOME THINGS TO CONSIDER BEFORE YOU BOOK A ROOM

Hotels

Accommodations in Miami during the winter season can be expensive by American standards, particularly if you want to stay in South Beach. It's also not uncommon for hotels to charge a weekend rate that is considerably higher than the weekday rate, even if you are already a guest.

Accommodations range from romantic suites to chain motel rooms, and there are hundreds of options. Prices run from $60 to $800 (and higher) per night; discounts for weekly rates. Rates vary enormously between the popular winter season (November to April) and the other months. Be sure to check if there is a convention or fair in town, as accommodation gets very booked up.

Hotels add an additional 5 percent on top of the 6.5 percent state sales tax, and an additional 2 percent tax on all food and beverages sold, so the final bill can come as a shock.

Bed & Breakfast Inns

There are a number of smaller, more traditional accommodation options in Greater Miami and the rest of South Florida. The following agencies will point you in the right direction:

Florida Bed and Breakfast Inns
www.bbonline.com/fl/fbbi
BedandBreakfast.com
www.bedandbreakfast.com
Key West Innkeeper's Association
Tel: (800) 492-1911
www.keywestinns.com

Camping

If you want to camp or park an RV there are two options:
Miami Everglades KOA
20675 SW 162nd Avenue
Tel: (305) 233-5300
Campsites for tents and RV hook-ups. Near Monkey Jungle south of Miami.
Larry and Penny Thompson Park
Operated by the Miami-Dade County Parks and Recreation Dept, 12451 SW 184th Street
Tel: (305) 232-1049.
Campsites for two or four people near Miami Metrozoo.

Condo & House Rentals

There are many real estate companies in the area that specialize in renting condominium apartments and houses to tourists. Lengths of stay can be anything from a week to a year, and options range from studio apartments to waterfront estates.

Most come fully equipped with furnishings and cookware; some even have maid service. Almost all require security deposits. For information, try:
Century 21, tel: (305) 235-2621 or (305) 264-6000.
Coconut Grove Realty, tel: (305) 448-4123.
Keyes, tel: (305) 443-7423.
Renters Paradise, tel: (305) 865-0200.

CHAIN HOTELS

These chain hotels are represented in the Miami area:
Best Western, tel: (800) 528-1234.
www.bestwestern.com
Days Inns of America, tel: (800) 325-2525.
www.daysinn.com
Hilton, tel: (800) HILTONS.
www.hilton.com
Holiday Inn, tel: (800) HOLIDAY.
www.holidayinn.miami.ichotelsgroup.com
Hyatt, tel: (800) 228-9000.
www.hyatt.com
Marriott, tel: (800) 228-9290.
www.marriott.com
Radisson, tel: (800) 333-3333.
www.radisson.com
Sheraton, tel: (800) 325-3535.
www.sheraton.com

ACCOMMODATIONS LISTINGS

SOUTH BEACH

Astor Hotel
956 Washington Avenue
Tel: (305) 531-8081,
(800) 270-4981
www.hotelastor.com.
Understated stylishness is the hallmark of this Deco hotel. Bedrooms – mostly suites – and their wall-to-wall marble bathrooms come in muted creams and beiges. The pool is striking, and Astor Place is one of South Beach's top restaurants. **$$$**

Avalon & Majestic
700 Ocean Drive
Tel: (305) 538-0133
www.southbeachhotels.com
Two of the less expensive, simpler Deco hotels on Ocean Drive – run as one single operation, popular with a young crowd. Bedrooms can be dated, but a fun bar in the Avalon there is a fun bar with a mermaid mural, and a good long-standing restaurant, A Fish Called Avalon. Rates are slightly lower in The Majestic next door. **$$**

Best Western South Beach
1050 Washington Avenue
Tel: (305) 674-1920,
(888) 343-1930
Fax: (305) 672-0646
www.bestwestern.com/southbeach
Within walking distance of Ocean Drive, shops, restaurants, nightclubs and the beach, this Art Deco-style hotel holds true to the architecture and colors of the 1930s with a series of little bungalows and 135 rooms and suites. Multilingual staff. **$$**

Breakwater Hotel
940 Ocean Drive
Tel: (305) 532-8250
www.breakwatercondohotel.com
Opened in 2006, another new luxury condo-hotel (a merge of the old Breakwater and Edison hotels) with self-contained rooms. The 95 guest rooms feature a mix of Art Deco and contemporary decor, each with a 42-inch plasma TV, all-marble bathroom, and Egyptian cotton bedding. Twin towers have rooftop sundecks. **$$$**

Cardozo Hotel
1300 Ocean Drive
Tel: (305) 535-6500,
(800) 782-6500
www.cardozohotel.com
Owned by Gloria Estefan, a Streamline Moderne masterpiece that is bathed in purple neon at night. A lively bar, seductive dining terrace, and eye-catching bedrooms with hardwood floors, iron beds and zebra-striped furniture. **$$**

Casa Grande
834 Ocean Drive
Tel: (305) 672-7003
Fax: (305) 673-3669
www.casagrandesuitehotel.com
Stunning, tropically decorated suites with original art, mahogany beds, Indonesian furniture and fully-kitted kitchens. The service is without fault. **$$$**

The Clay Hotel and International Hostel
1438 Washington Avenue
Tel: (305) 534-2988,
(800) 379 CLAY

www.clayhotel.com
This well-run hotel-cum-youth-hostel, once owned by Al Capone's gambling syndicate, takes up a large chunk of Española Way, with its 1920s Mediterranean Revival-style architecture. The bedrooms – some with shared, some with private bathrooms – and the small dormitories are basic but clean and well maintained. **$**

Delano Hotel
1685 Collins Avenue
Tel: (305) 672-2000,
(800) 555-5001
www.delano-hotel.com
Dubbed by some trendsetters as America's coolest hotel, this high-rise late-Deco block has been turned into a post-modern *tour de force* by New York entrepreneur Ian Schrager and French designer Philippe Starck. A catwalk of a lobby, a chic palm-fringed pool and clinically white minimalist bedrooms all delight and dazzle. **$$$**

Essex House
1001 Collins Avenue
Tel: (305) 673-6595,
(800) 553-7739
www.essexhotel.com
With porthole windows and a neon tower, this classic, salmon-pink Deco hotel has nautical echoes. It has undergone a faithful restoration, and is refreshingly unflashy inside, but a few guests have been underwhelmed. **$$**

European Guest House
721 Michigan Avenue
Tel: (305) 673-6665
Fax: (305) 672-7442
www.europeanguesthouse.com
South Beach's only gay B&B in the heart of the Art Deco district. Rooms furnished with Queen Anne furniture. Amenities include garden Jacuzzi and buffet breakfast. **$$**

The Hotel
801 Collins Avenue
Tel: (305) 531-2222
www.thehotelsouthbeach.com
American fashion designer Todd Oldham has turned the former Art Deco Tiffany Hotel into a glamourous pad that is utterly different from the competition. Instead of garish colors, he has chosen soothing blues, greens and yellows, and instead of paintings there are mirrors – ideal for the hotel's model-world clientele. Disarmingly informal except in tie-dyed shirts, and a slick rooftop pool. **$$$**

Hotel Victor
1144 Ocean Drive
Tel: (305) 438-1234
Fax: (305) 421-6281
www.victorhotelsouthbeach.com
Created by Parisian designer Jacques Garcia, the hotel retains the look and decadence

of the 1930s mixed with a sophisticated French style. Located next to the Versace Mansion. The hotel has a raised, rimless pool overlooking the Atlantic. **$$$**

The Kent
1131 Collins Avenue
Tel: (305) 604-5068,
(866) 826-KENT
www.thekenthotel.com
One of the best-value SoBe hotels. A trendy lobby (hip-hop music, burning joss-sticks), small but good-quality bedrooms, and a lovely jungle-like garden. **$$**

Loews Miami Beach Hotel
1601 Collins Avenue
Tel: (305) 604-1601
www.loewshotels.com
This luxury 800-room giant of a hotel occupies a new tower and a restored Deco block. Bedrooms are ordinary, but there is a fantastic pool, every conceivable facility, a children's club and direct beach access. Popular with conventioneers. **$$$**

Marlin Hotel
1200 Collins Avenue
Tel: (305) 604-3505
www.marlinhotel.com
This lilac-colored Art Deco building houses a hip, all-suite hotel and a recording studio (U2 and Aerosmith have made albums here). Rooms have outlandish "Afro-urban" décor (a combination of exotic furniture and stainless-steel kitchens). The bar often has live music in the evenings, which is quite a scene. **$$$**

National Hotel
1677 Collins Avenue
Tel: (305) 532-2311,
(800) 327-8370
www.nationalhotel.com
Landmark Art Deco

tower with one of SoBe's most stunning pools (pencil thin and nearly 70 yards/meters long). Rooms in the main building are understated, while those with terraces overlooking the pool are tropically themed. **$$$**

Park Central
640 Ocean Drive
Tel: (305) 538-1611,
(800) 727-5236
www.theparkcentral.com
This lilac and purple confection is one of South Beach's least snooty Deco hotels. It has 1930s furniture in the bedrooms and an original terrazzo floor in the lobby. **$$**

Pelican Hotel
826 Ocean Drive
Tel: (305) 673-3373,
(800) 773-5422
www.pelicanhotel.com
The wackiest hotel in South Beach. Each tongue-in-cheek bedroom in this 1950s motel is like a movie set: Psychedelic(ate) Girl could be from an *Austin Powers* film; Best Whorehouse from a spoof Western. The suites (the penthouse has nine TV screens, a giant fish tank and a Jacuzzi) are celebrity territory. **$$$**

Raleigh Hotel
1775 Collins Avenue
Tel: (305) 534-6300
(800) 848-1775
Fax: (305) 538-8140
www.raleighhotel.com
The ambience is sympathetic to the Art Deco architecture, and the hotel pool, with its distinctive shape and cascading waterfall, is one of the most beautiful in Miami. Poolside massages are another amenity. The Raleigh's understated elegance and relaxed atmosphere make the hotel very popular with a cool New York crowd. Free Raleigh bicycles for the use of guests; cabanas, hammocks and a private entrance to the beach. **$$$**

Royal Palm Resort
1545 Collins Avenue
Tel: (305) 604-5700,
(866) 821-5700
Fax: (305) 604-5700
www.royalpalm.com
One block from the stylish and sometimes quirky stores of Lincoln Road, and within walking distance of the Miami Beach Convention Center. One- and two-bedroom suites, many with an ocean view, and two swimming pools, one with an ocean view, one beachside. Art Deco lobby and multilingual staff. **$$–$$$**

The Standard Miami
40 Island Avenue
Tel: (305) 673-1717
Fax: (305) 673-8181
www.standardhotel.com
Located on lush Belle Isle, on the eastern edge of Venetian Causeway, this radical renovation of the old Lido Spa, by über-cool hotelier André Balazs, has

stunning views of Miami sunsets and, naturally, a distinctive array of water experiences for the bronzed and the beautiful. There's a shuttle service to its sister hotel, the Raleigh. **$$$**

The Tides
1220 Ocean Drive
Tel: (305) 604-5070,
(800) OUTPOST
www.thetideshotel.com
The sleek white oceanfront block contains a small luxury hotel of immaculate taste. The giant, minimalist bedrooms are really special, and the terrace provides wonderful viewing of the activities on Ocean Drive without having to be a part of it. Most rooms have uninterrupted views of the beach, with telescopes to watch the sea. There's also a good-sized swimming pool. **$$$**

The Winterhaven
1400 Ocean Drive
Tel: (305) 673-6595
(800) 553-7739
Fax: (305) 538-6387
www.winterhavenhotelsobe.com
A restored Art Deco hotel near the northern boundary of Ocean Drive, the Winterhaven has an elevated grand patio, a two-story lobby with polished terrazzoed floors, and a winding staircase with multi-level mezzanine. Most guest rooms have a view of the Atlantic. **$$–$$$**

PRICE CATEGORIES

Price categories are for a double room in winter (November–March):
$ = under $100
$$ = $100–250
$$$ = more than $250

MIAMI BEACH

Bal Harbour Sheraton
9701 Collins Avenue
Bal Harbour
Tel: (305) 865-7511
Fax: (305) 864-2601
www.sheraton.com/balharbour
A full-service luxury hotel on the beach, featuring several restaurants indoors and out, situated across the street from the chi-chi Bal Harbour Shops. A favorite spot for VIPs visiting the area. **$$$**

Bay Harbor Inn & Suites
9601 E Bay Harbor Drive
Bay Harbor Islands
Tel: (305) 868-4141
Fax: (305) 867-9094
www.bayharborinn.com
Situated beside Indian Creek, this is a pleasantly petite surprise among the area's big, brooding hotels. There are two excellent restaurants and several more in the neighborhood. **$$**

Beach House
9449 Collins Avenue, Surfside
Tel: (305) 535-8600,
(800) 327-6644
Fax: (305) 861-6596
www.thebeachhousehotel.com
Be in the lap of luxury yet just a short walk from the Bal Harbour Shops. With its own beach, you'll feel like you've escaped to a serene Caribbean island. **$$$**

Best Western Oceanfront Resort
9365 Collins Avenue, Surfside
Tel: (305) 864-2232
Fax: (305) 864-3045
www.bwoceanfront.com
A simple, newly renovated motel on the beach and within walking distance of Surfside's amenities. **$**

Casablanca on the Ocean
6345 Collins Avenue
Miami Beach
Tel: (305) 868-0010,
(800) 813-6676
Fax: (305) 861-7473
www.casablancaontheocean.com
Art Deco extended into the 1950s in true MiMo style, and the lobby holds true to that latter era with natural stone and open spaces. Condo-style rooms come with complete kitchens. Hotel overlooks the scenic and well-trafficked Intra-Coastal Waterway. **$$**

Deauville Beach Resort
6701 Collins Avenue
Miami Beach
Tel: (305) 865-8511,
(800) 327-6656
Fax: (305) 865-8154
www.deauvillebeachresort.com
An excellent example of MiMo architecture and the early glory of Miami Beach (attracting celebs from Hollywood stars to the Beatles, who performed on the *Ed Sullivan Show* from here), and now still a stylish place to stay. The on-site Arturo Sandoval Jazz Club continues the hotel's musical history. **$$$**

BELOW: the lobby of the Indian Creek Hotel.

Eden Roc Renaissance Resort & Spa
4525 Collins Avenue
Miami Beach
Tel: (305) 531-0000,
(800) 327-8337
www.edenrocresort.com
A stalwart of Miami Beach hotels, with 349 hotel rooms right on the beach and two ocean-front pools. The Italian marble and mahogany reception desk sets the MiMo style. **$$–$$$**

Fontainebleau Resort and Spa
4441 Collins Avenue
Miami Beach
Tel: (305) 538 2000
Fax: (800) 548-8886
www.fontainbleauresorts.com
Probably Miami Beach's most famous hotel, this extensively renovated 1950s landmark has every amenity you can imagine and one of the best swimming pools in the city. **$$$**

Indian Creek Hotel
2727 Indian Creek Drive
Tel: (305) 531 2727,
(800) 491 2772
www.indiancreekhotel.com
An Art-Deco delight built in 1936: unlike most of its competitors, it's decorated throughout with original period furniture. It also has a lovely

secluded garden and pool, but its hidden-away location is a slight drawback for anyone who expects to be nearer the beach or the bright lights of South Beach. There *is* a romantic restaurant. **$$**

The Jefferson House
1018 Jefferson Avenue
Tel: (305) 534-5247
www.thejeffersonhouse.com
B&B with 11 rooms and a pool in a quiet residential neighborhood not too far from the South Beach pulse. Gay friendly. **$$–$$$**

Sea View Hotel
Bal Harbour
9909 Collins Avenue
Bal Harbour
Tel: (305) 866-4441,
(800) 447-1010
www.seaview-hotel.com
A completely renovated 14-story English-style beachfront hotel with Mediterranean cabanas. Located directly across the street from the trendy Bal Harbour Shops. Includes a walking and jogging path. **$$**

Tropics Hotel & Hostel
1550 Collins Avenue
Miami Beach
Tel: (305) 531-0361
Fax: (305) 531-8676
Another clean space a block from the beach with a choice of dormitory or private rooms with fridges, stoves and ceiling fans. **$**

DOWNTOWN MIAMI

Courtyard by Marriott – Miami Downtown
200 SE 2nd Avenue
Tel: (305) 374-3000
Fax: (305) 374-5897
Full-service hotel with more than 230 guest-rooms, nearly all with balconies, including 25 one-bedroom suites. Located near Bayside Marketplace, Brickell Avenue and other key Downtown venues. **$$**

Hotel Inter-Continental
100 Chopin Plaza
Tel: (305) 577-1000,
(800) 327-3005
Fax: (305) 577-0384

www.intercontinental.com/miami
A soaring, high-rise hotel with 639 rooms, gourmet restaurants, pool, skyline views, fitness center and a jogging track on the bay in the heart of downtown Miami. **$$$**

Hyatt Regency
400 SE 2nd Avenue
Tel: (305) 358-1234
Fax: (305) 374-1728
www.miamiregency.hyatt.com
On the north bank of the Miami River, the Hyatt is a popular and well-run Downtown hotel for business travelers. **$$**

Miami River Inn B&B
118 SW South River Drive
Tel: (305) 325-0045
Fax: (305) 325-9227
www.miamiriverinn.com
Classic inn located on the Miami River built between 1906 and 1914, and restored in the 1980s by local preservationist Sallye Jude. The four wood-frame buildings house 40 antique-decorated rooms offering a cozy slice of Miami history. **$$**

Radisson Hotel Miami
1601 Biscayne Boulevard
Tel: (305) 374-0000,

(800) 333-3333
www.radison-miami.com
Overlooking Biscayne Bay and downtown Miami, with a Metrorail connection providing easy access around the city, plus a scheduled shuttle service to Bay-side Marketplace and South Beach. **$$**

CORAL GABLES, COCONUT GROVE AND KEY BISCAYNE

The Biltmore Hotel
1200 Anastasia Avenue
Coral Gables
Tel: (305) 445-1926,
(800) 727-1926
Fax: (305) 913-3159
www.biltmorehotel.com
A magnificent, historic hotel and resort with 278 rooms, a vast pool, fine restaurants, golf, tennis, health spa and lounge. **$$$**

Hotel Place St Michel
162 Alcazar Avenue
Coral Gables
Tel: (305) 444-1666
Fax: (305) 529-0074
www.hotelstmichel.com
Classic, small, historic hotel in the middle of the Coral Gables business district with antiques galore and an elegant French restaurant. **$$**

Mayfair Hotel & Spa
3000 Florida Avenue
Coconut Grove
Tel: (305) 441-0000
Fax: (305) 443-9284
www.mayfairhotelandspa.com
A European-style luxury

condo hotel with an indoor atrium. Each room has a private terrace with a Japanese hot tub. **$$$**

Mutiny Hotel
2951 S. Bayshore Drive
Coconut Grove
Tel: (305) 441-2100,
(888) 868-8469
Fax: (305) 441-2822
www.mutinyhotel.com
Located in Sailboat Bay on the edge of Coconut Grove, each of the rooms in this all-suite hotel have either a bay or a city view. **$$$**

Omni Colonnade Hotel
180 Aragon Avenue
Coral Gables
Tel: (305) 441-2600,
(800) 843-6664
Fax: (305) 445-3929
www.omnicolonnade.com
A prestigious hotel in downtown Coral Gables with 157 rooms and a pool, shops, Jacuzzi and small gym. **$$$**

Residence Inn by Marriott – Coconut Grove
2835 Tigertail Avenue

Coconut Grove
Tel: (305) 285-9303,
(800) 331-3131
www.residenceinn.com/miaco
This all-suite hotel is located near the shopping areas and within walking distance of all the popular places in the Grove. Complimentary breakfast included. **$$**

The Ritz-Carlton, Key Biscayne
455 Grand Bay Drive
Key Biscayne
Tel: (305) 365-4500,
(800) 241-3333
Fax: (305) 365-4501
www.ritzcarlton.com
This resort features a signature spa, two restaurants overlooking the Atlantic and a tennis court garden. **$$$**

Silver Sands Beach Resort
301 Ocean Drive
Key Biscayne
Tel: (305) 361-5441
Fax: (305) 361-5477
www.key-biscayne.com
An intimate, peaceful

setting for a 69-room hotel. Motel-like rooms with fridge, or four cottages with kitchen and living room. **$$**

Wyndham Grand Bay Hotel
2669 Bayshore Drive
Coconut Grove
Tel: (786) 206-7122
Fax: (786) 206-7123
www.wyndham.com
This modern building features luxurious rooms and bay views. **$$$**

PRICE CATEGORIES

Price categories are for a double room in winter (November–March):
$ = under $100
$$ = $100–250
$$$ = more than $250

EXCURSIONS

The Gold Coast

The Breakers
1 S County Road, Palm Beach
Tel: (561) 655-6611
www.thebreakers.com
One of the grand hotels of the 1920s, this ocean-front landmark has 572 luxurious rooms, pools, beach, croquet, golf, tennis and nightclub. **$$$**

Colony Hotel
525 E Atlantic Avenue
Del Ray Beach
Tel: (561) 276-4123
www.thecolonyhotel.com
This local landmark has been on the main street of Del Ray since 1926. A recent renovation has attracted a younger, wealthy set, who enjoy the private beach and oceanfront club with cabanas and a heated salt-water pool. **$$$**

Riverside Hotel
620 E Las Olas Boulevard
Fort Lauderdale
Tel: (954) 467-0671,
(800) 325-3280
www.riversidehotel.com
Located in the downtown shopping district, this historic hotel has 117 antique-furnished rooms, a pool, restaurants and lounge. **$$$**

West Coast

Ritz-Carlton Naples
280 Vanderbilt Beach Road
Naples
Tel: (239) 598-3300,
(800) 241-3333

PRICE CATEGORIES

Price categories are for a double room in winter (November–March):
$ = under $100
$$ = $100–250
$$$ = more than $250

www.ritzcarlton.com/naples
One of the more elegant hotels on the Gulf of Mexico, with 464 rooms, lavish public areas, pools, restaurants, tennis courts, golf course, fitness center, sailing and children's activities. **$$$**

South Seas Plantation Resort
South Seas Plantation Road
Captiva Island
Tel: (800) CAPTIVA
www.southseas.com
A 600-room resort on the beach with four restaurants, fishing, golf, tennis, pools, sailing school, children's programs and health club. **$$$**

Sundial Beach Resort
1451 Middle Gulf Drive
Sanibel Island
Tel: (800) 237-6000
www.sundialresort.com
The largest all-suite hotel on the island with Gulf views, 271 suites, pools, private beach, tennis, sailing and children's activities. **$$$**

Homestead

Tropical Paradise Bed & Breakfast
19801 SW 318th Street
Homestead
Tel: (305) 248-4181
Fax: (305) 245-0318
A small (one suite) and cozy home sitting in a tropical fruit grove 10 minutes from the Everglades and Biscayne National Parks. **$$**

The Florida Keys

Bay Cove Motel
MM 99.5, Key Largo
Tel: (305) 451-1686
www.baycovemotel.com

In the heart of Key Largo, the Bay Cove has cottages for two to four people, plus a house for eight people. Private sandy beach, as well as a dock and a boat ramp. **$$–$$$**

Cheeca Lodge
MM 82, Islamorada
Tel: (305) 664-4651
www.cheeca.com
Its main building features vast rooms with vast beds. Hurricane Donna leveled the first inn here in 1960, but its good beach (a rarity in the Keys) led super-market heiress "Chee-chee" Twitchell to rebuild the lodge. It has villas and a golf course. **$$$**

Jules' Undersea Lodge
MM103.2, Key Largo
Tel: (305) 451-2353
www.jul.com
Experience life underwater in this extraordinary, sub-aqua hotel. The only underwater lodgings in the world. **$$$**

Sunset Cove Motel
MM99 .5, Key Largo
Tel: (305) 451-0705
www.sunsetcovebeachresort.com
Traditional motel offering a taste of Old Florida. The rooms are in oceanfront cottages. **$–$$**

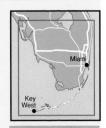

Key West

Casa Marina
1500 Reynolds Street
Tel: (305) 296-3535,
(800) 994-6597
www.casamarina.com
At the top end of the scale is this Spanish Renaissance-style hotel, one of Flagler's monuments to luxury. It has now been sympathetically restored and caters to a new generation of big spenders. **$$$**

Curry Mansion Inn
511 Caroline Street
Tel: (305) 294-5349,
(800) 253-3466
www.currymansion.com
A grand Victorian-style mansion turned into a charming 28-room inn with a pool and lush gardens. **$$**

Island City House Hotel
411 William Street
Tel: (305) 294-5702,
(800) 634-8230
www.islandcityhouse.com
Off the main strip, this tropical garden hotel has 24 suites with kitchens, swimming pool and Jacuzzi. **$$**

The Pier House
1 Duval Street
Tel: (305) 296-4600
www.pierhouse.com
This luxury resort feels like it's on its own private island, with a modern setting and a private (topless) beach. **$$$**

ACTIVITIES

THE ARTS, NIGHTLIFE, EVENTS, SHOPPING, SPORTS AND SIGHTSEEING TOURS

THE ARTS

Music & Dance

Ballet Flamenco La Rosa
13126 W. Dixie Highway
North Miami
Tel: (305) 899-7729
A professional flamenco/ballet troupe.

Florida Grand Opera
1200 Coral Way
Coral Gables
Tel: (800) 741-1010.
Miami's opera company that features artists from around the world. November–May.

Miami City Ballet Company
2200 Liberty Avenue
Miami Beach
Tel: (305) 929-7010.
Under the direction of former dancer Edward Villella, the Miami City Ballet has emerged as a provocative, stylish company. October–May.

Miami Symphony Orchestra
10300 SW 72nd Street, Suite 499, Miami
Tel: (305) 275-5666
Performs symphonic and lyric music of Spain and Latin America as well as the music of American and European composers.

New World Symphony
541 Lincoln Road
South Beach

Tel: (305) 673-3330.
An advanced training orchestra that presents gifted young musicians performing innovative concerts. October–May.

South Beach Chamber Ensemble
1300 Pennsylvania Avenue, Suite 8C, South Beach
Tel: (305) 673-2183
Chamber music performed by a core group of string quartet and piano. Performers are sometimes artists-in-residence at the Bass Museum of Art.

University of Miami, Frost School of Music
1314 Miller Drive
Coral Gables
Tel: (305) 284-2241
Presents approximately 250 concerts, recitals and various performances during the academic year (August–May).

Theater

There are several small and university-related repertory companies in the area with performances listed in the weekend section of the local press. There is no specific theater district in Miami.

Coconut Grove Playhouse
3500 Main Highway
Coconut Grove
Tel: (305) 442-4000.
Live performances in a Spanish Rococo-style theater built in the 1920s. October–June.

Colony Theater
1040 Lincoln Road
South Beach
Tel: (305) 674-1026.
Dance, music and live theater take place in this lovely, older South Beach property.

Dade County Auditorium
2901 W Flagler Street
Miami
Tel: (305) 547-5414.
A 2,500-seat auditorium staging opera, ballet and concerts.

Gusman Center for the Performing Arts
174 E Flagler Street
Downtown Miami
Tel: (305) 374-2444.
Built in 1926, the Gusman has an ornate palace interior and hosts various theater, dance and concert productions.

BUYING TICKETS

The easiest way to reserve and pay for tickets is to call the relevant box office and pay by credit card. Sometimes you will be required to make reservations through **Ticketmaster** – tel: (305) 358-5885 – which runs a pay-by-phone operation and also has outlets in some music and discount stores. Ticketmaster charges a commission fee of $2 or more above the normal ticket price.

Jackie Gleason Theater of the Performing Arts
1700 Washington Avenue
South Beach
Tel: (305) 673-7300.
Known locally as TOPA, the theater features concerts and theater productions from September–May.

Miami Performing Arts Center
1350 Biscayne Boulevard
Downtown Miami
Tel: (305) 949-6722.
The city's premier performance space. As well as state-of-the-art theaters and productions, the center is also the home of the Florida Grand Opera; the Miami City Ballet; the New World Symphony and the Concert Association of Florida.

ART GALLERIES

See pages 129–33 for more art galleries

Americas Collection
2440 Ponce de Leon Boulevard
Coral Gables
Tel: (305) 446-5578.

Bacardi Art Gallery
2100 Biscayne Boulevard
Tel: (305) 573-8511.
Works by local and international artists. Hours vary, call for information.

Britto Central
818 Lincoln Road
South Beach
Tel: (305) 531-8821.

Frederic Snitzer Gallery
2247 NW 1st Place
Tel: (305) 448-8976.

Miami International Airport Concourse Gallery
Concourse E
Great if you're killing time before a flight.

South Florida Art Center
924 Lincoln Road
South Beach
Tel: (305) 674-8278.
A center for new and established artists. Hours vary.

Virginia Miller Gallery
169 Madeira Avenue
Coral Gables
Tel: (305) 444-4493.

Cinema

In addition to many large chain theater complexes, there are a few independent movie houses in the area. Generally, afternoon matinées are less expensive than evening shows. Daily listings appear in local newspapers.

First-run Films

CocoWalk
3015 Grand Avenue
Coconut Grove
Tel: (305) 446-0450.

Fashion Island
18741 Biscayne Boulevard
North Miami Beach
Tel: (305) 466-0450.

South Beach 18
1100 Lincoln Road
South Beach
Tel: (305) 674-6766.

Sunset Place 24
5701 Sunset Drive, South Miami
Tel: (305) 466-0450.

Foreign and Art Films

Bill Cosford Cinema
University of Miami
Coral Gables
Tel: (305) 284-4861.

Miami Beach Cinematheque
512 Española Way
Tel: (305) 673-4567.

Miami-Dade Public Library
101 W. Flagler Street
Tel: (305) 375-1505.

NIGHTLIFE

Drinking

Miami has a rum-soaked, good-time reputation that is in fact warranted. Bars and clubs are scattered throughout the area. The legal drinking age is 21, and identification is required if there are any doubts. Alcoholic beverages, including beer, cannot be sold before 1pm on Sundays in some areas. Closing time for bars varies between midnight and 6am.

For complete listings of the nightlife and music scenes, refer to the *Miami Herald*'s Weekend section that comes out in Friday's paper. Also, look for the *New Times*, available in newspaper boxes on sidewalks.

Nightclubs

Amika
1532 Washington Avenue
South Beach
Tel: (305) 534-1499
Three separate areas, including a main room, a back lounge and an upstairs loft, with tasteful decor and pumping music.

Café Mystique
Days Inn Miami International Airport Hotel

TRANSPORTATION

7250 NW 11th Street
Tel: (350) 262-9500
A popular place for Miami-style salsa dancing. Cover charge on weekends for a live band.

Club Eclipse
Embassy Suites
Miami International Airport
3974 NW South River Drive
Tel: (305) 634-5000
Dancing and drinks, with room for a large crowd or a few friends.

crobar
1445 Washington Avenue
South Beach
Tel: (305) 672-8084
The huge space of the former Cameo Theater fills with party-goers, DJs, and performances from the fantastic to the kinky.

Gryphon Nightclub
5711 Seminole Way
Hollywood
Tel: (954) 581-5454
A European-style dance floor with two bars and an exclusive VIP section. Open very late.

Mansion
1235 Washington Avenue
South Beach
Tel: (305) 532-1524
A club formerly known as Prince-owned – when it was called Glam Slam. This is an old Art Deco theater converted into a giant lounge/nightclub catering to the glittering crowd, with music events and celebrity DJs.

Mango's Tropical Café
900 Ocean Drive
South Beach
Tel: (305) 673-4422
This high-octane club features a mural celebrating Haitian art and culture that has been in progress for more than a decade, as artists expand and change the mural, on and off the walls.

Nikki Beach Club
1 Ocean Drive
South Beach
Tel: (305) 538-1111
A hopping night spot described as the best club without walls, featuring DJs and beach parties. Sunday afternoons are the best.

Nocturnal Miami
50 NE 11th Street, Miami
Tel: (305) 576-6996

A casual but sophisticated atmosphere for dancing, dining or lounging on suede seats, backed by a tranquil waterfall.

Opium Garden
136 Collins Avenue
South Beach
Tel: (305) 531-5535
Open-air club with a strict door policy and featuring house and hip-hop music. Separate rooms for listening or dancing. A private, upstairs lounge caters for celebs and A-listers only.

Paradise Lounge
Howard Johnson Plaza Hotel –
Miami Airport
7707 NW 103rd Street
Tel: (305) 825-1000
Popular not only because of its location for those passing through, but also for a large space for groups and friends.

Bars

Automatic Slim's
1216 Washington Avenue
South Beach
Tel: (305) 695-8476
Popular bar with locals and well-situated on Washington Avenue, a major party thoroughfare. Open nightly with rotating DJs.

B.E.D.
929 Washington Avenue
South Beach
Tel: (305) 532-9070
An acronym for Beverage Entertainment Dining, this venue offers a chance to dine and lounge like Roman emperors, reclining on huge mattresses and pillows.

Blue
222 Española Way
South Beach
Tel: (305) 534-2274
One of the city's longest running bars, with a futuristic ambiance and blue decor.

Boom Box
423 16th Street
South Beach
Tel: (305) 538-8282
Promoter-theme parties and a variety of DJs feature Old Skool, hip-hop, reggae, indy, punk and retro.

Chamber Lounge
2940 Collins Avenue

South Beach
Tel: (305) 673-0338
Set in a hotel basement, but without the hotel. Trendy and popular, with a juke box and DJs.

Churchill's Hideaway
5501 NE 2nd Avenue
Little Haiti
Tel: (305) 757-1807
A bit seedy, but this is the place for local music in a neighborhood bar setting. Be alert at night.

Fallabella Bar
1650 James Avenue
Albion Hotel
South Beach
Tel: (305) 913-1000
Looks like a beauty salon, complete with chairs and hair dryers, but the drinks are popular and stylish. Resident DJs.

Laundry Bar
721 Lincoln Lane
South Beach
Tel: (305) 531-7700
Friendly DIY laundry with a bar. The drinks menu is almost as long as a laundry list, with music and friendly staff. Open late.

Mac's Club Deuce
222 14th Street
South Beach
Tel: (305) 531-6200
A local bar that's held its own despite the encroachment of SoBe's nightlife frenzy.

Playwright Irish Pub
1264 Washington Avenue
South Beach

ACCOMMODATIONS

ACTIVITIES

A – Z

Tel: (305) 534-0667
Casual place for a pint and a bite. Eight beers on tap plus classic Brit food like roast beef and fish 'n' chips.

Tobacco Road
626 S Miami Avenue
Tel: (305) 374-1198
Live "kick-ass" music nightly, featuring many local bands – jazz, blues and rock 'n' roll in an unpretentious setting.

Gay Clubs

Most South Beach clubs are a mix of gay, lesbian and straight. Check weekly publications for theme nights. The following places are predominantly gay and lesbian:

Score
727 Lincoln Road
South Beach
Tel: (305) 535-1111
Gay and mixed club hosting themed events – Sunday tea dance, Monday live cabaret with local drag queens, Tuesday gay Latin night.

Twist
1057 Washington Avenue
South Beach
Tel: (305) 53TWIS

EVENTS

Festivals occur all year round in warm-weather Miami. Specific dates change yearly but months usually remain constant.

January

Orange Bowl Classic (Jan 1). The big game between two nationally ranked college football teams at Dolphin Stadium on New Year's Day.

Art Deco Weekend (mid-Jan), Ocean Drive, between 5th and 14th streets. The heart of South Beach closes to motor vehicles, and visitors stroll along enjoying booths of collectibles and food, and street entertainers. Events include a week-long series of old

movies and lectures about Deco, and tours of the Art Deco district.

South Beach Dachshund Winterfest (mid-Jan). Held at Lummus Park, the event is complemented by the Tides Hotel on Ocean Drive, which puts on the dog festival, with champagne and plenty of photo opportunities.

Art Miami (Jan). Held in the Miami Beach Convention Center, this event attracts art dealers from 18 countries representing emerging artists. Displays include 20th-century and modern art – paintings, sculpture, photography.

Taste of the Grove (mid/late-January). Samples from Coconut Grove's finest restaurants, chef demonstrations, and jazz and rock performances fill the air with wondrous smells and sounds at Peacock Park, MacFarlane Road.

Beaux Arts Festival of Arts (mid/late-Jan). The University of Miami campus fills with artists whose works include watercolor, print, jewelry, ceramic, glass and wood, from around the country.

February

Coconut Grove Arts Festival (mid-Feb). The grandfather of the outdoor art scene; for three days Coconut Grove overflows with the works of hundreds of artists from all over the world. Includes a variety of food and music.

Miami Film Festival (mid-Feb). A week-long feast recognized as one of the leading American film festivals, held at the good-looking Gusman Center.

Miami International Boat Show (mid-Feb). Thousands of boats and the latest in marine accessories on display in marinas throughout the beach area and in the Miami Beach Convention Center, attracting international visitors.

Coral Gables Bluesfest (late Feb). Local and national blues bands perform in front of the Fritz & Franz Bierhaus bar. Austrian, German, American and Creole food add to the enjoyment.

March

The **NASDAQ-100 Open Tennis Championships** (late Feb–early March), held on Key Biscayne. Some of the best players in the world compete for millions of dollars in prize money. The glitterati crowd pay dearly for the championship's limited tickets.

Carnaval Miami/Calle Ocho Festival (early March). Miami's Latin flavor takes center stage. The festival includes 10 days of events and concerts culminating in the frenzy of the world's biggest block party on Little Havana's Calle Ocho.

Miami International Orchid Show (early March). More than 500,000 rare and exotic blooms from nearly 200 professional, amateur and orchid *aficionados* continue a long-running tradition. A cake-decorating competition is also held, with chefs decorating in orchid themes.

Winter Party Weekend (early March). A week filled with fun in the sun and some of the best parties for gays and lesbians in Miami. Funds are raised to support the Dade Human Rights Foundation, which fights discrimination against gays and lesbians.

Miami Riverday (late March). Held at José Martí Park, this celebration of the area's natural resources invites people to experience the Miami River with live music, boat tours, water taxis, historical re-enactments and environmental education booths. The food is local and good.

Miami Winter Music Conference (late March). Hundreds of parties are held in the city's clubs with non-stop dancing and networking. A showcase for new acts and the hottest DJs; some business deals even manage to take place in between the 24-hour, high-energy antics.

Miami Dade County Fair and Exposition (late March–early April). Carnival rides, home-grown food, circus acts, and student exhibits are featured at The Fair Expo Center.

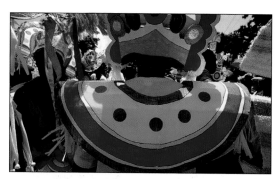

April

Merrick Festival (early April). Coral Gables hails its city founder, George Merrick, with French and Italian movies, "Taste of the Gables" cuisine, art exhibits and live performances.

Miami Gay and Lesbian Film Festival (late April). The Art Deco Colony Theater, along with various venues around town, hosts scores of full-length and short features from around the world with gay and lesbian themes.

May

Miami Fashion Week of the Americas (early May). Dozens of designers from Latin America, Asia, Europe and the Caribbean launch their latest creations at a fashion tent erected at 21st Street and Collins Avenue in South Beach, each vying for attention and awards.

June

Miami/Bahamas Goombay Festival (early June). Coconut Grove's Grand Avenue is turned into Nassau's Bay Street as colorful junkanoo dancers fill the air with Caribbean rhythms. There's lots of conch to consume in every form, plus island arts and crafts.

July

Everglades Music and Crafts Festival. The Miccosukee Indian Village, 30 miles (48 km) west of Miami on SW 8th Street, hosts this festival focusing on the many facets of American Indian heritage.

August

Miami Reggae Festival. One of the largest reggae events in the US, this is a day packed with local, national and international musicians, arts and crafts and food, held in downtown Miami's Bayfront Park.

September

Festival Miami (mid-Sept–late Oct). This month-long festival of sound features performances of chamber, orchestra, choral and solo repertoires, as well as jazz, contemporary and opera at Gusman Hall, on the University of Miami campus in Coral Gables.

Arabian Knights Festival. Set against the Moorish and Arabian backdrop of Opa-locka, this bazaar celebrates a diverse cultural heritage and features a parade, ethnic foods and entertainment.

October

Columbus Day Regatta (mid-Oct). One of the oldest and largest sailing competitions, this gathering has been called the Mardi Gras of sailing, with thousands of beer-swilling party-goers cheering on the 200 or so boats that sail through beautiful Biscayne Bay and Biscayne National Park.

November

Miami Book Fair International (mid-Nov). Lectures, readings, book exhibitions, sales and signings as respected authors from around the world gather to share their craft with half a million fans. The fair is held on the Downtown campus of Miami-Dade College.

South Miami Art Fair (mid-Nov). Yet another outdoor arts festival with entertainment and food on the streets of South Miami.

The White Party (mid-Nov). The culmination of a week of festivities to raise funds for the fight against HIV/Aids. The formal gala takes place at Vizcaya in Coconut Grove.

Banyan Arts and Crafts Fair. Another outdoor arts festival in fun-loving Coconut Grove, but not as massive as the one held here in February.

December

Art Basel Miami Beach (early Dec). Sister to Art Basel in Switzerland, the Florida version showcases art from more than 150 galleries throughout Miami and the US, Europe, Asia and Australia. The galleries celebrate with tours, wine and late hours.

King Mango Strut Festival (mid-Dec). This spoof of the traditional King Orange Jamboree Parade brings out the offbeat side of Miamians as they march down the streets of Coconut Grove.

Junior Orange Bowl Festival, (Oct–Dec). A series of sporting events that culminates in the New Year's Eve **King Orange Jamboree Parade**, along Biscayne Boulevard in downtown Miami, and a celebration in Bayfront Park, where at midnight the Big Orange signals the beginning of the New Year.

First Night Miami Beach (Dec 31). A New Year's Eve celebration of the performing arts for the entire family. Move from event to event – dance, opera, ethnic music, face painting, etc. – as you ring in the New Year with others in an alcohol-free environment, peaking with fireworks at midnight.

CLOTHING CHART

The chart listed below gives a comparison of United States, European and United Kingdom clothing sizes. It is always a good idea, however, to try on any article before buying it, as sizes between manufacturers can vary enormously.

● **Women's Dresses/Suits**

US	Continental	UK
6	38/34N	8/30
8	40/36N	10/32
10	42/38N	12/34
12	44/40N	14/36
14	46/42N	16/38
16	48/44N	18/40

● **Women's Shoes**

US	Continental	UK
4½	36	3
5½	37	4
6½	38	5
7½	39	6
8½	40	7
9½	41	8
10½	42	9

● **Men's Suits**

US	Continental	UK
34	44	34
—	46	36
38	48	38
—	50	40
42	52	42
—	54	44
46	56	46

● **Men's Shirts**

US	Continental	UK
14	36	14
14½	37	14½
15	38	15
15½	39	15½
16	40	16
16½	41	16½
17	42	17

● **Men's Shoes**

US	Continental	UK
6½	—	6
7½	40	7
8½	41	8
9½	42	9
10½	43	10
11½	44	11

SHOPPING

Where to Shop

There are several shopping areas in Greater Miami that range from exclusive indoor malls specializing in designer clothing to outdoor, waterfront marketplaces. Most are open seven days a week and offer entertainment, too. Many South Americans make regular trips to Miami just to shop *(see also pages 50–51)*.

Large purchases can usually be shipped home on major airlines by paying a small shipping fee. Should any problems arise in purchasing or shipping, contact the **Greater Miami Chamber of Commerce**, 1601 Biscayne Boulevard, tel: (305) 350-7700, or the **County Consumer Services Department**, 140 W Flagler Street, tel: (305) 468-5900.

Shopping Malls

Aventura Mall
19501 Biscayne Boulevard
Aventura
Tel: (305) 935-1110.
If you only have time for one mainstream mall, this is it. Recent expansion includes an indoor-outdoor piazza with a 24-screen theater, and more restaurants, anchored by all the major department stores.

Bal Harbour Shops
9700 Collins Avenue
Bal Harbour
Tel: (305) 866-0311.
Elegant shopping with designer stores in abundance.

Bayside Marketplace
401 Biscayne Boulevard
Tel: (305) 577-3344.
A festive waterfront arcade designed after Quincy Market in Boston. Dozens of restaurants and stores, boat rides and live entertainment.

Cauley Square
22400 Old Dixie Highway
Tel: (305) 258-3543.
South of Kendall, this cute space has antique and craft shops.

CocoWalk
3015 Grand Avenue
Coconut Grove
Tel: (305) 444-0777.
Major retailers along with specialty boutiques and outdoor cafés.

Dadeland Mall
7535 Kendall Drive
Tel: (305) 665-6226.
A homogenized US shopping mall with large chain stores like Saks Fifth Avenue and Lord & Taylor.

Design District
Bounded by NE 36th and 42nd streets and by NE 2nd and N Miami avenues, this is a collection of showrooms featuring furniture, antiques, accessories and art that cater to interior decorators and their clients.

Dolphin Mall
11401 NW 12th Street
Tel: (305) 365-7746.
A standard mix of shopping, dining and an entertainment complex, with more than 240 outlets, retail and speciality shops.

Downtown Miami
The neighborhood of Flagler Street and South Miami Avenue bustles with shopping traffic Monday through Saturday. This is the area to find the best buys in electronics and jewelry, with lots of haggling done in Spanish. If you're looking for jewelry check out the **Seybold Building** (36 NE 1st Street, tel: (305) 374-7922), which has one of the best selections of gold, diamonds and watches.

Española Way
An east/west street in South

Beach between 14th and 15th streets, Española is a colorful few blocks of art galleries, clothing stores and unusual shops.

The Falls
8888 SW 136th Street
Tel: (305) 255-4570.
An upscale center built around beautiful (man-made) waterfalls.

Lincoln Road
Located between 16th and 17th streets in South Beach, Lincoln Road is a pedestrian-friendly, fairly chic environment, full of boutiques, galleries, restaurants and outdoor cafés.

Mary Brickell Village
Named for a Miami pioneer, this mall in the downtown area is surrounded by banyan, live oak and mahogany trees.

Miracle Mile
In the heart of Coral Gables, this tree-lined thoroughfare features specialty shops, clothing boutiques and restaurants.

Prime Outlets at Florida City
250 E Palm Drive
Florida City
Tel: (305) 248-4727.
More than 60 factory outlet stores (including Levi's and Nike), about 30 minutes' drive south of downtown Miami.

Shops at Sunset Place
5701 Sunset Drive
South Miami
Tel: (305) 663-0482.
An open-air, three-level European streetscape anchored by a 24-theater multiplex, GameWorks, IMAX theater, NikeTown and Virgin Megastore.

South Beach
Boutiques and specialty shops line Collins Avenue, Washington Avenue and Ocean Drive. Along with designer fashions you can find funky clothes, collectibles and beach kitsch.

Village of Merrick Park Shops
358 San Lorenzo Avenue
Coral Gables
Tel: (305) 529-0200
A Mediterranean-style village, complete with garden and fountains, and more than 100 luxury boutiques and restaurants, including Nieman Marcus and Nordstrom.

SPORTS

Participant Sports

With year-round perfect weather, Miami is an outdoor sports city. Among the many choices are:

Boating

Officials say there are over 40,000 registered boats in the Miami area, many of which can be rented. From one-paddle canoes to crew-equipped yachts with every possible sailboat configuration in between, Miami can provide a rental to suit everyone's needs. Facilities are available at:

Beach Boat Rentals
2400 Collins Avenue
Miami Beach
Tel: (305) 534-4307.

Club Nautico
2560 S Bayshore Drive
Coconut Grove
Tel: (305) 858-6258.

Club Nautico
3621 Crandon Boulevard
Key Biscayne
Tel: (305) 361-9217.

Club Nautico
300 Alton Road
Miami Beach
Tel: (305) 673-2505.

Haulover Marine Center
15000 Collins Avenue
Miami-Dade
Tel: (305) 945-3934.

Watersports Club
Monty's Marina
Coconut Grove
Tel: (305) 856-6559.

Fishing

From bridges, boats, piers and the surf, fishing is a common diversion in Miami. While not as good as it was 20 years ago, deep-sea fishing is, nevertheless, still big business in the area. Boats are available from the MacArthur Causeway, Haulover Marina, Watson Island, Bayside Marketplace, Collins Avenue on Miami Beach and many area marinas. Most provide bait, tackle and someone to

remove your catch from the hook. The boats are available for half or full-day trips. Common catches include pompano, snapper, grouper and the occasional shark. Bring a sun hat. Freshwater fishing is available in the Everglades, but a license is required. For fishing off the shore, try the following piers:

Newport Beach Fishing Pier
16701 Collins Avenue,
Sunny Isles Beach
Tel: (305) 949-1300 ext. 1266.
Open 24 hours. Entrance fee.

Sunshine Pier
Government Cut,
Miami Beach
Open 24 hours. Free.

Golf

Since its early days, when Miami was designed to woo tourists from the frozen northeast, golf courses in the area have been abundant and important. Both 9- and 18-hole courses are open all year round. Green fees range from $8 to $40 and reservations are suggested at most. For general information on public courses, call the **Metro-Dade County Parks and Recreation Department**, tel: (305) 755-7800, or try one of the following courses:

Bayshore Golf Course
2301 Alton Road
Miami Beach
Tel: (305) 532-3350.

Briar Bay Golf Club
9373 SW 134th Street
Tel: (305) 235-6667.

Country Club of Miami
6801 NW 186th Street
Tel: (305) 829-4700.

CYCLING

There are about 100 miles (160 km) of flat, paved bicycle paths throughout Miami-Dade County, with dozens of bicycle rental shops listed in the telephone directory. For information, call the **Bicycle/Pedestrian Program of Miami-Dade County**, tel: (305) 375-1735.

Crandon Park Golf Course
6700 Crandon Boulevard
Key Biscayne
Tel: (305) 361-9129.
Don Shula's Hotel & Golf Club
7601 Miami Lakes Drive
Miami Lakes
Tel: (800) 24-SHULA.
Doral Golf Resort & Spa
4400 NW 87th Avenue
Tel: (305) 592-2000.
Fountainebleau Country Club
9603 Fountainebleau Boulevard
Tel: (305) 221-5181.
Granada Gold Course
2001 Granada Boulevard
Coral Gables
Tel: (305) 460-5367.
Greynolds Park Golf Course
17530 W Dixie Highway
North Miami Beach
Tel: (305) 949-1741.
Haulover Golf Course
10800 Collins Avenue

JET- AND WATER-SKIING

Although restricted to certain
areas in the Miami area, both
jet-skiing and water-skiing are
year-round sports. For more
information on rental of
equipment contact:
**Greater Miami Water-Ski
Club**
1800 NW 94th Avenue
Miami
Tel: (954) 704-0948.
Club Nautico
2560 S Bayshore Drive
Coconut Grove
Tel: (305) 858-6258.
Club Nautico
300 Alton Road
Miami Beach
Tel: (305) 673-2505.
Club Nautico
3621 Crandon Boulevard
Key Biscayne
Tel: (305) 361-9217.
Haulover Marine Center
15000 Collins Avenue
Miami-Dade
Tel: (305) 546-6833.
Key Biscayne Boat Rentals
3301 Rickenbacker Causeway
Key Biscayne
Tel: (305) 361-7368.

Miami Beach
Tel: (305) 940-6719.
Miami Springs Golf Club
650 Curtiss Parkway
Miami Springs
Tel: (305) 805-5180.
Normandy Shores Golf Course
2401 Biarritz Drive
Miami Beach
Tel: (305) 868-6502.
Par Three Course
2795 Prairie Avenue
Miami Beach
Tel: (305) 674-0305.
Palmetto
9300 Coral Reef Drive
Miami
Tel: (305) 238-2922.

Scuba Diving

Although the immediate Miami
area cannot compete with other
parts of Florida, there are a gen-
erous range of diving sites on
both natural and artificial reefs.
The Miami-Dade County Artificial
Reef Program, established in
1981, has constructed over 15
artificial reefs off Miami's coasts
that have increased the habitat
available for native marine life.

For information on this interesting artificial reef program, try
contacting the **Department of
Environmental Resources Man-
agement**, tel: (305) 375-3376.

For information on **scuba
lessons** or **rental of equipment**,
try contacting:
Divers Paradise
4000 Crandon Boulevard
Key Biscayne
Tel: (305) 361-3483.
H2O Scuba
160 Sunny Isles Boulevard
Sunny Isles Beach
Tel: (305) 956-3483.
South Beach Divers
850 Washington Avenue
Miami Beach
Tel: (305) 531-6110.
Tarpoon Lagoon
300 Alton Road
Miami Beach
Tel: (305) 532-1445.
Underwater Unlimited
4633 Le Jeune Road
Coral Gables
Tel: (305) 445-7837.

Swimming

Although many hotels in Miami
have their own pools and most
people prefer swimming in the
ocean anyway, there are several
Olympic-size public pools
throughout the area. Entrance
fees vary, but hours are usually
9am–6pm. Swimming lessons
and pool-based exercise
classes are available.
Flamingo Park Pool
1200 Jefferson Avenue
Miami Beach
Tel: (305) 673-7750.
José Martí Pool
351 SW 4th Street
Little Havana
Tel: (305) 575-5265.
Miami Shores Pool
10000 Biscayne Boulevard
Miami Shores
Tel: (305) 758-8105.
Normandy Isle Pool
7030 Trouville Esplanade
Miami Beach
Tel: (305) 993-2021.
Venetian Pool
2701 DeSoto Boulevard
Coral Gables
Tel: (305) 460-5356.

Tennis

Besides the hundreds of courts
on the grounds of hotels and private homes, Greater Miami has
over 25 public tennis parks listed
in the directory. Or call the
**Metro-Dade County Parks and
Recreation Department**, tel:
(305) 755-7800.

Most public courts charge
non-residents an hourly fee. For
general information, call the
Florida Tennis Association,
tel: (386) 671-8949, or try one of
the public courts:
Flamingo Tennis
1000 12th Street
Miami Beach
Tel: (305) 673-7761.
Haulover Tennis
10800 Collins Avenue
Miami Beach
Tel: (305) 940-6719.
Judge Arthur Snyder Center
16851 W Dixie Highway
North Miami Beach
Tel: (305) 948-2947.

Kirk Munroe
3101 Florida Avenue
Coconut Grove
Tel: (305) 442-0381.
Miami Shores Tennis Center
9617 Park Drive
Miami Shores
Tel: (305) 758-8122.
North Shore Tennis Center
350 73rd Street
Miami Beach
Tel: (305) 993-2022.
Salvadore Park Tennis Center
1120 Andalusia Avenue
Coral Gables
Tel: (305) 460-5333.
Sans Souci Tennis Center
1795 Sans Souci Boulevard
Tel: (305) 893-7130.
Surfside Tennis Center
8800 Collins Avenue
Surfside
Tel: (305) 866-5176.

Windsurfing

Calm waters and constant
breezes make this a Miami
favorite. Matheson Hammock
Park offers rentals and quiet
waters for lessons. Several rental
shops are located along the
Rickenbacker Causeway heading
over to Key Biscayne, including
Sailboards Miami, tel: (305)
361-7245.

Spectator Sports

Auto Racing

The Ford Championship Weekend, held in November, is when
the roar of the engines, and the
fans, fill the stands at the Homestead Miami Speedway. For information: tel: (305) 230-RACE;
www.homesteadmiamispeedway.com

Basketball

The Miami Heat are the city's
award-winning National Basketball Association team. Home
game season usually runs
November to May. Games are
played at the American Airlines
Arena, 601 Biscayne Boulevard.
For information: tel: (786) 777-
4000; www.heat.com, 38th Court,
tel: (305) 649-3000.

BASEBALL

The Florida Marlins, Miami's
professional baseball team,
play home games at Dolphin
Stadium. For ticket information: tel: (305) 626-7400;
www.floridamarlins.com

Football

The Miami Dolphins play home
games at Dolphin Stadium in
north Miami-Dade County at
2269 NW 199th Street. On game
days public transportation is
available. For ticket information:
tel: 1-888-346-7849; www.miami
dolphins.com. For info on transportation: tel: (305) 770-3131.

Jai-Alai

Originating in the Basque region
of Spain, Jai-Alai is considered
the world's fastest game, as
players try to catch the *pelotas*
(Jai-Alai balls) that can travel at
170 mph (270 kmph). Games are
played in a court called a *fronton*.
The Miami Jai-Alai Fronton is at
3500 NW 37th Avenue. For info:
tel: (305) 633-6400.

Soccer

The Miami FC is the team playing
in the United Soccer League,
with players from throughout
Central and South America.
Games are played at Tropical
Park Stadium, 7900 SW 40th St.
For ticket information, tel: (866)
57-MIAMI or visit www.miamifc.com

Tennis

The **NASDAQ-100 Open Tennis
Championships**, held on Key
Biscayne in late Feb–early Mar,
attracts the best players in the
world. Tickets are like gold-dust
and the spectators are starry.

SIGHTSEEING TOURS

Art Deco District Tours
1001 Ocean Drive
South Beach
Tel: (305) 531-3484.
Walking tours from the Miami
Design Preservation League.
Biscayne Helicopters
Tamiami Airport
Tel: (305) 252-3883.
Customized aerial tours.
Dragonfly Expeditions
1825 Ponce de Leon, S. 369
Coral Gables
Tel: (305) 774-9019.
**Historical Museum of
Southern Florida**
101 W Flagler Street
Tel: (305) 375-1492.
With the assistance of a local
historian, the museum offers
walking tours of several Miami
neighborhoods. Times vary; call
for information.
Island Queen
Tel: (305) 379-5119.
Departs from the Hyatt Regency
Hotel for a tour of Miami's million-
aire's row on Biscayne Bay. Daily
on the hour from 11am to 7pm.
Miami Duck Tours
1665 Washington Avenue
South Beach
Tel: (786) 276-8300.
Amphibious vehicles tour for 90
minutes of sightseeing and
duck jokes. Tours start on land,
go through Miami Beach and
downtown Miami, then splash
into Biscayne Bay and back.
Miami Nice Tours
5979 NW 151st Street, Suite 206
Miami Lakes
Tel: (305) 949-9180.
Two Foot Tours
5700 Collins Avenue, S. 98
South Beach
Tel: (305) 868-8433.

A – Z

A SUMMARY OF PRACTICAL INFORMATION, ARRANGED ALPHABETICALLY

Admission Fees

Fees to attractions vary, from as little as $2.50 to $12 or more. A few venues are free. Some museums offer one day or evening a week without a fixed admission fee but request a donation. If on a budget, call ahead to check.

Budgeting for Your Trip

While Miami has become an increasingly expensive city to visit, there are ways to enjoy the ambiance and amenities of this part of Florida without running out of money. Many motels and hotels near Miami International Airport offer rooms at a modest, less-expensive rate than the luxury,

Downtown and beach hotels. Fast food restaurants are everywhere. There are also a number of good, inexpensive restaurants and Cuban cafés throughout the city, although some of the staff do not speak much English. (They can also be extremely rude, but don't take it personally.) There are Automatic Teller Machines (ATMs) throughout the city which charge a fee of at least $2.50 per transaction, but the ATMs in Publix supermarkets are often free.

If money is really tight, visit Miami in May or September. These months are officially "out of season," but the weather is not intolerably hot. Not only will attractions be less crowded with visitors, but prices in hotels and

restaurants can drop by as much as 50 percent. This is also when the city begins to take on a more local – as opposed to tourist – feel, which is very pleasant.

Business Hours

Most offices and businesses are open Monday through Friday from 9am–5 or 5.30pm, with no closing hours for lunch. Banks are usually open from 9am–3pm Monday through Friday with some opening Saturday from 9am–noon. Most large shopping centers are open from 10am–9.30pm Monday through Saturday and from noon–6pm on Sunday. Many supermarkets and some restaurants stay open 24 hours.

CLIMATE CHART

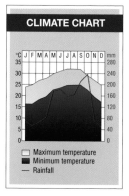

°C | J F M A M J J A S O N D | mm
35 | | 280
30 | | 240
25 | | 200
20 | | 160
15 | | 120
10 | | 80
5 | | 40
0 | | 0

☐ Maximum temperature
■ Minimum temperature
— Rainfall

C limate & Clothing

Although most Northerners cringe at the idea of a Miami summer, daytime temperatures are in fact no hotter than daytime summer temperatures in New York City. There is little variation between seasons and it is seldom cold. The average yearly temperature is 75°F (24°C), with a range from around 60°F in January to around 90°F in August (15–35°C). At night, in the summer, you will need air-conditioning or a fan to sleep in comfort. Due to the relatively mild winters, most Miami homes do not have heating systems, but erratic winter weather in recent years (including occasional snow flurries) has caught residents unprepared. Take a jacket and socks, just in case, even if you visit in January.

Definitely part of America's "Sunshine State," Miami sees sun almost 365 days a year. Summer is the rainy season, and brief but intense afternoon thundershowers can be expected almost daily in July and August. Lightning is also very common at this time of year.

Clothing

Casual, cool, lightweight and light colors are the norm. Formal clothes are rarely required. For men, a sports coat and open-necked shirt are usually acceptable at finer restaurants, with ties being optional. Shorts are acceptable for both men and women even on the streets of downtown Miami. In winter, a sweater or light jacket will usually be enough. Note that topless bathing is illegal on most beaches, but is more or less tolerated on South Beach.

If you intend to go clubbing, pack your bangles, spangles, highest heels or snazziest suits. Or just go shopping in Miami.

Children's Activities

Several of Miami's attractions are ideally suited for visiting with children. Try the **Miami Seaquarium**, **Monkey Jungle**, **Metrozoo**, **Miami Children's Museum**, and the **Miami Museum of Science & Planetarium**.

Others, such as the **Miami City Ballet**, **New World Symphony**, and **Florida Philharmonic Orchestra**, offer special performances geared toward children. And every March the **Miami-Dade County Youth Fair** features amusement rides, educational exhibits and concerts for children on fairgrounds a few miles west of the city.

Babysitters can be provided by the **International Nanny Service**, tel: (305) 949-0360.

Crime & Safety

For **police non-emergencies** in the City of Miami, tel: (305) 579-

6111; in Miami Beach or South Beach, tel: (305) 673-7900; in the rest of the county, tel: (305) 476-5423. Every municipality (e.g. Miami Beach, Coconut Grove, Bal Harbour) has its own police department, so find out which municipality you're staying in. For any areas not in a municipality, contact the Miami-Dade police.

If you report any incident, be sure to get a case number, and ask for a phone number so you can follow up on the status of your case.

While in the street, use common sense and act like a New Yorker. In other words, don't carry around large sums of money or expensive camera equipment, don't make eye contact with unwelcome strangers, and don't travel alone at night.

Although the city has definitely moved on from its *Miami Vice* days, a rash of crimes committed against tourists in the early 1990s forced the community to come up with effective safeguards to protect visitors from attacks. One of the most important is that car rental agencies have removed the special license plates which formerly earmarked rented cars, and replaced them with standard-issue plates.

A system of orange sunburst symbols on road signs has also been set up to help visitors stay on the main routes to and from the airport. If you're feeling jet-lagged, arrange to pick up your rented car near your hotel on the morning after you arrive rather than attempt to negotiate unfamiliar routes when tired. Many car rental agencies will deliver to your hotel for free, or for only a small extra charge.

Other tips: always park your car in a well-lit area, never in a shady back corner of a parking lot. Keep car doors locked and windows closed while driving through unfamiliar areas. If you're nervous coming from the airport, plot the route to your hotel in advance, with the aid of a map, or take advice from your car-rental agency.

CUSTOMS ALLOWANCE

Money: There is no limit on the amount of money – US or foreign traveler's checks or money orders – that you may bring into or take out of the US. But you must declare amounts exceeding $10,000 or the foreign currency equivalent.

Alcohol: Visitors over the age of 21 years are permitted to bring in 1 liter (34 fl oz) of alcohol (beer, wine or liquor) for their personal use. Excess quantities are subject to duty and tax.

Cigars and cigarettes: Visitors may bring in not more than 200 cigarettes (one carton), 50 cigars (as long as they are not Cuban) or 4.4 lbs (2 kg) of smoking tobacco, or proportionate amounts of each. An additional 100 cigars may be brought in under the gift exemption.

Gifts: As a visitor, you can claim up to $100 worth of merchandise, free of duty and tax, as gifts for other people. Such articles may have to be inspected, so do not gift-wrap them until after you have entered the country.

Customs Regulations

All articles brought into the US must be declared to Customs. You will be given a special form to fill in before you enter the country. Articles brought into the US are subject to duty or internal revenue tax, but visitors are given an allowance of exempted goods.

Prohibited Goods

Articles which visitors are forbidden to take into the US include:
• liquor-filled chocolates or candy
• dangerous drugs
• obscene publications
• hazardous articles (e.g. fireworks)
• most fresh food products,

unless you have an import permit
• narcotics – travelers using medicines containing narcotics (such as tranquilizers or cough medicine) should carry a prescription and/or a note from their doctor, and should take only the quantity required for a short stay.

Full details of customs requirements are available from your nearest US Embassy or Consulate.

D isabled Travelers

With an aging population, including tourists, more and more venues are prepared for travelers with disabilities. In addition, the American Disabilities Act requires equal access for the disabled at most places that cater to the public, including all government facilities.

Local agencies include the Miami-Dade Disability Services and Independent Living, 135 NW 14th Street, Miami, tel: (305) 547-5444, and also the Miami-Dade Office of ADA Coordination, 111 NW 1st Street, 12th Floor, Suite 348, Miami, tel: (305) 375-3566.

For information on apartments that cater to the disabled, go to Disabled Accommodations Miami, www.disabledapartments.com. Some hotels are making a deliberate effort to accommodate guests with disabilities, and some provide a diverse menu of services, such as the Wyndham Miami Airport Hotel, www.wyndham.com.

Deaf Services Bureau, tel: (305) 560-2866.

Miami Lighthouse for the Blind, tel: (305) 856-2288.

Miami-Dade Office of Americans with Disabilities Act Coordination, tel: (800) 514-0301.

E mergencies

All emergencies, tel: 911.
A&E Dentists, 11400 N. Kendall Drive, Mega Bank Building, Miami, tel: (305) 271-2777.
Crisis Intervention, tel: (305) 358-4357.
Dental Referral Service, tel: (800) 577-7322.
Poison Information Center, tel: (800) 282-3171.
Visitors Medical Hotline, tel: (305) 674-2222.

Entry Regulations

Most foreign visitors are required to have a passport (which should be valid for at least six months longer than their intended stay) and a visa to enter the US. You should also be able to provide evidence that you intend to leave the US after your visit is over (usually in the form of a return or onward ticket), and visitors from some countries need an international vaccination certificate.

Certain foreign nationals are exempt from the normal visa requirements. Canadian citizens with a valid Canadian passport need no visa. Nor do Mexican citizens provided they have a Mexican passport and a US Border Crossing Card (Form I-186 or I-586), and as long as they are residents of Mexico.

Since 2005, visitors from a number of countries, including the UK, who are staying for less than 90 days (you will need to be able to prove that), can waive the US visa through the Visa Waiver Pilot Program. If you are staying for more than 90 days, you will need to obtain a visa to allow you to enter the US.

EMBASSIES & CONSULATES

Bahamas: 25 SE 2nd Avenue, tel: (305) 373-6295.
Canada: 200 S Biscayne Boulevard, tel: (305) 579-1600.
Great Britain: 1001 S Bayshore Drive, tel: (305) 374-1522.

Israel: 100 N Biscayne Boulevard, tel: (305) 925-9400.
Jamaica: 25 SE 2nd Avenue, tel: (305) 374-8431.
Netherlands: 701 Brickell Avenue, tel: (786) 866-0480.

ELECTRICITY

The US uses flat two- or three-pronged plugs at 110–115 volts.

Anyone requiring a visa or visa information can apply to the US Embassy or Consulate nearest their home.

Vaccination requirements vary, but proof of immunization against smallpox or cholera may occasionally be necessary.

G ay & Lesbian Travelers

The South Beach area is well-known for its welcoming and tolerant atmosphere and is a magnet for gay and lesbian travelers, who spend over $100 million here every year. The two big events are the **White Party** (at Vizcaya on the Sunday after Thanksgiving), and the **Winter Party** (on South Beach in March), when locals and visitors go even wilder than usual.

Useful Numbers

The **Switchboard of Miami**, tel: (305) 358-4357, is a 24-hour information, referral and crisis line that can answer questions.
Gay & Lesbian Chamber of Commerce
2121 Park Avenue, Miami

Tel: (305) 673-7530
www.gogaymiami.com
Another potential resource is
www.pinkweb.com

H ealth Insurance

Most visitors to Miami will have few health problems during their stay: sunburn and mosquito bites in summer are the main nuisances. The city's medical facilities are considered some of the best in the country. In case of any medical emergency, telephone **911** and assistance will be available.

As the US has no socialized medicine and all medical care must be paid for by the individual, you should never leave home without travel insurance to cover both yourself and your belongings. Your own insurance company or travel agent can advise on policies, but shop around since rates vary. Make sure you are covered for accidental death, emergency medical care, trip cancellation and luggage or document loss.

See page 238 for more information on medical treatment and health hazards.

I nternet & Websites

WiFi (wireless Internet facility) is fast becoming available in many areas of the city. More and more hotels are gearing up to provide WiFi in their guestrooms, and some may provide a keyboard and link for a small charge. Many large hotels also have business centers that provide Internet access for a fee. E-mail can be sent from most branches of FedEx/Kinko's copy shops (many open 24 hours a day); from coffee bars and lounges; or from computers in most public libraries.

Cyber Cafes

d'Vine Cyber Lounge, 910 Collins Avenue, South Beach, tel: (305) 534-1414.
Kafka's Cybercafe & Bookstore, 1464 Washington Avenue, South Beach, tel: (305) 673-9669.

Oasis Internet Cafe, 2977 McFarlane Road, 100-A, Coconut Grove 33133, tel:(305) 446-6565
e-mail: oasisinternet@hotmail.com.

Useful websites

Greater Miami Convention & Visitors Bureau
www.MiamiandBeaches.com
Coconut Grove Chamber of Commerce
www.coconutgrove.com
Downtown Miami Welcome Center
www.downtownmiami.com
Miami Beach Latin Chamber of Commerce Visitor Information Center
www.miamibeach.org
Miami Beach Visitor Center
www.miamibeachchamber.com
Sunny Isles Beach Resort Association Visitor Information Center
www.sunnyislesfla.com
Surfside Tourist Bureau
www.townofsurfside.gov
Tropical Everglades Visitor Association
www.tropicalevergldes.com
World's Best Bars
www.worldsbestbars.com
Miami Beach 411
www.miamibeach411.com
South Beach USA
www.southbeach-usa.com

L ost Property

For lost property, depending on your length of stay, contact: Miami International Airport, tel: (305) 876-8388, or Miami-Date Transit, tel: (305) 770-3131.

M edia

Newspapers

The *Miami Herald* (www.herald.com) is Florida's most respected daily paper. It offers sound coverage of local, state and Latin American news. Its Friday edition offers a useful what-to-do weekend tabloid section. A Spanish-language sister paper, *El Nuevo Herald* (www.elherald.com), is published daily. You can usually pick up *USA Today* from dispensers in the street, while good news-stands and certain bookshops sell other national and foreign papers. The News Café, at 800 Ocean Drive in South Beach, has a large selection.

Miami New Times (www.miami newtimes.com), a free alternative weekly, delivers an offbeat view of the city. Its calendar of events rivals the *Miami Herald*'s and lets visitors know what's hot and happening. *Diario Las Americas* is a Spanish-language daily in which coverage emphasizes Cuban/Central American news, with a political bias toward the right. *Miami Times* is a weekly paper that covers news from the black community.

Television & Radio

A weekly TV guide is published on Sunday in the *Miami Herald*. Cable television stations are abundant, including many that are available in hotels and motels. The national network channels are: 2 (WPBT-PBS), 4 (WFOR-CBS), 6 (WTVJ-NBC), 7 (WSVN-FOX), 10 (WPLG-ABC). There are many Miami area channels, including locally pro-duced 69 WAMI, and several Spanish-language stations such as 23 Univision and 51 Tele-mundo. On the radio, AM fre-quencies in Miami tend to carry more talk shows and commer-cials. FM stations offer a wider range of programs and higher-quality stereo sound.

Medical Services

There are several walk-in medical and dental care offices in the Miami area. These are listed in the telephone directory under "Clinics." For dentist referrals, tel: (305) 667 3647. A 24-hour pharmacy can be found by calling Walgreens Pharmacy, tel: (305) 595-3326. *See page 236* for a list of emergency numbers.

Clinics

Around the Clock Medical Services, 1380 Miami Gardens

HOSPITALS

Baptist Hospital, 8900 N Kendall Drive, tel: (786) 596-1960.
Coral Gables Hospital, 3100 Douglas Road, Coral Gables, tel: (305) 445-8461.
Columbia Aventura Hospital, 20900 Biscayne Boulevard, Aventura, tel: (305) 682-7000.
Jackson Memorial Hospital, 1611 NW 12th Avenue, tel: (305) 585-1111.
Mercy Hospital, 3663 S Miami Avenue, Coconut Grove, tel: (305) 854-4400.
South Shore Hospital, 630 Alton Road, Miami Beach, tel: (305) 672-2100.

Drive, North Miami Beach, tel: (305) 940-9300.
Clinicaro Medical Center, 1540 Washington Avenue, Miami Beach, tel: (305) 531-6859.
Today's Woman Medical Center, 3250 S Dixie Highway, Coconut Grove, tel: (305) 441-0304.

Health Hazards

Sunburn
Severe cases of sunburn are common among visitors. The glare from the azure seas and white sands increases the sun's intensity. Use a high-factor sun-screen all the time on exposed areas and especially while swim-ming, even on cloudy days. You are most vulnerable during the first few days of a trip.

See page 239 for more tips on safety at the seaside.

Insects
During the summer, mosquitoes can be a nuisance. Sand-flies – or "no-see-ums," as locals call them – will bite at the beach in the evening; insect repellent can help. Fire ants – tiny red ants that live in mounds of dirt in grassy areas – can inflict stings that will occasionally cause an allergic reaction, so look before you sit down.

Money

Foreign visitors are advised to take US dollar traveler's checks to Miami, since exchanging for-eign currency – whether as cash or checks – can prove problem-atic. An increasing number of banks, including the First Union National Bank, Nations Bank and Sun Bank chains, offer foreign exchange facilities, but this prac-tice is not widespread. Some large department store chains offer foreign currency exchange.

Most stores, restaurants and other establishments accept traveler's checks in US dollars and will give change in cash. Alternatively, checks can be con-verted into cash at the bank, but be sure to take your passport.

Credit Cards

Credit cards are very much part of daily life in Miami, as in other parts of the US. They can be used to pay for pretty much any-thing, and it is also common for car rental firms and hotels to take an imprint of your card as a deposit. Rental companies may oblige you to pay a large deposit in cash if you do not have a card.

You can also use your credit card to withdraw cash from ATMs. Before you leave home, make sure you know your PIN and find out which ATM system will accept your card. The most widely accepted cards are Visa, American Express, MasterCard, Diners Club, Japanese Credit Bureau and Discovery.

P ostal Services

Information on Miami's postal facilities can be gleaned by tele-phoning (800) 275-8777. Post offices in Miami-Dade County are open 8.30am–5pm Monday through Friday, with most open on Saturday 8.30am–noon. Stamps are also sold at many hotels and drugstores. Overnight and express mail services are available at all post office branches, along with a general delivery service that allows out-of-towners to receive mail and parcels. Express Mail guarantees next-day delivery within the US and delivery within two or three days elsewhere in the world. Speedy delivery to most places around the world is offered by courier services such as the following:

Federal Express: tel: (800) 238-5355.
DHL: tel: (800) 345-2727.
UPS: tel: (800) 742-5877.

Post Offices

Airport Mail Facility, Miami International Airport, Miami, tel: (305) 871-3918.
Biscayne (Downtown) Branch, 2 S Biscayne Boulevard, Miami, tel: (305) 599-1744.
Coconut Grove Branch, 3191 Grand Avenue, Coconut Grove, tel: (305) 599-1750.
Coral Gables Branch, 251 Valencia Avenue, Coral Gables, tel: (305) 599-1795.
Key Biscayne Branch, 951 Crandon Boulevard, Key Biscayne, tel: (305) 361-7884.
Miami Beach Branch, 1300 Washington Avenue, Miami Beach, tel: (305) 599-1787.
Surfside Branch, 250 95th Street, Surfside, tel: (305) 639-5520.

Public Holidays

During the public holidays listed below, some or all government offices, businesses and banks may be closed. School is also in recess during these times, so local beaches and family attractions around Miami are usually pretty crowded.

January 1 New Year's Day
January 15 Martin Luther King's Birthday
February (third Monday) President's Day
May (last Monday) Memorial Day
July 4 Independence Day
September (first Monday) Labor Day
October (second Monday) Columbus Day
November 11 Veterans' Day
November (fourth Thursday) Thanksgiving
December 25 Christmas Day

R eligious Services

The following places conduct services of worship. For a larger selection, check the *Yellow Pages* under Churches or Synagogues.
St Frances De Sales (Catholic), 600 Lenox Avenue, Miami Beach, tel: (305) 672-0093.
Coral Gables Congregational Church (United Church of Christ), 3010 DeSoto Boulevard, Coral Gables, tel: (305) 448-7421.
First Church of Christ Scientist (Christian Science), 410 Andalusia Avenue, Coral Gables, tel: (305) 443-1427.
First Spanish Baptist Church (Baptist), 1790 NE 2nd Court, Miami Beach, tel: (305) 374-2766.
Ismaili Cultural Center (Muslim), 2045 NE 151st Street, North Miami Beach, tel: (954) 923-1837.
J. W. Kingdom Hall (Jehovah's Witness), 300 W 40th Street, Miami Beach, tel: (305) 532-8588.
Temple Emanu-El (Synagogue), 1701 Washington Avenue, Miami Beach, tel: (305) 538-2503.

SAFETY BY THE SEASIDE

Most people will enjoy a trouble-free time on the beach, but here are a few natural occurrences to be on the look-out for:
Marine life: if you brush against a jellyfish in the water, you will receive only a short-lived sting. But stingrays, which move close to shore in August and September to mate, can deliver a very nasty one. Seek medical help if the barb stays in the skin.

All popular beaches have lifeguards, who can advise on wave conditions. There is also a flag warning system:
● green: good swimming conditions.
● yellow: caution.
● red: danger from currents, winds or lightning.
● blue: hazardous marine life (e.g. jellyfish).
Sea currents: the waters off Miami are not dangerous, but rough surf and strong currents do occur. Most rescue operations happen when tired swimmers try to swim against a riptide or undertow and become too exhausted to continue. If you're caught in either, stay calm and don't swim against it, but instead, flow with the current.

S moking

Smoking is banned in all public buildings in Greater Miami. Hotels offer non-smoking rooms, and an increasing number are becoming no-smoking establishments. Smoking is not allowed in any place that serves food, although it's often possible to eat and smoke on outdoor terraces. Bars, lounges and cigar bars remain among the few indoor oases for smokers. Miami's balmy weather, and tropical ambiance, however, mean that it's usually possible to find pleasant outdoor spaces in which to light up.

Student Travelers

Many museums, attractions and theaters offer a discounted student rate. A student ID card is usually required although not necessarily one from the United States. Resources for obtaining an international student ID include the International Youth Travel Corp., www.isecard.com, and the International Student Travel Confederation, www.istc.org

 elecommunications

Making calls

The **305** prefix area code covers the metropolitan Miami area and the Florida Keys, and must be included in every local call. Bell South has recently added the newer area code of **786** to the Miami and Miami Beach area. Fort Lauderdale's area code is **954**, Palm Beach's area code is **561**.

To ask an operator for a Miami area number, telephone 411. To ask for a number outside of Miami but in the 305 area code, telephone 1-305-555-1212. For long-distance or international assistance, dial 0. Toll-free numbers for various businesses and services are indicated by the prefix 800. The toll-free information number is (800) 555-1212.

Public Phones

Public phones are located in numerous public places. A local call will cost 25¢ for three minutes. For long-distance calls, it is easier to use a phonecard or credit card. Credit cards can be used at any phone: dial 1-800-CALLATT, key in your credit card number and wait to be connected.

Cell Phones

European phones will not work on the American tri-band system. If you plan to stay for several weeks and are going to use a phone regularly, look into buying or renting a local cell phone. There are many retail outlets in the downtown Miami area.

Miami is on Eastern Standard Time, which is the same time zone as New York, 3 hours ahead of San Francisco and 5 hours behind Greenwich Mean Time (GMT).

Fax/Telex/Telegrams

Dozens of businesses offering communication services are listed in the telephone directory. Many are open 24 hours a day. **Kinkos,** 600 Brickell Avenue, tel: (305) 373-4910. **Western Union,** tel: (800) 325-6000.

Tipping

Tips are usually not included on most restaurant bills and the suggested rate is 15 to 20 percent. The same rate is normal for taxi drivers. Porters are readily available at the airport; a tip of $1–1.50 per suitcase is customary. Moderate hotel tipping for bellboys is about 50¢ per bag handled. You should tip a doorman if he parks your car or performs any other services.

Tourist Offices

Art Deco Welcome Center, 1001 Ocean Drive, Miami Beach, tel: (305) 672-2014**.**
Coconut Grove Chamber of Commerce, 2121 Park Avenue, tel: (305) 673-7530.
Coral Gables Chamber of Commerce, 224 Catalonia Avenue, Coral Gables, tel: (305) 446-1657.
Greater Homestead/Florida City Chamber of Commerce, 43 N Krome Avenue, Homestead, tel: (305) 247-2332, www.chamberin action.com
Greater Miami Chamber of Commerce, 1601 Biscayne Boulevard, Miami, tel: (305) 350-7700, www.greatermiami.com
Miami Beach Chamber of Commerce, 1920 Meridian Ave, Miami Beach, tel: (305) 672-1270, www.miamibeachchamber.com

Greater Miami Convention & Visitors Bureau, 701 Brickell Avenue, tel: (305) 539-3000 or (800) 933-8448, www.gmcvb.com or www.TropicoolMiami.com
Miami Beach Visitors Center, 1920 Meridian, Miami, tel: (305) 672-1270.
Sunny Isles Beach Resort Association, 17100 Collins Avenue, Sunny Isles Beach, tel: (305) 947-5826, www.sunnyislesfla.com
Surfside Tourist Board, 9301 Collins Avenue, Surfside, tel: (305) 864-0722, www.town.surfside.fl.us
Tropical Everglades Visitor Association, 160 US 1, Florida City, tel: (800) 388-9669, www.tropicaleverglades.com
Florida Division of Tourism, Tallahassee, tel: (888) 735-2872, www.flausa.com

U seful Addresses

Marriages

Marriage License Bureau, 140 W Flagler Street, tel: (305) 275-1155.

Immigration Office

District Headquarters, 7880 Biscayne Boulevard, Miami, tel: (800) 375-5283, www.usas.gov

W eights & Measures

The US uses the Imperial system of weights and measures. Metric is rarely used. A conversion chart is provided here:
1 inch = 2.54 centimeters
1 foot = 30.48 centimeters
1 mile = 1.609 kilometers
1 quart = 1.136 liters
1 ounce = 28.4 grams
1 pound = .453 kilograms
1 yard = .9144 meters

What to Bring

Everything you could possibly need can be bought inexpensively in Miami. Some basic suggestions, however, include sunscreen, a sun hat, an umbrella, a swim suit, and any prescription medications.

WHAT TO READ

History & Culture

Black Miami in the Twentieth Century by Marvin Dunn, University Press of Florida (1997). A 100-year history from the pirates of Biscayne Bay to Miami's golden era between the World Wars to the Miami civil rights movement.

City on the Edge by Alejandro Portes and Alex Stepick, University of California Press (1993). A pair of sociologists explore the ethnic influences that shaped Miami. Using demographic data, newspaper articles, interviews and anecdotal evidence, they profile the culturally diverse city of Miami.

Deco Delights by Barbara Baer Capitman, E.P. Dutton (1988). An interesting read by the champion of the Art Deco District, though the pictures of South Beach now look rather dated. She describes the struggle between pressure for development and necessity of preservation.

Havana USA: Cuban Exiles and Cuban Americans in South Florida 1959–1994 by María Cristína García, University of California Press (1997). An account of the post-revolution Cuban migration and the cultural, economic and political evolution of Florida's Cuban community.

Miami by Joan Didion, Vintage (1998). Known for her sharp eye for the realities of American life, Didion captures the essence of a city of glamor, racial tension and fast money with a culture, history and state of mind inextricably linked with Cuba, only 90 miles (145 km) away.

Miami: A Sense of Place edited by Arva Moore Parks, Greater Miami Convention and Tourist Bureau (2004). Local historians write loving accounts of the city's heritage buildings in a neighborhood by neighborhood format.

Miami: In Our Own Words Miami Herald Publishing Co. (1995). An insightful collection of portraits, in words and photos, by *Miami Herald* writers and photographers, of some of Miami's living or recently deceased movers and shakers in all walks of life.

Miami: Then & Now by Arva Moore Parks, Thunder Bay Press (2003). A look at the history of Miami through a collection of contemporary and historic photographs and captions that describe the birth and growth of the city. One of a series.

Miami Beach: A History by Howard Kleinberg, Centennial Press (1994). One of the most complete histories of Miami Beach available; Miami journalist and historian Kleinberg writes a comprehensive and entertaining work to the beach.

Miami Beach Memories: A Nostalgic Chronicle of Days Gone By by Joann Biondi, Globe Pequot Press (2006). Full of vintage photographs, this collection of first-hand interviews with 100 people – strippers, comedians, maids, architects, lawyers – paints a vivid portrait of Miami Beach from the 1920s to the 1960s.

MiMo Miami Modern Revealed Chronicle Books (2004). The first comprehensive survey of the rich post-World War II architecture that symbolizes the romance and energy of Miami. Scores of photographs reflect

the influences from the days of the nightclub acts and swank hotels to the emergence of the downtown skyscrapers.

The Making Of Miami Beach – 1933–1941: The Architecture of Lawrence Murray Dixon by Kean Francois Lejeune, Rizzoli Publishers (2001). This look at Miami's history is drawn from Dixon's collection of drawings and photographs at the Bass Museum of Art, featuring the landmark buildings.

South Beach Style by Laura Cerwinske, Harry Abrams (2002). A more focused look at the trendy corner of Miami before it became an international playground of the pretty and the pampered. The book looks at the physicality of South Beach – the architecture, the gardens, the courtyards and bay-front gardens.

Landscape & Natural History

The Everglades: River of Grass by Marjory Stoneman Douglas, Pineapple Press (1997). This seminal work describing the magic of the Everglades, first published in 1947, contributed to the establishment of the Everglades National Park. This complete history of the unique environmental treasure became an impassioned plea for saving the wilderness.

Birds of Florida by Frances W. Hall, Great Outdoors (1994). The definitive guide to Florida's feathered inhabitants.

Diver's Guide to Florida and the Florida Keys by Jim Stachowicz, Windward Publishing, Miami (1994). A guide to underwater Florida.

Fiction Set in Florida

Edna Buchanan: winner of the Pulitzer prize for her crime reporting for the *Miami Herald*, Edna Buchanan has also written a series of excellent thrillers. Try *Miami, it's Murder* (Random House, 1994), *Margin of Error* (Hyperion, 1997), *Shadows* (2005), *Cold Case Squad* (2004) and *The Ice Maiden: A Britt Montero Mystery* (2003). Her first work remains her best, based on her sidewalk-pounding search for the truth through detail, *The Corpse Had a Familiar Face* (Random House 1987).

James W. Hall: the author of excellent Florida-based thrillers. Titles include *Tropical Freeze, Bones of Coral, Hard Aground, Mean High Tide,* and his latest *Body Language* (St. Martins, 1998).

Carl Hiaasen: another *Miami Herald* journalist, Hiaasen is the author of many comic thrillers set in Florida. They include: *Native Tongue* (1992), which makes fun of the world of theme parks; *Skin Tight* (1990), in which he turns his wit against plastic surgery in Miami; and *Lucky You* (1998), a wacky look at lottery winners. *Striptease* (1993) was made into a film, but his stories are best appreciated in print. His latest include *Flush* (2005), *Hoot* (2004), released in 2006 as a film, *Skinny Dip* (2004) and *Native Tongue* (2004).

Paul Levine: a lawyer turned novelist, Levine has written a series of novels based on the trials and tribulations of Jake Lassiter, Miami Dolphins football player turned lawyer. Titles include *Flesh & Bones* (William Morrow, 1996), *Fool Me Twice, Mortal Sin* and *To Speak for the Dead*.

Les Standiford: gives us the adventures of building contractor and sleuth John Deal in *Raw Deal* (1995), *Deal on Ice* (1998) and *Presidential Deal* (Harper Collins, 1999).

Carl Hiaasen's portrayal of a macabre, off-kilter Florida has influenced a number of fiction writers. Other recent books include *Whale Season* by **N.M. Kelb**y (Shayne Areheart Books 2006) about a second generation Cuban who thinks he is Jesus Christ, and *Florida Road Kill* by **Tim Dorsey** (Harper Paperback 2006), with two bad guys, including one who is obsessed with Florida history, chasing missing money.

Cookbooks

Eat at Joe's: The Joe's Stone Crab Restaurant Cookbook by Jo Ann Bass and Richard Sax, Clarkson Potter (2000). Get a bit of South Beach history with these mouthwatering recipes. A great way to recapture the meal you had in this world-famous eatery.

The Food of Miami: Authentic Recipes from South Florida and the Keys by Caroline Stuart, Peripus Editions (1999). These recipes are recounted with passion and a particular mix of favorites from the author and South Florida chefs.

Three Guys from Miami Cookbook, Gibb Smith (2003). Latin food in general, and Cuban food specifically, is enjoying a renaissance in Florida, and this book provides the flavor of the ethnic tastes and techniques of creating, and enjoying, the food that has influenced South Florida taste buds. Easy to follow recipes.

Other Insight Guides

The 500 titles in the *Insight Guides* range cover every continent and include comprehensive coverage of the US. Destinations in this region include: *Insight Guide: Florida, Orlando, Caribbean, Bermuda, Bahamas* and *Cuba*.

There are also over 120 *Insight Pocket Guides*, with an itinerary-based approach designed to assist the traveler with a limited amount of time to spend in a destination. Each comes with a full-size fold-out map. Titles include: *Florida*, the *Florida Keys*, and *Bahamas*.

Insight Compact Guides offer a highly portable encyclopedic travel guide packed with carefully cross-referenced text, photographs and maps. Titles include: *Insight Compact Guide: Florida, Florida Keys, Bahamas, and Cuba*.

Insight Fleximaps combine clear detailed cartography with essential travel information. The laminated finish makes the maps durable, waterproof and easy to fold. Titles in the region include: *Florida, Orlando, Cuba,* and the *Bahamas*.

MIAMI STREET ATLAS

The key map shows the area of Miami covered by the atlas section. An index of street names and places of interest shown on the maps can be found on the following pages. For each entry there is a page number and grid reference.

Map Legend

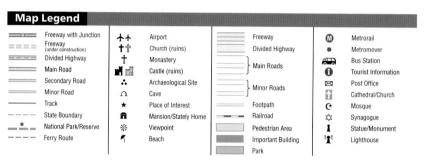

Freeway with Junction	Airport
Freeway (under construction)	Church (ruins)
Divided Highway	Monastery
Main Road	Castle (ruins)
Secondary Road	Archaeological Site
Minor Road	Cave
Track	Place of Interest
State Boundary	Mansion/Stately Home
National Park/Reserve	Viewpoint
Ferry Route	Beach

Freeway	Metrorail
Divided Highway	Metromover
Main Roads	Bus Station
Minor Roads	Tourist Information
Footpath	Post Office
Railroad	Cathedral/Church
Pedestrian Area	Mosque
Important Building	Synagogue
Park	Statue/Monument
	Lighthouse

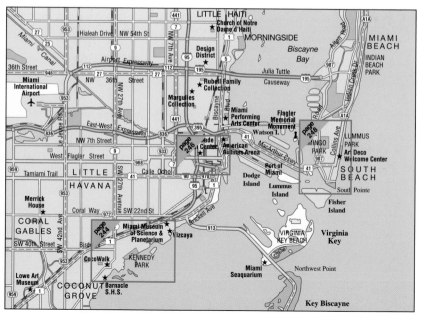

A   B

1

THE PINES

SILVER BLUFF ESTATES

SW 24th St
SW 24th St
SW 24th St
SW 24th Terr
SW 24th Terr
SW 24th Terr
SW 25th St
SW 25th St
SW 25th
SW 25th Terr
SW 25th
SW 26th St
SW 26th
SW 26th
SW 26th St

SOUTH BAY ESTATES

SW 27th St
SW 29th Ct
SW 29th Pl
SW 27th
SW 27th

SW 27th
SW 27th Way
SW 27th Terr
La
Coconut Grove La

Coral Gables

SW 27th
SW 28th
SW 27th
SW 27th
Terr. Ave

M   South Dixie Highway

2

SW 28th
SW 28th Terr
SW 28th
SW 28th

SW 28th Terr
SW 28th

South Dixie Highway
SW 29th

SW 35th
SW 34th

W Trade Ave

Virginia   Coconut
Catalina
Whitehead
Louise St
Center St
Ave

OCEAN VIEW HEIGHTS

Andros
Abaco
Jefferson
Lucaya
Calusa
Kirk
Feather

Inagua
Aviation
Swanson
Trapp

Bird Rd
Bird Rd
Bird
Rd
Washington
SW 27th Ave

Jackson
Matilda
LINCOLN PARK
BLANCHE PARK

Shipping Ave
Shipping Ave

Blaine
Lincoln

3

Carter
Hibiscus
New York
Elizabeth
Ohio
Indiana
Orange St
Ruth   Naomi
St   St
Center
St
SW 27th Ave

Day Ave
Day Ave

Darwin
Tiger Tail Ave

ELIZABETH VIRRICK PARK
Percival Ave
Lime
Ct
Coconut Grove Tennis Courts

Oak Ave
Lamb
Ct
Gifford
KIRK MUNROE PARK
Oak Ave

Doubletree

Tiger Tail
Ave
Greenwood Rd
Grapeland Blvd

Marine Commercial Development

Biscayne Bay Yacht Club

Frow   Ave
Frow Ave
Florida   Ave
Florida Ave

McDonald
Florida St
Matilda St
CocoWalk
Mayfair
Virginia

Mary St
Grand Bay

Pan American Dr

Dinner Key Marina

Grand Ave
Grand Ave

Clipper
Circle

Thomas
William
Charles
Franklin

Elizabeth
Margaret
Ave
Ave
Ave
Ave

Commodore
Plaza
Florida
St
Main Highway
McFarlane Rd

Coconut Grove Public Library
Chamber of Commerce

BAYSIDE PARK

South Bayshore Dr
Miami City Hall
Coconut Grove Exhibition Center

Yacht Basin

4

COCONUT GROVE
Coconut Grove Playhouse

PEACOCK PARK
Coconut Grove Sailing Club

DINNER KEY PICNIC ISLANDS

Loquat Ave
Avocado Ave
Palmetto Ave
Hibiscus
Oleon
Banyan Trees
Main Highway
Royal Rd
The Barnacle State Historic Site

Plymouth Congregational Church

A   B

SW 24th St

SW 18th Ave

Ave

Ave

Ave

SW 24th Terr

SW 19th St

SW 21st Terr

SW 1st St

SW 1st Ave

SW 1st Ave

SW 1st Ave

South Dixie Highway

Dixie Highway

Wakeena Dr.

Talupa Dr.

Opechee Dr.

Noc-A-Tee

Dr.

Espanola Dr.

Secoffee St

Chucunantah Rd

Crystal Terr

Seminole St

Natoma St

Crystal Dr.

All-We-Wa

Tiger Tail

DOUGLAS

Micanopy St

Caacoochee St

Farisle St

Vista Ct

Crystal View Ct

SW 17th

South Bayshore Dr.

S Bayshore La

Sky Lime Dr.

Rockerman Rd

KENNEDY

ELIZABETH STEELE PARK

Hiawatha Ave

W Fairview St

E Fairview St

Fairhaven Pl

W Glencoe

E Glencoe

W Glencoe

Grove Isle

Nethia Dr.

Hallsee

Onaway Dr.

Hilola St

Shore Dr.

Bay Heights Dr.

Alaka St

Shore Dr. S

BAY HEIGHTS

Pina Rd

Samana Dr.

Dr. W

Dr. E

Shore Dr. S

South Miami Ave

South Miami Ave

South Miami Ave

Miami Museum of Science

Planetarium

VIZCAYA PARK

Vizcaya Art Museum

Ermita de la Caridad

Mercy Hospital

Heliport

Biscayne Bay

Picnic Island

N

| 0 | 400 yards |
| 0 | 400 m |

A

Sunset Islands
No 2
W 27th St
W 25th St

No 3
W 24th St
W 23rd St

Sunset Lake

No 4
W 21st St

BAYSHORE MUNICIPAL GOLF COURSE

MUNICIPAL GOLF COURSE
Lake Pancoast

Pine Tree Dr
Collins Ave
Miami Beach Ave

Bayshore

Miami City Ballet
Holiday Inn-Oceanside

22nd St
Bass Museum of Art
Regional Library
21st St

Rivo Alto Island

ISLAND VIEW PARK

20th St

Miami Beach Visitors Center
Convention Center
Holocaust Memorial

19th St

COLLINS PARK

Shelborne

Venetian Causeway (Toll)

Belle Isle

Venetian Islands

Bay Rd
Purdy Ave

Dade Blvd
Collins Canal

18th St

17th St

City Hall

Lincoln Rd Arts District
Lincoln Rd
Colony Theater
Lincoln Rd Mall
South Florida Arts Center

Alton Rd
West Ave
Lenox Ave
Michigan Ave
Jefferson Ave

16th St
15th Terr
15th St

Espanola Way

FLAMINGO PARK

14th

13th St
Memorial Field

12th St

11th St

10th St

9th St

8th St

7th St

6th St

Jackie Gleason Theater of Performing Arts
Lincoln Theatre

The Raleigh
Delano
Loew's

Pennsylvania Ave
Euclid Ave
Drexel Ave
Washington Ave

ART DECO

Clay

NATIONAL

Old City Hall

HISTORIC

DISTRICT

Cameo Theater
Cavalier
Carlton
Cardozo
LUMMUS
Leslie

Casa Casuarina (Versace Mansion)
Wolfsonian Foundation
Art Deco Welcome Center
Ocean Front Auditorium
Beach Patrol Headquarters
Waldorf Towers
The Hotel
PARK
Colony

ATLANTIC OCEAN

BUDY PARK

Star Island

Lenox Ave
Michigan Ave
Jefferson Ave
Meridian Ave
Collins Ave
Ocean Dr

907
10th St

Bridge Rd

Fisher Island Ferry Terminal

Terminal Island

MacArthur Causeway
A1A

US Coast Guard Base

Marina

Meloy Channel

Causeway Island

Main Channel

Lummus Island

Miami Beach Drive (5th St)
41

4th St
3rd St
2nd St
1st St

Biscayne St

Jewish Museum of Florida

OCEAN BEACH PARK

WASHINGTON PARK

PIER PARK

Port Blvd

South Pointe Tower

0   800 yards
0   800 m

Fisher Island

Inlet Blvd
SOUTH POINTE PARK

Government Cut

University of Miami Marine Laboratory

N

STREET INDEX

ART & PHOTO CREDITS

GENERAL INDEX